Overcoming Anxiety

FOR

DUMMIES®

2ND EDITION

**by Charles H. Elliott, PhD, and
Laura L. Smith, PhD**

WILEY

Wiley Publishing, Inc.

Overcoming Anxiety For Dummies®, 2nd Edition

Published by
Wiley Publishing, Inc.
111 River St.
Hoboken, NJ 07030-5774
www.wiley.com

For general information on our other products and services, please contact our Customer Care Department within the U.S. at 877-762-2974, outside the U.S. at 317-572-3993, or fax 317-572-4002.

For technical support, please visit www.wiley.com/techsupport.

Wiley also publishes its books in a variety of electronic formats. Some content that appears in print may not be available in electronic books.

Library of Congress Control Number: 2010924567

ISBN: 978-0-470-57441-6

Manufactured in the United States of America

10 9 8 7 6 5 4 3 2

WILEY

About the Authors

Charles H. Elliott, PhD, is a clinical psychologist and a Founding Fellow in the Academy of Cognitive Therapy. He is also a member of the faculty at Fielding Graduate University. He specializes in the treatment of children, adolescents, and adults with obsessive-compulsive disorder, anxiety, anger, depression, and personality disorders. Dr. Elliott has authored many professional articles and book chapters in the area of cognitive behavior therapies. He presents nationally and internationally on new developments in the assessment and therapy of emotional disorders.

Laura L. Smith, PhD, is a clinical psychologist and adjunct faculty member at Fielding Graduate University. She specializes in the assessment and treatment of adults and children with obsessive-compulsive disorder, as well as personality disorders, depression, anxiety, attention-deficit hyperactivity disorder, and learning disorders. She often provides consultations to attorneys, school districts, and governmental agencies. She presents workshops on cognitive therapy and mental-health issues to national and international audiences. Dr. Smith is a widely published author of popular and professional articles and books.

Together, Drs. Elliott and Smith have written *Borderline Personality Disorder For Dummies, Obsessive-Compulsive Disorder For Dummies, Seasonal Affective Disorder For Dummies, Anxiety and Depression Workbook For Dummies, Depression For Dummies, Hollow Kids: Recapturing the Soul of a Generation Lost to the Self-Esteem Myth,* and *Why Can't I Be the Parent I Want to Be?* They are members of the Board of Directors of the New Mexico Psychological Association and affiliated training faculty at the Cognitive Behavioral Institute of Albuquerque. Their work has been featured in various periodicals, including *Family Circle, Parents, Child,* and *Better Homes and Gardens,* as well as popular publications like the *New York Post, The Washington Times,* the *Daily Telegraph* (London), and *The Christian Science Monitor.*

They have been speakers at numerous conferences, including those of the National Alliance for the Mentally Ill (NAMI), the Association for Behavioral and Cognitive Therapies, the International Association for Cognitive Psychotherapy, and the National Association of School Psychologists. They have appeared on TV networks such as CNN and Canada AM, and, in radio, they're often featured as experts on various NPR programs, as well as *You: The Owner's Manual Radio Show, Doctor Radio* on Sirius Satellite Radio, the *Frankie Boyer Radio Show,* and *The Four Seasons Radio Show.* They've committed their professional lives to making the science of psychology relevant and accessible to the public. Drs. Smith and Elliott are available for speaking engagements, expert interviews, and workshops. You can visit their Web site at www.psychology4people.com or their blog, "Anxiety & OCD Exposed," at http://blogs.psychcentral.com/anxiety.

Dedication

We dedicate this book to our growing, changing families — Brian, Alli, Sara, and Trevor. And of course to our grandchildren: Cade, Carter, Alaina, and Lauren. Thanks for the excitement — of course, *enough is enough* sometimes!

Authors' Acknowledgments

We'd like to thank our excellent editors at Wiley: Project Editor extraordinaire Vicki Adang, Acquisitions Editor Michael Lewis, and masterful Copy Editor Christy Pingleton, as well as our agents Elizabeth and Ed Knappman. We are also grateful to Dr. Scott Bea from the Cleveland Clinic for reviewing our work and making insightful suggestions.

We also wish to thank our publicity and marketing team, which includes David Hobson and Adrienne Fontaine at Wiley. Thanks also to Alan Rubin, MD, and all the other Dummies authors for a great conference and inspiration.

Thanks to Bob Elliott for all the savvy advice and Mathew Raikes at www.darn-computer.com for his expertise on computers and Web site support. Thanks to Trevor Wolfe and Kate Guerin for keeping us up on pop culture, social media, blogging, and tweeting on Twitter.

We want to thank Deborah Wearn, Pamela Hargrove, Tracie Antonuk, and Geoff Smith for their continued interest. Thanks to Matt Lewis for keeping our view great. And a special thanks to Sadie and Murphy for taking us on much-needed walks.

To Drs. Brad Richards and Jeanne Czajka from the Cognitive Behavioral Institute of Albuquerque, thanks for including us on your affiliated training faculty. To Dr. Brenda Wolfe and her husband, Ken, thanks for including us in your voyage. We're still eager to see your next book.

Finally, we are especially grateful to our many clients we've seen, both those with anxiety disorders and those without. They helped us understand psychological issues in general, as well as anxiety. They also taught us about courage and persistence.

Publisher's Acknowledgments

We're proud of this book; please send us your comments at http://dummies.custhelp.com. For other comments, please contact our Customer Care Department within the U.S. at 877-762-2974, outside the U.S. at 317-572-3993, or fax 317-572-4002.

Some of the people who helped bring this book to market include the following:

Acquisitions, Editorial, and Media Development

Project Editor: Victoria M. Adang
  (Previous Edition: Norm Crampton)

Acquisitions Editor: Michael Lewis
  (Previous Edition: Natasha Graf)

Copy Editor: Christine Pingleton
  (Previous Edition: Esmerelda St. Clair)

Assistant Editor: Erin Calligan Mooney

Senior Editorial Assistant: David Lutton

Technical Editor: Scott M. Bea, PsyD

Editorial Manager: Michelle Hacker

Editorial Assistant: Jennette ElNaggar

Cover Photos: iStock

Cartoons: Rich Tennant
  (www.the5thwave.com)

Composition Services

Project Coordinator: Patrick Redmond

Layout and Graphics: Ashley Chamberlain, Joyce Haughey, Christine Williams

Proofreaders: Laura Albert, Evelyn C. Gibson

Indexer: Steve Rath

Publishing and Editorial for Consumer Dummies

  Diane Graves Steele, Vice President and Publisher, Consumer Dummies

  Kristin Ferguson-Wagstaffe, Product Development Director, Consumer Dummies

  Ensley Eikenburg, Associate Publisher, Travel

  Kelly Regan, Editorial Director, Travel

Publishing for Technology Dummies

  Andy Cummings, Vice President and Publisher, Dummies Technology/General User

Composition Services

  Debbie Stailey, Director of Composition Services

Contents at a Glance

Table of Contents

Introduction

· ·

*T*he idea of a self-help book on anxiety in the *For Dummies* series germi-
nated in the summer of 2001. At the time, we wondered how the audience would react to a book with a title like *Overcoming Anxiety For Dummies.*
Would potential readers feel turned off or insulted by the title? Would they
think such a book would be condescending and "dummied down?"

A few people did respond negatively, and a couple of e-mails made us a tad
anxious. Like most folks, we find that criticism stings. But we were surprised
and gratified at the overwhelmingly positive responses we got from the
majority of readers who contacted us.

People all over the world e-mailed us to say that they had found this book to
be one of the most comprehensive and accessible books on anxiety they had
ever read. Some told us that for the first time in their lives, anxiety no longer
dominated their lives. We were also thrilled to discover that many counselors, therapists, and psychologists reported using the book as a supplement
to psychotherapy sessions for their anxious patients.

When our editors approached us about updating *Overcoming Anxiety For
Dummies,* we took some time to think about what had happened in the world
since we wrote the first edition. As we reflected on this issue, we realized that
the world has changed a lot in the nine years since the first edition appeared
on bookshelves. We have more to worry about than ever. Because of these
growing, emerging sources of worry, we felt a need to include information in
this book that addresses them.

For example, some airport security areas now have equipment that takes a
virtual naked picture of you as you enter. We've suffered through what's currently called the Great Recession, and at the time of this writing, it's unclear
where the world economy is headed. People worry about getting jobs, keeping jobs, and fragile dreams of retirement. The globalization of economies
and travel have made the spread of pandemics faster and potentially more
deadly than ever. Environmental worries have escalated; the viciousness of
Mother Nature has frequently flashed across our computer and TV screens.
The spread of nuclear weapons continues, and worries abound about war,
crime, and terror. Children are frightened by stories about abuse and violence on the Internet and TV, while their worried parents increasingly restrict
their lives.

So today's world gives us plenty to worry about, as it always has. But just as we don't want to become victims of terror, we can't let ourselves become victims of anxiety. Anxiety clouds our thinking and weakens our resolve to live life to the fullest. We realize that some anxiety is realistic and inescapable; yet, we can keep it from dominating our lives. Even under duress, we can preserve a degree of serenity; we can hold onto our humanity, vigor, and zest for life. We can love and laugh.

Because we believe in our collective resilience, we take a humorous, and at times irreverent, approach to conquering anxiety. Our message is based on sound, scientifically proven methods. But we don't bore you with the scientific details. Instead, we present a clear, rapid-fire set of strategies for beating back anxiety and winning the war against worry.

About This Book

We have three goals in writing this book. First, we want you to understand just what anxiety is and the different forms it can take. Second, we think that knowing what's good about anxiety and what's bad about it is good for you. Finally, we cover what you're probably most interested in — discovering the latest techniques for overcoming your anxiety and helping someone else who has anxiety.

Unlike most books, you don't have to start on page 1 and read straight through. Use the extensive table of contents to pick and choose what you want to read. Don't worry about reading parts in any particular order. For example, if you really don't want much information about the who, what, when, where, and why of anxiety and whether you have it, go ahead and skip Part I. However, we encourage you to at least skim Part I, because it contains fascinating facts and information as well as ideas for getting started.

An Important Message to Our Readers

Since the first edition of *Overcoming Anxiety For Dummies,* we've made a point of commenting on our use of humor in these books. Although topics like anxiety, depression, obsessive-compulsive disorder, and borderline personality disorder are serious, painful subjects, we believe that laughter, like a little sugar, helps the medicine go down and the message come through. We hope you agree.

This book is meant to be a guide to overcoming a mental state or disorder called anxiety. It should be used to give support and information to our readers. Everyone alive suffers from anxiety from time to time. However, if your anxiety greatly interferes with your day-to-day life, restricts your activities, and robs you of pleasure, we urge you to seek professional mental healthcare.

Conventions Used in This Book

We use a lot of case examples to illustrate our points throughout this book. Please realize that these examples represent composites of people with various types of anxiety disorders. None of the examples is about real people we've seen or known. Any resemblance to a particular person is entirely coincidental. We **bold** the names of people in our examples to indicate that a case example is starting.

Psychologists use lots of jargon and acronyms. We try our best to keep these to a minimum, but sometimes we can't avoid them. When we do use a new term, we *italicize* and define it.

We also use **boldface** text to indicate keywords in a bulleted list or to highlight action parts of numbered steps. Finally, when we direct you to a Web site for additional information, it's printed in `monofont`.

What You're Not to Read

Not only do you not have to read each and every chapter in order (or at all, for that matter), you don't have to read each and every icon or sidebar (the text in the gray boxes). We try to give you plenty of current information and facts about anxiety. Some may not interest you — so don't get too anxious about skipping around.

Foolish Assumptions

Who might pick up this book? We assume, probably foolishly, that you or someone you love suffers from some type of problem with anxiety or worry. But it's also possible that you simply find the topic of anxiety interesting. We imagine that you may be curious about a variety of helpful strategies to choose from that can fit your lifestyle and personality. Finally, you may be a mental-health professional who's interested in finding a friendly resource for your clients who suffer from anxiety or worry.

How This Book Is Organized

Overcoming Anxiety For Dummies is organized into 6 parts and 23 chapters. Right now, we tell you a little about each part.

Part 1: Detecting and Exposing Anxiety

In the first two chapters, you find out a great deal about anxiety — from who gets it to why people become anxious. We explain the different kinds of anxiety disorders — they're not all the same — and we tell you who is most susceptible and why.

In Chapter 3, we review the biological aspects of anxiety disorders — from the toll they take on the body to the underlying biochemical processes involved.

Chapter 4 helps you clear the roadblocks to change. You discover the most common reasons that people resist working on their anxiety and what to do if you find yourself stuck.

Part II: Battling Anxiety

In Part II, we give you an array of proven, specific strategies for battling and overcoming anxiety. We show you strategies for transforming anxious thoughts into calm thoughts. And you discover how the words that you use can increase anxiety and how simply changing your vocabulary decreases anxiety.

One of the best ways to tackle anxiety is by taking action. No wimps here. We show you how to stare your fears in the face and conquer them. In addition, we take a look at how medication can sometimes alleviate anxiety disorders. We also review the most recent biological alternatives for reducing anxiety.

Part III: Letting Go of the Battle

These chapters take a look at ways of dealing with anxiety indirectly. Changes in lifestyle such as staying connected with others, exercising, getting enough sleep, and maintaining a proper diet all help. Learning to relax through breathing exercises, muscle exercises, or conjuring up calm images can relieve anxiety passively.

Chapter 13 takes a mindful approach to managing anxiety. Mindfulness has emerged as a highly popular as well as empirically supported approach to improving emotional well-being.

Part IV: Zeroing in on Specific Worries

Part IV is a brand new part in this edition of *Overcoming Anxiety For Dummies*. The chapters in this part focus on anxieties about finances, terrorism, natural disasters, and health. You can't live a meaningful life without having some concern about issues such as these. This part gives you ways of preparing for unexpected calamities and ideas about how to accept uncertainty in an uncertain world.

Part V: Helping Others with Anxiety

What do you do when someone you love worries too much? First, we look at how you can help a significant adult in your life with anxiety. As a coach or simply a cheerleader, you can help your friend or family member conquer anxiety. In this new, expanded portion of the book, we also give you the tools to understand the differences between normal fear and anxiety in children. We also provide some simple guidelines to help out anxious kids. In addition, we talk about who to go to for help with your child and what to expect.

Part VI: The Part of Tens

If you're looking for a quick fix or a simple review, take a look at these helpful lists. You can read about ten ways to stop anxiety in its tracks, ten ways to handle relapse, and ten signs that professional help is in order.

Finally, the appendix lists books and Web sites for obtaining more information about the topics we cover in this book.

Icons Used in This Book

For Dummies books use little pictures, called *icons,* in the margins to get your attention. Here's what they mean:

The Anxiety Ax icon represents a particular action you can take to help get rid of anxiety.

 The Remember icon appears when we want your attention. Please read the text associated with it for critical information.

 The Tip icon alerts you to important insights or clarifications.

 Warning icons appear when you need to be careful or seek professional help.

Where to Go from Here

Overcoming Anxiety For Dummies offers you the best, most up-to-date advice based on scientific research on anxiety disorders. If you want help controlling your negative thoughts, turn to Chapters 5, 6, and 7. You say you just want to relax? Try the techniques in Chapter 11. Or if you're worried about your job and finances, in Chapter 14 we provide tips for finding your next job and pinching pennies. If you practice the techniques and strategies provided throughout, you're likely to feel calmer. For many people, this book should be a complete guide to fighting frenzy and fear.

However, some stubborn forms of anxiety need more care and attention. If your anxiety and worry significantly get in the way of work or play, get help. Start with your family doctor to rule out physical causes. Then consult with a mental-health professional. Anxiety can be conquered; don't give up.

Part I
Detecting and Exposing Anxiety

The 5th Wave

By Rich Tennant

"I think she's getting better. She bought three 'Life is Good' T-shirts yesterday."

In this part . . .

We explore the ins and outs of anxiety, discussing the anxiety epidemic that's going around and showing how anxiety affects the entire body. In this part, you can find all the major categories of anxiety disorders, along with an overview of what you can do to reduce anxiety. You discover how you can easily get stuck tackling your anxiety, and we tell you how to keep that from happening.

Chapter 1

Analyzing and Attacking Anxiety

- -

- -

Stroll down the street and about one in four of the people you walk by either has an anxiety disorder or will at some point in their lives experience one. And almost half of the people you encounter will struggle with anxiety to one degree or another, although they may not have a full-blown anxiety disorder. The rate of anxiety disorders has climbed for many decades, and no end is in sight.

The world watches in fear as disasters, terrorism, financial collapse, pandemics, crime, and war threaten the security of home and family. Anxiety creates havoc in the home, destroys relationships, causes employees to lose time from work, and prevents people from living full, productive lives.

In this chapter, you find out how to recognize the symptoms of anxiety. We clarify the costs of anxiety — both personal and societal. We provide a brief overview of the treatments presented in greater detail in later chapters. You also get a glimpse of how to help if someone you care about or your child has anxiety. If you worry too much or care for someone who has serious problems with anxiety, this book is here to help!

Anxiety: Everybody's Doing It

Anxiety involves feelings of uneasiness, worry, apprehension, and/or fear, and it's the most common of all the so-called mental disorders. In other words, you definitely aren't alone if you have unwanted anxiety. And the numbers have grown over the years. At no time in history has anxiety tormented more people than it does today. Why?

Life has never been as complicated as it is today. The workweek has grown longer rather than shorter. Broken and blended families create increased stresses to manage. Computer screens and television news bring the latest horrors into your living room in real time. Newspapers, blogs, tweets, and magazines chronicle crime, war, and corruption. Terrorism has crossed the globe and escalated to new heights. The media's portrayal of these modern plagues includes full-color images with unprecedented, graphic detail. Let's face it, fear sells.

Unfortunately, as stressful and anxiety-arousing as the world is today, only a minority of those suffering from anxiety seek treatment. That's a problem, because anxiety causes not only emotional pain and distress but also physical strain and even death, given that anxiety extracts a serious toll on the body and sometimes even contributes to suicide. Furthermore, anxiety costs society as a whole, to the tune of billions of dollars.

When people talk about what anxiety feels like, you may hear any or all of the following descriptions:

- When my panic attacks begin, I feel tightness in my chest. It's as though I'm drowning or suffocating, and I begin to sweat; the fear is overwhelming. I feel like I'm going to die, and I have to sit down because I may faint.

- I've always been painfully shy. I want friends, but I'm too embarrassed to call anyone. I guess I feel like anyone I call will think I'm not worth talking to.

- I wake with worry every day, even on the weekends. Ever since I lost my job, I worry all the time. Sometimes, when it's really bad, I think about going to sleep and never waking up.

- Ever since my accident, I have nightmares and constant images racing through my mind about glass breaking, tires screeching, and passengers screaming. I'm so jumpy and irritable that I can barely get through the day.

- I'm so afraid of flying that I can't travel, even though I'd like to.

- I worry about germs and contamination so much that I wash my hands about 30 times a day — my hands are raw and bleeding. I just can't stop.

As you can see, anxiety results in all sorts of thoughts, behaviors, and feelings. When your anxiety begins to interfere with day-to-day life, you need to find ways to put your fears and worries at ease.

Tabulating the Costs of Anxiety

Anxiety costs. It costs the sufferer in emotional, physical, and financial terms. But it doesn't stop there. Anxiety also incurs a financial burden for everyone. Stress, worry, and anxiety disrupt relationships, work, and family.

The heartbreak of anxiety

Two studies have found a critical relationship between anxiety and heart disease. One investigation at Duke University divided cardiac patients into three groups: an exercise group, a stress management group, and a care-as-usual group. After five years, the stress management group had fewer additional heart-related problems than the other two groups. Although this was a small study, one researcher concluded that managing stress and anxiety is one of the most powerful tools in fighting heart disease. The other study, published in the January 2002 issue of the journal *Stroke,* found that men who suffer from anxiety and depression are much more likely to die from strokes than those without these psychological problems.

What does anxiety cost you?

Obviously, if you have a problem with anxiety, you experience the cost of distressed, anxious feelings. Anxiety feels lousy. You don't need to read a book to know that. But did you know that untreated anxiety runs up a tab in other ways as well? These costs include

- **A physical toll:** Higher blood pressure, tension headaches, and gastrointestinal symptoms can affect your body. In fact, recent research found that certain types of chronic anxiety disorders change the makeup of your brain's structures.

- **A toll on your kids:** Parents with anxiety more often have anxious children. This is due in part to genetics, but it's also because kids learn from observation. Anxious kids may be so stressed that they can't pay attention in school.

- **Fat!:** Anxiety and stress increase the stress hormone known as cortisol. *Cortisol* causes fat storage in the abdominal area, thus increasing the risk of heart disease and stroke. Stress also leads to increased eating.

- **More trips to the doctor:** That's because those with anxiety frequently experience worrisome physical symptoms. In addition, anxious people often worry a great deal about their health.

- **Relationship problems:** People with anxiety frequently feel irritable. Sometimes, they withdraw emotionally or do the opposite and dependently cling to their partners.

- **Downtime:** Those with anxiety disorders miss work more often than other people, usually as an effort to temporarily quell their distress.

Adding up the cost to society

Anxiety costs many billions of dollars worldwide. A U.S. government report says that anxiety costs more than depression, schizophrenia, or any other emotional problem. The annual tab is estimated at more than $65 billion. The United Kingdom spent 32 billion pounds (approximately $53 billion) on mental healthcare in 2002, a huge portion of which was spent on anxiety-related problems. Even countries that spend little on mental healthcare incur substantial costs from anxiety disorders. These costs include

- Decreased productivity
- Healthcare costs
- Medications

Decreased productivity is sometimes due to health problems made worse by anxiety. But the financial loss from downtime and healthcare costs doesn't include the dollars lost to substance abuse, which many of those with anxiety disorders turn to in order to deal with their anxiety. Thus, directly and indirectly, anxiety extracts a colossal toll on both the person who experiences it and society at large.

Recognizing the Symptoms of Anxiety

You may not know if you suffer from anxiety or an anxiety disorder. That's because anxiety involves a wide range of symptoms. Each person experiences a slightly different constellation of these symptoms. And your specific constellation determines what kind of anxiety disorder you may have. We discuss the various types of anxiety disorders in detail in Chapter 2.

For now, you should know that some signs of anxiety appear in the form of thoughts or beliefs. Other indications of anxiety manifest themselves in bodily sensations. Still other symptoms show up in various kinds of anxious behaviors. Some people experience anxiety signs in all three ways, while others only perceive their anxiety in one or two areas.

Thinking anxiously

Folks with anxiety generally think in ways that differ from the ways that other people think. You're probably thinking anxiously if you experience

- **Approval addiction:** If you're an approval addict, you worry a great deal about what other people think about you.

Name that phobia!

Phobias are one of the most common types of anxiety disorder, and we discuss them in detail in Chapter 2. A *phobia* is an excessive, disproportionate fear of a relatively harmless situation or thing. Sometimes, the phobia poses some risk, but the person's reaction clearly exceeds the danger. Do you know the technical names for phobias? Draw arrows from the common name of each phobia to the corresponding technical name. See how many you get right. The answers are printed upside down at the bottom.

Be careful if you have *triskaidekaphobia* (fear of the number 13), because we're giving you 13 phobias to match!

Technical Name	Means a Fear of This
1. Ophidiophobia	A. Growing old
2. Zoophobia	B. Sleep
3. Gerascophobia	C. The mind
4. Acrophobia	D. Imperfection
5. Lachanophobia	E. Snakes
6. Hypnophobia	F. Fear
7. Atelophobia	G. New things
8. Phobophobia	H. Animals
9. Sesquipedalophobia	I. Small things
10. Neophobia	J. Mirrors
11. Psychophobia	K. Heights
12. Tapinophobia	L. Long words
13. Eisoptrophobia	M. Vegetables

Answers: 1. E, 2. H, 3. A, 4. K, 5. M, 6. B, 7. D, 8. F, 9. L, 10. G, 11. C, 12. I, 13. J

✔ **Living in the future and predicting the worst:** When you do this, you think about everything that lies ahead and assume the worst possible outcome.

✔ **Magnification:** People who magnify the importance of negative events usually feel more anxious than other people do.

✔ **Perfectionism:** If you're a perfectionist, you assume that any mistake means total failure.

✔ **Poor concentration:** Anxious people routinely report that they struggle with focusing their thoughts. Short-term memory sometimes suffers as well.

✔ **Racing thoughts:** Thoughts zip through your mind in a stream of almost uncontrollable worry and concern.

We discuss anxious thinking in great detail in Chapters 5, 6, and 7.

Behaving anxiously

We have three words to describe anxious behavior — avoidance, avoidance, and avoidance. Anxious people inevitably attempt to stay away from the things that make them anxious. Whether it's snakes, heights, crowds, freeways, parties, paying bills, reminders of bad times, or public speaking, anxious people search for ways out.

In the short run, avoidance lowers anxiety. It makes you feel a little better. However, in the long run, avoidance actually maintains and heightens anxiety. We give you ways of dismantling avoidance in Chapter 8.

One of the most common and obvious examples of anxiety-induced avoidance is how people react to their phobias. Have you ever seen the response of a spider phobic when confronting one of the critters? Usually, such folks hastily retreat.

Finding anxiety in your body

Almost all people with severe anxiety experience a range of physical effects. These sensations don't simply occur in your head; they're as real as this book you're holding. The responses to anxiety vary considerably from person to person and include

- Accelerated heartbeat
- A spike in blood pressure
- Dizziness
- Fatigue
- Gastrointestinal upset
- General aches and pains
- Muscle tension or spasms
- Sweating

These are simply the temporary effects that anxiety exerts on your body. Chronic anxiety left untreated poses serious risks to your health as well. We discuss the general health effects in greater detail in Chapter 2.

Seeking Help for Your Anxiety

As we say earlier in this chapter, most people simply choose to live with anxiety rather than seek help. Some people worry that treatment won't work. Or they believe that the only effective treatment out there is medication, and they hate the possibility of side effects. Others fret about the costs of getting help. And still others have concerns that tackling their anxiety would cause their fears to increase so much that they wouldn't be able to stand it.

Well, stop adding worry to worry. You can significantly reduce your anxiety through a variety of interesting strategies. Many of these don't have to cost a single cent. And if one doesn't work, you can try another. Most people find that at least a couple of the approaches that we review work for them. The following sections provide an overview of treatment options and give you some guidance on what to do if your self-help efforts fall short.

Untreated anxiety may cause long-term health problems. It doesn't make sense to avoid doing something about your anxiety.

Matching symptoms and therapies

Anxiety symptoms appear in three different spheres, as follows (see the earlier section "Recognizing the Symptoms of Anxiety" for more details on these symptoms):

- ✔ Thinking symptoms: The thoughts that run through your mind
- ✔ Behaving symptoms: The things you do in response to anxiety
- ✔ Feeling symptoms: How your body reacts to anxiety

Treatment corresponds to each of these three areas, as we discuss in the following three sections.

Thinking therapies

One of the most effective treatments for a wide range of emotional problems, known as *cognitive therapy,* deals with the way you think about, perceive, and interpret everything that's important to you, including

- ✔ Your views about yourself
- ✔ The events that happen to you in life
- ✔ Your future

Ten dubious duds

This book is designed to give you ideas on how to beat anxiety. Beware the following things, which make anxiety worse:

✓ **Avoidance:** Avoiding what scares you makes anxiety worse. For example, if you're afraid of driving on a freeway and only use side streets, your fear of driving on crowded, fast roads will get worse.

✓ **Whining and complaining:** People love to do this, but it only makes things worse.

✓ **Seeking reassurance:** When people give you reassurance, it feels good. But the effects are short-lived, and reassurance can actually make anxiety worse.

✓ **Seeking quick fixes:** The Internet is full of quick fixes, but we don't know of any that have really been proven to work.

✓ **Psychoanalysis:** This approach to therapy works for some problems, but it hasn't collected much support in alleviating anxiety.

✓ **Drinking or illegal drugs:** Substances may relieve anxiety for a short while, but they actually increase anxiety in the long run.

✓ **Trying too hard:** If you push yourself too hard and feel anxious about your progress, you're just going to make things worse. Slow down a little.

✓ **Sipping herbal drinks:** There's nothing wrong with using these as a short-term crutch, but don't count on them to cure your problem.

✓ **Hoping for miracles:** Hope is good — miracles do happen — but it's not a good idea to sit around and wait for one to come along.

✓ **Taking medication as a sole solution:** Some medications help *some* people with *some* anxiety problems, *some* of the time. But the strategies and therapies described in this book have proven to be more reliable and effective in the long run.

When people feel unusually anxious and worried, they almost inevitably distort the way they think about these things. That distortion actually causes much of their anxiety. In the following example, Luann has both physical symptoms and cognitive symptoms of anxiety. Her therapist chooses a cognitive approach to help her.

> **Luann,** a junior in college, gets physically ill before every exam. She throws up, has diarrhea, and her heart races. She fantasizes that she will fail each and every test she takes and that eventually, the college will dismiss her. Yet, her lowest grade to date has been a B–.
>
> The cognitive approach her therapist uses helps her capture the negative predictions and catastrophic outcomes that run through her mind. It then guides her to search for evidence about her true performance and a more realistic appraisal of the chances of her actually failing.

As simple as this approach sounds, hundreds of studies have found that it works well to reduce anxiety. Part II of this book describes various cognitive or thinking therapy techniques.

Behaving therapies

Another highly effective type of therapy is known as *behavior therapy*. As the name suggests, this approach deals with actions you can take and behaviors you can incorporate to alleviate your anxiety. Some actions are fairly straightforward, like getting more exercise and sleep and managing your responsibilities. You can get good ideas on those actions in Chapter 10.

On the other hand, one type of action that targets anxiety and can feel a little scary is *exposure* — breaking your fears down into small steps and facing them one at a time. We cover exposure in Chapter 8.

Some people, with the advice of their doctor, choose to take medications for their anxiety. If you're considering that option, be sure to see Chapter 9 to help you make an informed decision.

Feeling therapies — soothing the inner storm

Anxiety sets off a storm of distressing physical symptoms, such as a racing heartbeat, upset stomach, muscle tension, sweating, dizziness, and so on. We have a variety of suggestions, including breathing and relaxation techniques, for helping quell this turmoil. You may choose to make changes in your lifestyle (see Chapter 10), give the relaxation strategies we cover in Chapters 11 and 12 a try, or employ mindfulness, an approach that teaches you to connect with present moment experiences (see Chapter 13).

Choosing where to start

We organize this book so you can start anywhere you want, but you may wonder whether one set of strategies would work better for you than another. Although we can't predict with certainty what will work best for you, we do have a guide for helping you choose the approach that may feel most compatible for your initial efforts. On the other hand, if you just want to read the book from front to back, that's fine, too.

In the following anxiety quiz, check all the items that apply to you. If you check off more items in one category than the others, you may consider starting with the part of this book that applies to it. For example, Chapters 5, 6, and 7 are designed especially for thinkers and present the thinking therapies, also known as *cognitive therapy;* Chapter 8 is aimed at doers and provides the essentials of *behavior therapy*. Part III focuses on feelers who may profit most by starting with strategies for quelling troubling bodily sensations and feelings through relaxation, diet, exercise, meditation, better sleep habits, and mindfulness. If you check an equal number of items in two or more categories, ask yourself which one seems most like you and start there.

Thinkers (see Chapters 5, 6, and 7)

___I like to analyze problems.

___I like to carefully consider pros and cons.

___I enjoy dealing with facts.

___I like to be logical.

___I like to plan things in advance.

Doers (see Chapter 8)

___If I have a problem, I take action right away.

___I love getting things done.

___I'm energetic.

___I'm an active person.

___I hate sitting still with nothing to do.

Feelers (see Part III)

___I am always aware of every discomfort in my body.

___I hate the feeling of anxiety.

___I love to immerse myself in the arts.

___Music speaks to me.

___I love the feeling of a massage or a hot bath.

Finding the right help

We suppose it's not too presumptuous to assume that because you're reading this book, you or someone you know suffers from anxiety. And you'd probably like to tackle anxiety on your own. This *is* a self-help book, after all.

The good news is that self-help does work. A number of studies support the idea that people can deal with important, difficult problems without seeking the services of a professional. People clearly benefit from self-help. They get better and stay better.

Then again, sometimes self-help efforts fall short. Chapter 23 provides ten critical signs that indicate a likely need for professional help. See Chapter 4 for information about finding the right professional for you.

If you do need professional consultation, many qualified therapists will work with you on the ideas contained in this book. That's because most mental-health professionals will appreciate the comprehensive nature of the material and the fact that most of the strategies are based on well-proven methods. If research has yet to support the value of a particular approach, we take care to let you know that. We happen to think you're much better off sticking with strategies known to work and avoiding those that don't.

In Chapters 18, 19, and 20, we discuss how to help a child or an adult loved one who has anxiety. If you're working with a friend or family member, you both may want to read Part V, and possibly more, of this book. Sometimes, friends and family can help those who are also working with a professional and making their own efforts.

Whichever sources, techniques, or strategies you select, overcoming anxiety will be one of the most rewarding challenges that you ever undertake. The endeavor may scare you at first, and the going may start slow and have its ups and downs. But if you stick with it, we believe that you'll find a way out of the quicksand of anxiety and onto the solid ground of serenity.

Chapter 2

Examining Anxiety: What's Normal, What's Not

Anxious feelings sprout up for most folks here and there and are completely normal. In certain situations, anxiety is a perfectly understandable reaction. For example, if you're driving in a snowstorm and your car starts to spin out of control, feeling anxious makes sense. But sometimes anxiety signals something more serious.

To get a feel for the difference between something as serious as an anxiety disorder and a normal reaction, read the following description and imagine ten minutes in the life of Tiffany.

> **Tiffany** feels restless and shifts her weight from foot to foot. Walking forward a little, she notices a slight tightening in her chest. Her breathing quickens. She feels an odd mixture of excitement and mounting tension. She sits down and does her best to relax, but the anxiety continues to intensify. Her body suddenly jerks forward; she grips the sides of her seat and clenches her teeth to choke back a scream. Her stomach feels like it might come up through her throat. She feels her heart race and her face flush. Tiffany's emotions run wild. Dizziness, fear, and a rushing sensation overtake her. The feelings all come in waves — one after the other.

You may wonder what's wrong with poor Tiffany. Maybe she has an anxiety disorder. Or possibly she's suffering a nervous breakdown. Perhaps she's going crazy. No, Tiffany actually *wanted* to feel scared and anxious!

You see, she was at an amusement park. She handed her ticket to the attendant and buckled herself into a roller coaster. After that, you probably understand the rest of her experience. Tiffany doesn't have an anxiety disorder, she isn't suffering a nervous breakdown, and she isn't going crazy. As her story illustrates, the symptoms of anxiety can be ordinary reactions to life.

In this chapter, we help you figure out whether you're suffering from an anxiety disorder, everyday anxiety, or something else. We take a close look at all the different forms and symptoms of anxiety. Then we discuss some of the other emotional disorders that often accompany anxiety.

Knowing When Anxiety Is a Help and When It's a Hindrance

Imagine a life with no anxiety at all. How wonderful! You awaken every morning anticipating nothing but pleasant experiences. You fear nothing. The future holds only sweet security and joy.

Think again. With no anxiety, when the guy in the car in front of you slams on the brakes, your response will be slower and you'll crash. With no worries about the future, your retirement may end up bleak. The total absence of anxiety may cause you to walk into a work presentation unprepared.

Anxiety is good for you! It prepares you to take action. It mobilizes your body for emergencies. It warns you about danger. Be *glad* you have some anxiety. Your anxiety helps you stay out of trouble.

Anxiety poses a problem for you when

- **It lasts uncomfortably long or occurs too often.** For example, if you have anxiety most days for more than a few weeks, you have reason for concern.

- **It interferes with doing what you want to do.** Thus, if anxiety wakes you up at night, causes you to make mistakes at work, or keeps you from going where you want to go, it's getting in the way.

- **It exceeds the level of actual danger or risk.** For example, if your body and mind feel like an avalanche is about to bury you but all you're doing is taking a test for school, your anxiety has gone too far.

- **You struggle to control your worries, but they keep on coming.** Regardless of what you do, anxious thoughts pop up over and over.

Presenting the Seven Types of Anxiety

Anxiety comes in various forms. The word "anxious" is a derivative of the Latin word *angere,* meaning to strangle or choke. A sense of choking or tightening in the throat or chest is a common symptom of anxiety. However, anxiety also involves other symptoms, such as sweating, trembling, nausea, and a racing heartbeat. Anxiety may also involve fears — fear of losing control and fear of illness or dying. In addition, people with excessive anxiety avoid various situations, people, animals, or objects to an unnecessary degree.

Psychologists and psychiatrists have compiled a list of seven major categories of anxiety disorders as follows:

- ✔ Generalized anxiety disorder (GAD)
- ✔ Social phobia
- ✔ Panic disorder
- ✔ Agoraphobia
- ✔ Specific phobias
- ✔ Post-traumatic stress disorder (PTSD)
- ✔ Obsessive-compulsive disorder (OCD)

You don't need a full-blown diagnosis to feel that you have some trouble with anxiety. Many people have more anxiety than they want but don't completely fit the category of having an official anxiety disorder.

Only a mental-health professional can tell you for certain what type of anxiety you have, because various other disorders can look similar.

Generalized anxiety disorder: The common cold of anxiety

Some people refer to *generalized anxiety disorder* (GAD) as the common cold of anxiety disorders because it afflicts more people throughout the world than any other anxiety disorder. GAD involves a long-lasting, almost constant state of tension and worry. Realistic worries don't mean you have GAD. For example, if you worry about money and you've just lost your job, that's not GAD; it's a real-life problem. But if you constantly worry about money and your name is Bill Gates or Warren Buffet, you just may have GAD!

You may have GAD if your anxiety has shown up almost every day for the last six months. You try to stop worrying but you just can't, *and* you frequently experience a number of the following problems:

> ✔ You feel restless, often irritable, on edge, fidgety, or keyed up.
>
> ✔ You get tired easily.
>
> ✔ Your muscles feel tense, especially in your back, neck, or shoulders.
>
> ✔ You have difficulty concentrating, falling asleep, or staying asleep.

Not everyone experiences anxiety in exactly the same way. Some people complain about other problems — such as twitching, trembling, shortness of breath, sweating, dry mouth, stomach upset, feeling shaky, being easily startled, and having difficulty swallowing — and fail to realize that they actually suffer from GAD.

The following profile offers an example of what GAD is all about.

> In a subway, **Brian** taps his foot nervously. He slept only a few hours last night, tossing, turning, and ruminating about the economy. He's sure that he's next in line to lose his job. Even though his boss says that he's safe, Brian can't stop worrying. He believes that he may end up broke and homeless.
>
> His back is killing him; he shrugs his shoulders trying to loosen up his tight muscles. He struggles to concentrate on the blog that he's looking at and realizes that he can't remember what he just read. He notices his shirt feels damp. He thinks he might be sick. He *is* sick — with worry.
>
> Brian has worked steadily at the same company since graduating from college six years ago. His work is highly technical. Most of the senior executives depend on his technology know-how. He has stashed away a nice amount of money for emergencies. Nevertheless, his anxiety has increased over the last year to the point that he notices that he's making mistakes. He can't think; he feels horrible and is in a constant state of distress. Brian suffers from GAD.

The economy can make anyone anxious at times. But Brian's worries seem out of proportion to his real situation. It seems unlikely that he's in danger of losing his job. However, his extreme anxiety may, in fact, cause him to get in trouble at work. People with overwhelming anxiety often make careless mistakes because of problems with attention and concentration. GAD takes everyday worries and turns up the volume to full blast.

Social phobia: Avoiding people

Those with *social phobia* fear exposure to public scrutiny. They frequently dread performing, speaking, going to parties, meeting new people, entering groups, using the telephone, writing a check in front of others, eating in public, and/or interacting with those in authority. They see these situations as painful because they expect to receive humiliating or shameful judgments from others. Social phobics believe they're somehow defective and inadequate; they assume they'll bungle their lines, spill their drinks, shake hands with clammy palms, or commit any number of social faux pas and thus embarrass themselves. They also worry about what others are thinking about them — so much that they don't listen well enough to keep a conversation going.

Everyone feels uncomfortable or nervous from time to time, especially in new situations. For example, if you've been experiencing social fears for less than six months, you may not have social phobia. A short-term fear of socializing may be a temporary reaction to a new stress such as moving to a new neighborhood or getting a new job. However, you may have social phobia if you experience the following symptoms for a prolonged period:

✔ You fear situations with unfamiliar people or ones where you may be observed or evaluated in some way.

✔ When forced into an uncomfortable social situation, your anxiety increases powerfully. For example, if you fear public speaking, your voice shakes and your knees tremble the moment that you start your speech.

✔ You realize that your fear is greater than the situation really warrants. For example, if you fear meeting new people, logically you know nothing horrible will happen, but tidal waves of adrenaline and fearful anticipation course through your veins.

✔ You avoid fearful situations as much as you can or endure them only with great distress.

Check out the following prime example of a social phobic and see whether any of it seems familiar.

Quinton, a 35-year-old bachelor, wants a serious relationship. Women consider him attractive and he has a high-paying job. Quinton's friends invite him to parties and other social events in an effort to set him up with women. Unfortunately, he detests the idea of going. Quinton conjures up a number of good excuses for backing out. However, his desire to meet potential dates eventually wins. Whenever he imagines scenes of meeting women, he feels intense, anxious anticipation.

When Quinton arrives at the party, he heads to the bar to quell his mounting anxiety. His hands shake as he picks up his first drink. Quickly downing the drink, he orders another in hopes of numbing his emotions. After an hour of nonstop drinking, he feels much braver. He interrupts a cluster of attractive women and spews out a string of jokes that he has memorized for the occasion. Then he approaches various women throughout the night, sometimes making flirtatious, suggestive comments. His silly, drunken behavior doesn't get him any dates. The following day, he's embarrassed and ashamed.

Quinton has social phobia. Drug and alcohol abuse often accompany social phobia because people with social phobia feel desperate to quell their anxious feelings. And drugs and alcohol offer a quick fix. Unfortunately, that fix often turns into an addiction.

Panic disorder: Way beyond everyday anxiety

Of course, everyone feels a little panicked from time to time. People often say they feel panicked about an upcoming deadline, an impending presentation, or planning for a party. You're likely to hear the term used to describe concerns about rather mundane events such as these.

But people who suffer with *panic disorder* are talking about entirely different phenomena. They have periods of stunningly intense fear and anxiety. If you've never had a panic attack, trust us, you don't want one. The attacks usually last about ten minutes, and many people who have them fully believe that they will die during the attack. Not exactly the best ten minutes of their lives. Panic attacks normally include a range of robust, attention-grabbing symptoms, such as

- An irregular, rapid, or pounding heartbeat
- Perspiring
- A sense of choking, suffocation, or shortness of breath
- Vertigo or lightheadedness
- Pain or other discomfort in the chest
- A feeling that events are unreal or a sense of detachment
- Numbness or tingling
- Hot or cold flashes
- A fear of impending death, though without basis in fact
- Stomach nausea or upset
- Thoughts of going insane or completely losing control

Panic attacks begin with an event that triggers some kind of sensation, such as physical exertion or normal variations in physiological reactions. This triggering event induces physiological responses, such as increased levels of adrenaline. No problem so far.

But the otherwise normal process goes awry at the next step — when the person who suffers from panic attacks misinterprets the meaning of the physical symptoms. Rather than viewing the physical symptoms as normal, the person with panic disorder sees them as a signal that something dangerous is happening, such as a heart attack or stroke. That interpretation causes escalating fear and thus more physical arousal. Fortunately, the body can sustain such heightened physical responses only for a while, so it eventually calms down.

Professionals say that in order to have full-blown panic disorder, panic attacks must occur more than once. People with panic disorder worry about when the next panic attack will come and whether they'll lose control. They often start changing their lives by avoiding certain places or activities.

The good news: Many people have a single panic attack and never have another one. So don't panic if you have a panic attack. Maria's story is a good example of a one-time panic attack.

> **Maria** resolves to lose 20 pounds by exercising and watching what she eats. On her third visit to the gym, she sets the treadmill to a level six. Almost immediately, her heart rate accelerates. Alarmed, she decreases the level to three. She starts taking rapid, shallow breaths but feels she can't get enough air. Sweating profusely and feeling nauseous, she stops the machine and staggers to the locker room. She sits down; the symptoms intensify and her chest tightens. She wants to scream but can't get enough air. She's sure that she'll pass out and hopes someone will find her before she dies of a heart attack. She hears someone and weakly calls for help. An ambulance whisks her to a nearby emergency room.
>
> At the ER, Maria's symptoms subside, and the doctor explains the results of her examination. He says that she has apparently experienced a panic attack and inquires about what may have set it off. She answers that she was exercising because of concerns about her weight and health.
>
> "Ah, that explains it," the doctor reassures. "Your concerns about health made you hypersensitive to any bodily symptom. When your heart rate naturally increased on the treadmill, you became alarmed. That fear caused your body to produce more adrenaline, which in turn created more symptoms. The more symptoms you had, the more your fear and adrenaline increased. Knowing how this works may help you; hopefully, in the future, your body's normal physical variations won't frighten you. Your heart's in great shape. Go back to exercising.
>
> "Also, you might try some simple relaxation techniques; I'll have the nurse come in and tell you about those. I have every reason to believe that you won't have another episode like this one. Finally, you may want to read *Overcoming Anxiety For Dummies* by Drs. Charles Elliott and Laura Smith (Wiley); it's a great book!"

Maria doesn't have a diagnosis of panic disorder because she hasn't experienced more than one attack, and she may never have an attack again. If she believes the doctor and takes his advice, the next time her heart races, she probably won't get so scared. She may even use the relaxation techniques that the nurse explained to her.

Help! I'm dying!

Panic attack symptoms, such as chest pain, shortness of breath, nausea, and intense fear, often mimic heart attacks. Alarmed, those who experience these terrifying episodes take off in the direction of the nearest emergency room. Then, after numerous tests come back negative, overworked doctors tell the victim of a panic attack in so many words that "It's all in your head." Many patients with panic attacks doubt the judgment of the physician and strongly suspect that something important was missed or wasn't found.

The next time an attack occurs, panic attack victims are likely to return to the ER for another opinion again and again. The repeat visits frustrate people with panic attacks as well as ER staff. However, a simple 20- or 30-minute psychological intervention in the emergency room decreases the repeat visits dramatically. The intervention is pretty simple — just providing education about what the disorder is all about and describing a few deep relaxation techniques to try when panic hits.

Agoraphobia: Panic's companion

Approximately half of those who suffer from a panic disorder have an accompanying problem: a*goraphobia.* Unlike most fears or phobias, this strange disorder usually begins in adulthood. Individuals with agoraphobia live in terror of being trapped. In addition, they worry about having a panic attack, throwing up, or having diarrhea in public. They desperately avoid situations from which they can't readily escape, and they also fear places where help may not be readily forthcoming should they need it.

The agoraphobic may start with one fear, such as being in a crowd, but in many cases the feared situations multiply to the point that the person fears even leaving home. As agoraphobia teams up with panic, the double-barreled fears of not getting help and of feeling entombed with no way out can lead to paralyzing isolation.

You or someone you love may have agoraphobia if

- ✔ You worry about being somewhere where you can't get out or can't get help in case something bad happens, like a panic attack.

- ✔ You tremble over everyday things like leaving home, being in large groups of people, or traveling.

- ✔ Because of your anxiety, you avoid the places that you fear so much that it takes over your life, and you become a prisoner of your fear.

You may have concerns about feeling trapped or have anxiety about crowds and leaving home. Many people do. But if your life goes on without major changes or constraints, you're probably not agoraphobic.

For example, imagine that you quake at the thought of entering large sports stadiums. You see images of crowds pushing and shoving, causing you to fall over the railing, landing below, only to be trampled by the mob as you cry out. You may be able to live an entire blissful life avoiding sports stadiums. On the other hand, if you love watching live sports events, or you just got a job as a sports reporter, this fear could be *really bad*.

Patricia's story, which follows, demonstrates the overwhelming anxiety that often traps agoraphobics.

> **Patricia** celebrates her 40th birthday without having experienced significant emotional problems. She has gone through the usual bumps in the road of life like losing a parent, her child having a learning disability, and a divorce ten years earlier. She prides herself in coping with whatever cards life deals her.
>
> Lately, she feels stressed when shopping at the mall on weekends because of the crowds. She finds a parking spot at the end of a row. As she enters the mall, her sweaty hands leave a smudge on the revolving glass door. She feels as though the crowd of shoppers is crushing in on her, and she feels trapped. She's so scared that she flees the store.
>
> Over the next few months, her fears spread. Although they started at the mall, fear and anxiety now overwhelm her in crowded grocery stores as well. Later, simply driving in traffic scares her. Patricia suffers from agoraphobia. If not treated, Patricia could end up housebound.

Many times, panic, agoraphobia, and anxiety strike people who are otherwise devoid of serious, deep-seated emotional problems. So if you suffer from anxiety, it doesn't necessarily mean you'll need years of psychotherapy. You may not like the anxiety, but you don't have to think you're nuts!

Specific phobias: Spiders, snakes, airplanes, and other scary things

Many fears appear to be hard-wired into the human brain. Cave men and women had good reasons to fear snakes, strangers, heights, darkness, open spaces, and the sight of blood — snakes could be poisonous, strangers could be enemies, a person could fall from a height, darkness could harbor unknown hazards, open spaces could leave a primitive tribe vulnerable to attack from all sides, and the sight of blood could signal a crisis, even potential death. Fear fuels caution and avoidance of harm. Those with these fears had a better chance of survival than the naively brave.

That's why many of the most common fears today reflect the dangers of the world thousands of years ago. Even today, it makes sense to cautiously identify a spider before you pick it up. However, sometimes fears rise to a disabling level. You may have a *specific phobia* if

✔ You have an exaggerated fear of a specific situation or object.

✔ When you're in a fearful situation, you experience excessive anxiety immediately. Your anxiety *may* include sweating, rapid heartbeat, a desire to flee, tightness in the chest or throat, or images of something awful happening.

✔ You know the fear is unreasonable. However, kids with specific phobias don't always know that their phobia is unreasonable. For example, they may really think that *all* dogs bite. (See Chapter 19 for more on specific phobias in children.)

✔ You avoid your feared object or situation as much as you possibly can.

✔ Because your fear is so intense, you go so far as to change your day-to-day behavior at work, at home, or in relationships. Thus, your fear inconveniences you and perhaps others, and it restricts your life.

Almost two thirds of people fear one thing or another. For the most part, those fears don't significantly interfere with everyday life. For example, if you fear snakes but don't run into too many snakes, then your fear can't really be considered a phobia. However, if your snake fear makes it impossible for you to walk around in your neighborhood, go on a picnic, or enjoy other activities, then it may be a specific phobia.

The following description of Ted's life is a prime picture of what someone with a specific phobia goes through.

> **Ted** trudges up eight flights of stairs each morning to get to his office and tells everyone that he loves the exercise. When Ted passes the elevators on the way to the stairwell, his heart pounds, and he feels a sense of doom. Ted envisions being boxed inside the elevator — the doors slide shut, and there's no escape. In his mind, the elevator box rises on rusty cables, makes sudden jerks up and down, falls freely, and crashes into the basement.

> Ted has never experienced anything like his fantasy, nor has anyone he knows had this experience. Ted has never liked elevators, but he didn't start avoiding them until the past few years. It seems that the longer he stays away from riding them, the stronger his fear grows. He used to feel okay on escalators, but now he finds himself avoiding those as well. Several weeks ago at the airport, he had no alternative but to take the escalator. He managed to get on but became so frightened that he had to sit down for a while after he reached the second floor.

> One afternoon, Ted rushed down the stairs after work, running late for an appointment. He slipped and fell, breaking his leg. Now in a cast, Ted faces the challenge of his life — with a broken leg, he now must take the elevator to get to his office. Ted has a specific phobia.

Ted's story illustrates how a specific phobia often starts out small and spreads. Such phobias gradually grow and affect one's life increasingly over time.

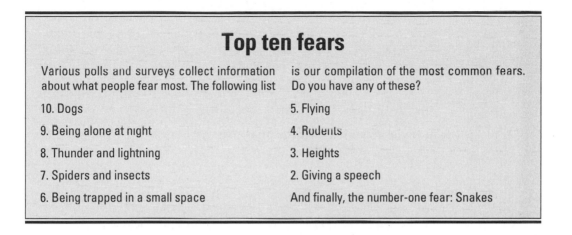

Top ten fears

Various polls and surveys collect information about what people fear most. The following list is our compilation of the most common fears. Do you have any of these?

10. Dogs

9. Being alone at night

8. Thunder and lightning

7. Spiders and insects

6. Being trapped in a small space

5. Flying

4. Rodents

3. Heights

2. Giving a speech

And finally, the number-one fear: Snakes

Post-traumatic stress disorder:
Feeling the aftermath

Tragically, war, rape, terror, crashes, brutality, torture, and natural disasters are a part of life. You or someone you know may have experienced one of life's traumas. No one knows why for sure, but some people seem to recover from these events without disabling symptoms. However, many others suffer considerably after their tragedy, sometimes for a lifetime. *Post-traumatic stress disorder (PTSD)* sometimes results from such shocks.

More often than not, trauma causes at least a few uncomfortable emotional and/or physical reactions for a while. These responses can show up immediately after the disaster, or, sometimes, they emerge years later. These symptoms are the way that the body and mind deal with and process what happened. If an extremely unfortunate event occurs, it's normal to react strongly.

You may have PTSD if you experience or witness an event that you perceive as potentially life-threatening or causing serious injury and you feel terror, horror, or helplessness. In order to have a diagnosis of PTSD, *three types of problems* must also occur:

✔ **You relive the event** in one or more ways:

- Having unwanted memories or flashbacks during the day or in your dreams

- Feeling the trauma is happening again

- Experiencing physical or emotional reactions when reminded of the event

✔ **You avoid anything that reminds you of the trauma** and try to suppress or numb your feelings in several ways:

- Trying to block out thinking or talking about the event because you get upset when you remember what happened

- Staying away from people or places that remind you of the trauma

- Losing interest in life or feeling distant from people

- Sensing somehow that you don't have a long future

- Feeling numb or detached

✔ **You feel on guard and stirred up** in several ways:

- Becoming startled more easily

- Losing your temper quickly and feeling irritable

- Feeling unable to concentrate as well as before

- Sleeping poorly

The diagnosis of PTSD is complicated. If you suspect that you may have it, you should seek professional help. On the other hand, you may realize that you have a few of these symptoms but not the full diagnosis. If so, and if your problem feels mild and doesn't interfere with your life, you may want to try working on the difficulty on your own for a while. But seek help if you don't feel better soon.

The following example of Wayne illustrates what living with PTSD is like. Wayne struggles daily with his demons.

> **Wayne** was late for work. He started the long trek from his car to his office at the Pentagon, and he heard the loud engine of an airplane just overhead. He was shocked to see how low the plane was flying. The next thing he knew, he was thrown to the ground by a loud explosion and a burst of wind. He remembers people streaming out of the building screaming and crying, some injured. Wayne can't recall many of the details of that day. He was told that his late arrival certainly saved his life. Many friends and co-workers weren't so lucky.

> Wayne believes he should be more grateful. Physically he was banged up a little. But his emotional injuries were extensive. Wayne has trouble sleeping. He tries to block the memories of that horrible day, but they seem to flood his brain. He can't concentrate, and he feels like he's in another world detached from others. He can't face going to work and takes an early retirement.

Wayne has PTSD. Like many others with the disorder, he witnessed a horrible event that his mind doesn't know how to cope with. Many veterans returning from active duty suffer from PTSD. Treatment can be very effective. See Chapter 8 for strategies.

Obsessive-compulsive disorder: Over and over and over again

Obsessive-compulsive disorder (OCD) wreaks incredible havoc on people's lives because OCD frustrates and confuses not only the people afflicted with it but their families and loved ones as well. If untreated, it's likely to last a lifetime. Even with treatment, symptoms often recur. That's the bad news. Thankfully, highly effective treatments are available. For much more information, read our book *Obsessive-Compulsive Disorder For Dummies* (Wiley).

Distinguishing between obsessions and compulsions

A person with OCD may exhibit behaviors that include an obsession, a compulsion, or both. So what's the difference between obsessions and compulsions?

Obsessions are unwelcome, disturbing, and repetitive images, impulses, or thoughts that jump into the mind. For example, a religious man may have a thought urging him to shout obscenities during a church service, or a caring mother may have intrusive thoughts of causing harm to her baby. Thankfully, people with OCD don't carry out these kinds of thoughts, but the obsessions haunt those who have them. Most people who have OCD know that their obsessions are not entirely realistic but can't seem to stop believing them.

Compulsions are repetitive actions or mental strategies carried out to temporarily reduce anxiety or distress. Sometimes, an obsessive thought causes the anxiety; at other times, the anxiety relates to some feared event or situation that triggers the compulsion.

For example, a woman may wash her hands literally hundreds of times each day in order to reduce her anxiety about germs, or a man may have an elaborate nighttime ritual of touching certain objects, lining up clothes in a specific way, arranging his wallet next to his keys in a special position, stacking his change, getting into bed in precisely the correct manner, and reading one section of the Bible before turning out the light. And if he performs any part of the ritual in less than the "perfect" way, he feels compelled to start all over until he gets it right. Otherwise, he worries that he won't be able to sleep and that something bad may happen to those he cares about.

Table 2-1 presents some common obsessions and compulsions experienced by those with OCD.

Table 2-1	Common Obsessions and Compulsions
Obsessions	*Compulsions*
Worry about contamination, such as from dirt, germs, radiation, and chemicals	Excessive hand-washing or cleaning due to the obsessive fear of contamination
Doubts about having remembered to turn the stove off, lock the doors, and so on	Checking and rechecking to see that the stove is off, doors are locked, and so on
Perverted sexual imagery that causes shame or thoughts that urge one to behave in a socially unacceptable way	Counting or repeating phrases or prayers to prevent oneself from carrying out shameful acts
Unwanted thoughts of harming someone	Repeating rituals over and over again, such as touching things in a particular sequence
Worries about death, bad luck, and catastrophes	Avoiding certain numbers, words, and places associated with death and bad luck
Worries that everything must be "just so"	Arranging items in particular patterns, alphabetically, or in some symmetrical order

Seeing OCD when it isn't there

You may recall walking to school with your friends and avoiding cracks in the sidewalk. If you stepped on one, perhaps someone chided, "If you step on a crack, you'll break your mother's back!" And sometimes you walked to school by yourself and that same thought occurred to you, so you avoided stepping on the cracks. Obviously, you knew that stepping on a crack wouldn't break your mother's back. So not stepping on cracks almost qualifies as a compulsion. That's because you may have done it repeatedly while knowing that it wouldn't stop anything bad from happening. If you did it simply as a game and it didn't bother you that much, avoiding cracks was no big deal, and it wasn't OCD. Besides, kids often have magical or superstitious thinking, which they usually outgrow.

On the other hand, if some part of you really worried that your mother might suffer if you stepped on a crack and if you sometimes couldn't even get to school because of your worry, you probably had a full-blown compulsion. Many people check the locks more than once, go back to make sure the coffeepot is turned off a couple of extra times, or count stairs or steps unnecessarily. It's only when doing these things starts taking too much time and interferes with relationships, work, or everyday life that you really have a problem.

Lisa's story depicts someone with OCD who worries about contamination. Like many people with OCD, her fears have some chance of coming true, but she greatly exaggerates the risks.

> **Lisa** likes a neat and clean home. In college, she ended up staying in a single dorm room because she couldn't stand the mess of other students. Now, married and with a new baby, Lisa spends hours cleaning and straightening the house. Her husband doesn't seem to mind. He works very long hours and likes coming home to a neat house and a hot meal.

> Lisa's television is usually on during the day while she cleans and tends to the baby. She first hears about a possible flu outbreak on cable news. The death of a toddler in a nearby state frightens her, and she begins obsessing about a worldwide pandemic. She believes that by sanitizing her house, she will keep the virus from infecting her family. Lisa orders her groceries and cleaning supplies over the Internet so that she can avoid leaving the house, fearing contamination. She now spends most of the day cleaning except when she is feeding the baby. Her husband, starting to get concerned, asks her if maybe she's becoming a bit too uptight about germs.

Like many people with OCD, Lisa's fear of germs starts off with a normal tendency to be clean and neat. However, OCD takes over her life when she can't seem to clean enough and constantly worries about getting the flu.

Seeing How Anxiety Differs from Other Disorders

Anxious symptoms sometimes travel with other company. Thus, you may have anxiety along with other emotional disorders. In fact, about half of those with anxiety disorders develop depression, especially if their anxiety goes untreated. Recognizing the difference between anxiety and other emotional problems is important because the treatments differ somewhat.

- **Depression:** Depression can feel like life in slow motion. You lose interest in activities that used to bring you pleasure. You feel sad. Most likely, you feel tired, and you sleep fitfully. Your appetite may wane, and your sex drive may droop. Similar to anxiety, you may find it difficult to concentrate or plan ahead. But unlike anxiety, depression saps your drive and motivation. For more information, see our book *Depression For Dummies* (Wiley).

- **Bipolar disorder:** If you have bipolar disorder, you seesaw between ups and downs. At times, you feel that you're on top of the world. You believe your ideas are unusually important and need little sleep for days at a time. You may feel more special than other people. You may invest in risky schemes, shop recklessly, engage in sexual escapades, or lose your good judgment in other ways. You may start working frantically on important projects or find ideas streaming through your mind. Then suddenly you crash and burn. Your mood turns sour and depression sets in. (Check out *Bipolar Disorder For Dummies* by Candida Fink, MD, and Joe Kraynak [Wiley] for more about this disorder.)

✓ **Psychosis:** Not only may psychosis make you feel anxious, but the symptoms also profoundly disrupt your life. Psychosis weaves hallucinations into everyday life. For example, some people hear voices talking to them or see shadowy figures when no one is around. Delusions, another feature of psychosis, also distort reality. Common psychotic delusions include believing that the CIA or aliens are tracking your whereabouts. Other delusions involve grandiose, exaggerated beliefs, such as thinking you're Jesus Christ or that you have a special mission to save the world.

If you think you hear the phone ringing when you're drying your hair or in the shower, only to discover that it wasn't, you're not psychotic. Most people occasionally hear or see trivial things that aren't there. Psychosis becomes a concern only when these perceptions seriously depart from reality. Fortunately, anxiety disorders don't lead to psychosis.

✓ **Substance abuse:** When people develop a dependency on drugs or alcohol, withdrawal may create serious anxiety. The symptoms of drug or alcohol withdrawal include tremors, disrupted sleep, sweating, increased heartbeat, agitation, and tension. However, if these symptoms only come on in response to a recent cessation of substance use, they don't constitute an anxiety disorder.

Those with anxiety disorders sometimes abuse substances in a misguided attempt to control their anxiety. If you think you have an anxiety disorder, be very careful about your use of drugs or alcohol. Talk to your doctor if you have concerns.

Chapter 3

Sorting Through the Brain and Biology

Most people with anxiety describe uncomfortable physical symptoms that go along with their worries. They may experience heart palpitations, nausea, dizziness, sweats, or muscle tension. Those symptoms are evidence that anxiety is truly a disorder of both the mind and the body.

In this chapter, we review some of the biological roots of anxiety, as well as the consequences of chronic stress on health. Then we tell you about medications or food that can actually make you feel anxious. Finally, we discuss how some illnesses can cause or mimic anxiety.

Examining the Anxious Brain

The brain takes in information about the world through sight, taste, smell, sound, and touch. Constantly scanning the world for meaning, the brain integrates information from the past with the present and plans what actions to take. For most people, most of the time, the brain does a pretty good job. But for those with chronic anxiety, something goes awry.

Billions of nerve cells *(neurons)* reside in the brain. They're organized into a variety of complex structures or circuits. Some of these structures are particularly involved in producing feelings of anxiety, fear, and stress. These brain structures communicate with one another by sending chemical messengers, known as *neurotransmitters,* back and forth among them.

In the following sections, we explain how the brain interprets information and what role the brain's chemicals play in making you anxious.

Seeing how the brain's circuits are connected

Think of the brain as having many interconnected circuits. One circuit involves the *limbic system* and the *frontal lobes.* The limbic system (particularly the *amygdala*) registers danger and threats and gives rise to reflexive fear responses. The frontal lobes use thought and reason to process incoming information. For example, the limbic system could set off alarms reflexively upon seeing a snake. However, the frontal lobes may signal the system to calm down as it processes the fact that the snake is in a glass cage.

In anxiety disorders, either the limbic system or the frontal lobes (or both) may fail to function properly. Thus, the limbic system may trigger fear responses too easily and too often, or the frontal lobes may fail to use logic to quell the fears set off by the limbic system. When the brain signals danger, the body responds by getting ready for action. The next section explains the chemical aspects of fear.

Communicating chemicals

Neurotransmitters help nerve cells communicate feelings, fears, emotions, thoughts, and actions through an intricate orchestration. Four major neurotransmitter systems and some of their functions include

- **The noradrenergic system,** which produces norepinephrine and epinephrine. It also stimulates organs required in the fight-or-flight response (see the following section).
- **The cholinergic system,** which activates the noradrenergic neurotransmitters and facilitates formation of memories.
- **The dopaminergic system,** which is involved in movement and is also related to feelings of pleasure and reward. Dopamine disruptions cause problems with attention, motivation, and alertness, and appear to be quite important in the development of fear responses.
- **The serotonergic system,** which is related to moods, anxiety, and aggression.

As these neurotransmitters pulse through your brain, the brain circuitry involved in fear and anxiety lights up. Your body then responds with a full-system alert known as the fight-or-flight response.

Preparing to Fight or Flee

When danger presents itself, you reflexively prepare to stand and fight or run like you've never run before. Your body mobilizes for peril in complex and fantastic ways. Figure 3-1 gives you the picture.

Your body responds to threats by preparing for action in three different ways: physically, mentally, and behaviorally.

> ✔ **Physically:** The brain sends signals through your nervous system to go on high alert. It tells the adrenal glands to rev up production of adrenaline and noradrenaline. These hormones stimulate the body in various ways. Your heart pounds faster and you start breathing more rapidly, sending increased oxygen to your lungs while blood flows to the large muscles, preparing them to fight or flee from danger.

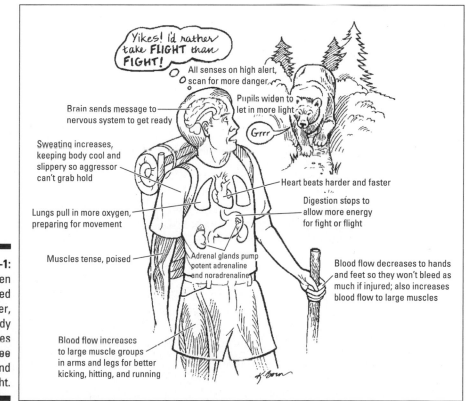

Figure 3-1: When presented with danger, your body prepares itself to flee or stand and fight.

Stress and the common cold

Research has shown that the way people perceive things — possibly more than what's happening in reality — affects the immune system and the tendency to come down with colds.

Psychologist Dr. Sheldon Cohen and colleagues have conducted research on the role of stress in susceptibility to the common cold virus. In one of his earlier studies, Dr. Cohen asked volunteers to describe their stress levels in the previous months. He then exposed the participants to the cold virus. Those who reported high stress came down with colds at far higher rates than the volunteers who reported having low stress.

A more recent study reported in the journal *Health Psychology* (2008) found that people's self-reported sense of their socioeconomic status also predicted who would come down with a cold after exposure to the virus. Those who felt themselves to be at a lower status level got sick more frequently than the others. Interestingly, objective measures of socioeconomic status were not so predictive of who would get colds. Thus, it seems it's people's perception of their socioeconomic ranking that matters, not the actual ranking itself.

These studies show that the mind and body have an intricate relationship. Other research has been consistent with this idea, showing that stress also slows wound healing, diminishes the effectiveness of vaccinations, and increases inflammation. In other words, the way people think about things that happen to them strongly affects their bodies.

Digestion slows to preserve energy for meeting the challenge, and pupils dilate to improve vision. Blood flow decreases to hands and feet to minimize blood loss if injured and keep up the blood supply to the large muscles. Sweating increases to keep the body cool, and it makes you slippery so aggressors can't grab hold of you. All your muscles tense to spring into action.

✔ **Mentally:** You automatically scan your surroundings intensely. Your attention focuses on the threat at hand. In fact, you can't attend to much of anything else.

✔ **Behaviorally:** You're now ready to run or fight. You need that preparation in the face of danger. When you have to take on a bear, a lion, or a warrior, you'd better have all your resources on high alert.

Granted, in today's world, you're not very likely to encounter lions and bears. Unfortunately, your body reacts too easily with the same preparation to fight traffic, meet deadlines, speak in public, and cope with other everyday worries.

When human beings have nothing to fight or run from, all that energy has to be released in other ways. So you may feel the urge to fidget by moving your feet and hands. You may feel like jumping out of your skin. Or you may impulsively rant or rave with those around you.

Most experts believe that experiencing these physical effects of anxiety on a frequent, chronic basis doesn't do you any good. Various studies have suggested that chronic anxiety and stress contribute to a variety of physical problems, such as abnormal heart rhythms, high blood pressure, irritable bowel syndrome, asthma, ulcers, stomach upset, acid reflux, chronic muscle spasms, tremors, chronic back pain, tension headaches, a depressed immune system, and even hair loss. Figure 3-2 illustrates the toll of chronic anxiety on the body.

Before you get too anxious about your anxiety, please realize that chronic anxiety contributes to many of these problems, but we don't know for sure that it's a major cause of them. Nevertheless, enough studies have suggested that anxiety or stress can make these disorders worse to warrant taking chronic anxiety seriously. In other words, be concerned, but don't panic.

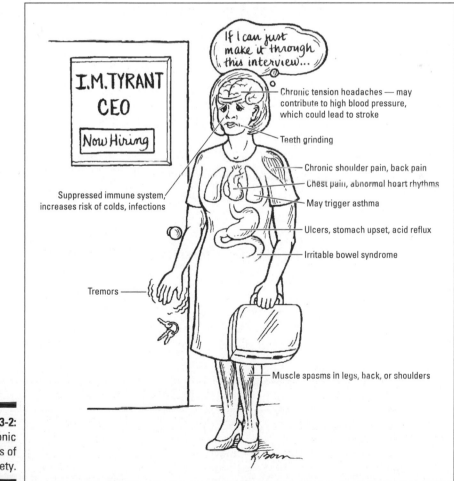

Figure 3-2:
The chronic effects of anxiety.

Defending against diabetes

As if the misery of chronic anxiety isn't enough, excess stress can deliver another wallop: People with long-lasting stress are significantly more likely to develop type 2 diabetes. This isn't surprising, because stress increases the levels of glucose (sugar) in the bloodstream.

Researchers at Duke University conducted a study with over 100 subjects and found that when stress management was added to the care of adults with diabetes, their blood sugar readings actually went down. These techniques weren't complex or time-consuming. In fact, many of them are the same techniques that you can read about in this book.

The amazing result of this study was that the glucose levels of those who found out how to calm down dropped as much as would have been expected had the subjects been taking an extra diabetes-control drug. So if you don't have diabetes, protect yourself by overcoming anxiety, and if you do have diabetes, know that calm thoughts may help you control the disease.

Mimicking Anxiety: Drugs, Diet, and Diseases

As common as anxiety disorders are, believing that you're suffering from anxiety when you're not is all too easy. Prescription drugs may have a variety of side effects, some of which mimic some of the symptoms of anxiety. Sometimes what you eat or drink can make you feel anxious. Various medical conditions also produce symptoms that imitate the signs of anxiety. We look at these anxiety imitators in the following sections.

Exploring anxiety-mimicking drugs

The pharmaceutical industry reports on the most widely prescribed categories of medications every year. To show you how easily medication side effects can resemble the symptoms of anxiety, we list ten of the most widely prescribed types of drugs and their anxiety-mimicking side effects in Table 3-1. These medications have many other side effects that we don't list here.

Table 3-1	Angst in the Medicine Cabinet	
Drug Name or Category	*Purpose*	*Anxiety-Like Side Effects*
Angiotensin-converting enzyme (ACE) inhibitors	Reduce high blood pressure	Impotence, dizziness, insomnia, headaches, nausea, vomiting, weakness

Drug Name or Category	Purpose	Anxiety-Like Side Effects
Anti-arthritic and anti-inflammatory medications	Treat arthritis and pain	Fatigue, anxiety, dizziness, nervousness, insomnia, nausea, vomiting, sweating, tremors, confusion, shortness of breath
Anti-ulcerants	Treatment of ulcers	Dizziness, anxiety, confusion, headache, weakness, diarrhea, flushing, sweating, tremors
Benzodiazepines	Treat anxiety	Dizziness, headache, anxiety, tremors, stimulation, insomnia, nausea, diarrhea
Beta blockers	Reduce angina and high blood pressure, treat dysrhythmia	Dizziness, diarrhea, nausea, palpitations, impotence, disorientation
Calcium channel blockers	Stabilize angina and reduce high blood pressure	Dizziness, flushing, palpitations, diarrhea, gastric upset, insomnia, anxiety, confusion, lightheadedness, fatigue
Codeine	Alleviate pain and manage nonproductive cough	Agitation, dizziness, nausea, decreased appetite, palpitations, flushing, restlessness
Selective serotonin reuptake inhibitors (SSRIs)	Treatment of depression, anxiety, and bulimia	Headache, insomnia, anxiety, tremor, dizziness, nervousness, fatigue, poor concentration, agitation, nausea, diarrhea, decreased appetite, sweating, hot flashes, palpitations, twitching, impotence
Statins	Cholesterol reduction	Headache, dizziness, diarrhea, nausea, muscle cramps, tremor
Thyroid replacement medications	Treatment of hypothyroidism	Hives, chest pain, irregular heartbeat, nervousness, shortness of breath

Interesting, isn't it? Even medications for the treatment of anxiety can produce anxiety-like side effects. Of course, most people don't experience such side effects with these medications, but they do occur. If you're taking one or more of these drugs and feel anxious, check with your doctor.

Angst from over the counter

One of the most common ingredients in over-the-counter cold medications is pseudoephedrine, a popular and effective decongestant that stimulates the body somewhat like adrenaline. I, Dr. Charles Elliott, specialize in the treatment of panic and anxiety disorders. A few years ago, I had a bad cold and cough for longer than usual. I treated it with the strongest over-the-counter medications that I could find. Not only that, I took a little more than the label called for during the day so I could see clients without coughing through sessions. One day, I noticed an unusually rapid heartbeat and considerable tightness in breathing. I wondered if I was

having a panic attack. It didn't seem possible, but the symptoms stared me in the face. Could I possibly have caught a panic disorder from my clients?

Not exactly. I realized that perhaps I'd taken more than just a little too much of the cold medication containing pseudoephedrine. I stopped taking the medication, and the symptoms disappeared, never to return.

So, be careful with over-the-counter medications. Read the directions carefully. Don't try to be your own doctor like I did!

In addition, various over-the-counter medications sometimes have anxiety-mimicking side effects. These include cold remedies, bronchodilators (for asthma), and decongestants. Also, many types of aspirin contain caffeine, which can produce symptoms of anxiety if consumed excessively. These medications can cause restlessness, heart palpitations, tension, shortness of breath, and irritability.

Ingesting anxiety from your diet

Stress and anxiety often provoke people to binge on unhealthy foods and substances, which may lead to increased anxiety over the long run. In Chapter 10, we discuss foods that may help you calm your moods and alleviate your anxiety. Here we tell you how to avoid foods or drinks that may worsen problems with anxiety.

Notice whether you have special sensitivities to certain types of food. Whenever you feel out of sorts or especially anxious for no particular reason, ask yourself what you've eaten in the past couple hours. Take notes for a few weeks. Although food sensitivities aren't generally a major cause of anxiety, some people have adverse reactions to certain foods, such as nuts, wheat, dairy, shellfish, or soy. If your notes say that's true for you, avoid these foods!

The chicken or the egg: Irritable bowel syndrome

Irritable bowel syndrome (IBS) is a common condition that involves a variety of related problems, usually including cramps or pain in the abdomen, diarrhea, and/or constipation. These occur in people with no known physical problems in their digestive systems. For many years, doctors told most of their patients that irritable bowel syndrome was caused by stress, worry, and anxiety.

In 1999, Catherine Woodman, MD, and colleagues discovered a mutated gene in patients with IBS more often than in those without it. Interestingly, that same rogue gene also occurs more often in those with panic disorders. Other possible physical causes of IBS may have to do with poor communication between muscles and nerves in the colon.

Various medications have been found to decrease some of the worst symptoms of IBS. In addition, psychotherapy that teaches relaxation techniques, biofeedback, and techniques for coping with anxiety and stress also improves IBS symptoms. So at this point, no one really knows to what extent IBS is caused by physical causes, anxiety, or stress. It's more likely, however, that the mind and body interact in important ways that can't always be separated.

Limit or avoid alcohol, which can make you feel tense in the long run. Alcohol may relax you in small quantities, so many people try to self-medicate by imbibing. However, people with anxiety disorders easily become addicted to it. Furthermore, in excess, alcohol can lead to a variety of anxiety-like symptoms. For example, after a night of heavy drinking, alcohol can leave you feeling more anxious because it clears the system quickly and the body craves more. That craving can lead to addiction over time.

Caffeine can also spell trouble. Some people seem to thrive on triple espressos, but others find themselves up all night with the jitters. Caffeine lurks in most energy drinks as well as chocolate, so be careful if you're sensitive to the effects of caffeine.

Speaking of energy drinks, these sometimes contain unusually large quantities of not only caffeine but also other stimulants. You'll see herbal stimulants such as taurine, guarana (loaded with caffeine), ginseng, and ginkgo biloba, among others. Reported adverse effects include nervousness, sleeplessness, abnormal heart rhythms, and seizures. If you have excessive anxiety, you don't want to be chugging down these concoctions.

Finally, lots of people get nervous after eating too much sugar. Watch kids at birthday parties or Halloween. Adults can have the same reaction. Furthermore, sugar is bad for your body in a variety of ways, such as spiking blood glucose levels and contributing to metabolic syndrome (a condition that often leads to high blood pressure and diabetes).

Investigating medical anxiety imposters

More than a few types of diseases and medical conditions can create anxiety-like symptoms. That's why we strongly recommend that you visit your doctor, especially if you're experiencing significant anxiety for the first time. Your doctor can help you sort out whether you have a physical problem, a reaction to a medication, an emotionally based anxiety problem, or some combination of these. Table 3-2 lists some medical conditions that produce anxiety symptoms.

Getting sick can cause anxiety, too. For example, if you receive a serious diagnosis of heart disease, cancer, or a chronic progressive disorder, you may develop anxiety about dealing with the consequences of what you've been told. The techniques we give you for dealing with anxiety throughout this book can help you manage this type of anxiety as well.

Table 3-2	Medical Imposters	
Medical Condition	**What It Is**	**Anxiety-Like Symptoms**
Hypoglycemia	Low blood sugar; sometimes associated with other disorders or can occur by itself. A common complication of diabetes.	Confusion; irritability; trembling; sweating; rapid heartbeat; weakness; cold, clammy feeling
Hyperthyroidism	Excess amount of thyroid hormone. Various causes.	Nervousness, restlessness, sweating, fatigue, sleep disturbance, nausea, tremor, diarrhea
Other hormonal imbalances	Various conditions associated with fluctuations in hormone levels, such as premenstrual syndrome (PMS), menopause, or postpartum. Highly variable symptoms.	Tension, irritability, headaches, mood swings, compulsive behavior, fatigue, panic
Lupus	An autoimmune disease in which the patient's immune system attacks certain types of its own cells.	Anxiety, poor concentration, irritability, headaches, irregular heartbeat, impaired memory
Mitral valve prolapse	The mitral valve of the heart fails to close properly, allowing blood to flow back into the left atrium. Often confused with panic attacks in making the diagnosis.	Palpitations, shortness of breath, fatigue, chest pain, difficulty breathing
Ménière's syndrome	An inner ear disorder that includes vertigo, loss of hearing, and ringing or other noises in the ear.	Vertigo that includes abnormal sensations associated with movement, dizziness, nausea, vomiting, and sweating

Chapter 4

Clearing the Roadblocks to Change

*T*he odds are that if you're reading this book, you want to do something about your own anxiety or help someone you love. If so, you should know that sometimes people start on the path to change with the best intentions, but as they move along, they suddenly encounter icy conditions, lose traction, spin their wheels, and slide off the road.

This chapter gives you ways to throw salt and sand on the ice and keep moving forward. First, we explain where anxiety comes from. When you understand the origins of anxiety, you can move from self-blame to self-acceptance, thus allowing yourself to direct your energy away from self-abuse and toward more productive activities. Next, we show you the other big barriers that block the way to change. We give you effective strategies to keep you safely on the road to overcoming anxiety. And finally, if you need some outside support, we give you suggestions on how to find professional help.

Digging Out the Roots of Anxiety

Anxiety doesn't come out of nowhere; rather, it typically stems from some combination of three major contributing factors. The primary villains underlying anxiety are

✔ **Genetics:** Your biological inheritance

✔ **Parenting:** The way that you were raised

✔ **Trauma:** Horrific events that sometimes happen

Studies show that of those people who experience an unanticipated trauma, only a minority end up with severe anxiety. That's because anxiety stems from a combination of causes — perhaps genes and trauma, trauma and parenting, or even all three factors may gang up to induce anxiety. Some people seem almost immune to developing anxiety, yet it's possible that life could deal them a blow that challenges their coping abilities in a way they couldn't expect. In the story that follows, Bonnie shows how someone can show resilience for many years yet be tipped over the edge by a single traumatic event.

> **Bonnie** manages to grow up in a drug war zone without developing terribly distressing symptoms. One night, bullets whiz through her bedroom window and one pierces her abdomen. She shows surprising resilience during her recovery. Surely, she must have some robust anti-anxiety genes and perhaps some pretty good parents in order to successfully endure such an experience. However, when she is raped at the age of 16, she develops post-traumatic stress disorder (PTSD; see Chapter 2 for more information). Bonnie has sustained one trauma too many.

Thus, as Bonnie's example illustrates, you can never know for certain the exact cause of anyone's anxiety with absolute certainty. However, if you examine someone's childhood relationship with her parents, family history, and the various events in her life (such as accidents, war, disease, and so on), you can generally come up with good ideas as to why anxiety now causes problems. If you have anxiety, think about which of the causes of anxiety have contributed to your troubles.

What difference does it make where your anxiety comes from? Overcoming anxiety doesn't absolutely require knowledge of where it originated. The remedies change little whether you were born with anxiety or acquired it much later in your life.

The benefit of identifying the source of your anxiety lies in helping you realize anxiety isn't something you brought on yourself. Anxiety develops for a number of good, solid reasons, which we elaborate on in the following sections. The blame doesn't belong with the person who has anxiety.

Guilt and self-blame only sap you of energy. They drain resources and keep your focus away from the effort required for challenging anxiety. By contrast, self-forgiveness and self-acceptance energize and even motivate your efforts (we cover these ideas later in the chapter).

It's in my genes!

If you suffer from excessive worries and tension, look at the rest of your family. Of those who have an anxiety disorder, typically about a quarter of their relatives suffer along with them. So your Uncle Ralph may not struggle with anxiety, but Aunt Melinda or your sister Charlene just might.

Maybe you're able to make the argument that Uncle Ralph, Aunt Melinda, and your sister Charlene all had to live with Grandma, who'd make anyone anxious. In other words, they lived in an anxiety-inducing environment. Maybe it has nothing to do with their genes.

Various researchers have studied siblings and twins who live together to verify that genes do play an important role as to how people experience and cope with anxiety. As predicted, identical twins were far more similar to each other in terms of anxiety than fraternal twins or other siblings. But even if you're born with a genetic predisposition toward anxiety, other factors — such as environment, peers, and how your parents raised you — enter into the mix.

It's how I was raised!

Blaming parents for almost anything that ails you is easy. Parents usually do the best they can. Raising children poses a formidable task. So in most cases, parents don't deserve as much blame as they receive. However, they do hold responsibility for the way that you were brought up to the extent that it may have contributed to your woes.

Three parenting styles appear to foster anxiety in children:

- ✔ **Over-protectors:** These parents shield their kids from every imaginable stress or harm. If their kids stumble, they swoop them up before they even hit the ground. When their kids get upset, they fix the problem. Not surprisingly, their kids fail to find out how to tolerate fear, anxiety, or frustration.

- ✔ **Over-controllers:** These parents micro-manage all their children's activities. They direct every detail from how they should play to what they should wear to how they solve arithmetic problems. They discourage independence and fertilize dependency and anxiety.

- ✔ **Inconsistent responders:** The parents in this group provide their kids with erratic rules and limits. One day, they respond with understanding when their kids have trouble with their homework; the next day, they explode when their kids ask for help. These kids fail to discover the connection between their own efforts and a predictable outcome. Therefore, they feel that they have little control over what happens in life. It's no wonder that they feel anxious.

If you recognize your own parenting style in any of these descriptions and worry that your behavior may be affecting your child, flip to Chapter 20 to see how you can help your child overcome her anxiety.

It's the world's fault!

The world today moves at a faster pace than ever, and the workweek has gradually inched upward rather than the other way around. Modern life is filled with both complexity and danger. Perhaps that's why mental-health workers see more people with anxiety-related problems than ever before. Four specific types of events can trigger a problem with anxiety, even in someone who has never suffered from it much before:

- ✔ **Unanticipated threats:** Predictability and stability counteract anxiety; uncertainty and chaos fuel it. For example, Calvin works long hours to make a decent living. Nevertheless, he lives from paycheck to paycheck with little left for savings. A freak slip on an icy patch of sidewalk disables him for six weeks, and he has insufficient sick leave to cover his absence. He now worries obsessively over his ability to pay bills. Even when he returns to work, he worries more than ever about the next financial booby trap that awaits him.

- ✔ **Escalating demands:** Having too much responsibility piled on your plate can make you anxious. Jake initially thinks that nothing is better than a promotion when his supervisor hands him a once-in-a-lifetime opportunity to direct the new high-risk research and development division at work. Jake never expected such a lofty position or the doubling of his salary this early in his career. Of course, new duties, expectations, and responsibilities come along for the ride. Jake now begins to fret and worry. What if he fails to meet the challenge? Anxiety starts taking over his life.

- ✔ **Confidence killers:** Unexpected criticisms and rejections can certainly trigger anxiety. Tricia is on top of the world. She has a good job and feels ecstatic about her upcoming wedding. However, she is stunned when her fiancé backs out of the proposal. Now, she worries incessantly that something is wrong with her; perhaps she'll never have the life she envisioned for herself.

- ✔ **Terrorizing trauma:** No one ever wants to experience a horrifying or even life-threatening experience. Unfortunately, these bitter pills do happen. Horrific accidents, acts of terrorism, pandemics, natural disasters, battlefield injuries, and violence have occurred for centuries, and we suspect they always will. When they do, severe problems with anxiety often emerge. Thus, survivors of tsunamis often have residual anxiety or PTSD (see Chapters 2 and 8) for years because of the totally unexpected nature of the event.

Finding Self-Acceptance

Time and again, we see our worried, tense clients suffer from another need-less source of pain. Their anxiety is bad enough, but they also pound on themselves *because* they have anxiety. Such self-abuse involves harsh, critical judgments. If you do this to yourself, we suggest that you try the following approach to self-acceptance.

Start by making a list of all the likely causes of your problems with anxiety. First, list any possible genetic contributions that you can think of in your relatives who may suffer from anxiety. Then review how your parents may have either modeled anxiety or instilled it in you because of their harsh or unpredictable parenting style. Then review events in your world from the distant to recent past that were highly anxiety-arousing. Finally, after you list the likely culprits that led to your distress, ask yourself some questions like the ones that follow:

- ✔ Did I ask for my anxiety?
- ✔ Was there ever a time in my life that I actually wanted to feel anxious?
- ✔ Am I primarily to blame for my worries?
- ✔ What percentage of the blame can I realistically assign to myself as opposed to genes, parenting, and events, both old and new?
- ✔ If a couple of friends of mine had troubles with anxiety, what would I say to them?
  - • Would I think they were to blame?
  - • Would I think as ill of them as I do myself?
- ✔ Does thinking badly about myself help me to get over my anxiety?
- ✔ If I decided to stop pummeling myself, would I have more energy for tackling my problems?

These questions can help you move toward self-acceptance and discover that having anxiety has nothing to do with your worth or value as a human being. Then you just might lighten up on yourself a little. We recommend it highly. Mind you, people get down on themselves at times. But chronic, unrelenting self-abuse is another matter. If you find yourself completely unable to let go of self-abuse, you may want to seek professional help (see the related section at the end of this chapter). You can read more about self-acceptance in Chapter 13.

Gary's story illustrates how reviewing the causes of your anxiety, followed by asking yourself those important questions, can help you acquire self-acceptance.

Anxiety among the rich and famous

So many of our clients seem to think that they're the only people in the world who struggle with anxiety. But we let them know that many millions of Americans suffer from anxiety. Perhaps you won't feel quite so alone if you consider some of the famous people throughout history who've suffered from one or more of the various anxiety disorders discussed in this book.

Reportedly, Albert Einstein and Eleanor Roosevelt both suffered from fears of social situations. Further, Charles Darwin eventually became a virtual hermit because of his disabling agoraphobia (see Chapter 2). Robert Frost also battled anxiety.

Billionaire Howard Hughes had many emotional problems — among them, apparently, a severe case of obsessive-compulsive disorder (see Chapter 2). Hughes insisted on having three copies of a magazine delivered to him. When delivered, Hughes removed the middle magazine with his hands covered in tissue paper. Then he would instruct an assistant to burn the other two magazines. In addition, Hughes had other bizarre compulsions involving preparation of his food, the handling of objects, and toileting.

Finally, a search on the Internet shows you that hundreds of celebrities reputedly suffer from all kinds of severe problems with anxiety. Use a search engine and type in "famous people and anxiety." You'll be surprised by what you find.

Gary has developed panic disorder. His attacks of feeling nauseous, dizzy, and thinking he's going crazy have increased recently. He feels shame that someone like him has this problem. When he starts having panic attacks at work, he seeks help. He tells his psychologist that a real man would never have this kind of problem. His psychologist helps Gary to be more self-forgiving. He asks Gary to write down the causes of his anxiety. He tells him to thoroughly review his life and come up with as many contributors to his anxiety as he can. Table 4-1 shows what Gary comes up with.

Table 4-1	Gary's Anxiety Causes	
Possible Genetic Influences	*Parenting*	*Events: Old and New*
My Aunt Mary hardly ever leaves her house. Maybe she has something like I do.	Well, my father had quite an unpredictable temper. I never knew when he'd blow.	When I was 6, we had a terrible car accident, and I spent three days in the hospital. I was very scared.

Possible Genetic Influences	Parenting	Events: Old and New
My mother is very high-strung.	My mother's moods bounced all over the place. I could never tell how she'd react when I asked her for something.	My middle school was in a terrible neighborhood. Gangs ruled. I had to look over my shoulder at every turn.
My cousin Margarite seems very shy. Maybe she has a lot of anxiety.		My first marriage ended when I caught my wife cheating. Even though I trust my new wife, I worry too much about her faithfulness.
My brother worries all the time. He seems totally stressed.		Two years ago, I was diagnosed with diabetes. I worry a lot about my health.

By reviewing the causes of his anxiety and asking himself the questions listed earlier in this section, Gary moves from self-abuse to self-acceptance. Now he's ready to work on overcoming his anxiety.

Having Second Thoughts about Change

Clearly, no one likes feeling anxious, tense, and nervous, and sometimes anxiety climbs to such heights that it overwhelms personal resources and the capacity to cope. Chronic, severe anxiety not infrequently serves as a prelude to serious depression. Obviously, anyone experiencing this torment would jump at the chance to do something about it.

With good intentions, people buy self-help books, attend workshops, and even seek therapy. They fully intend to make meaningful changes in their lives. But have you ever gone to a health club in January? It's packed with new, enthusiastic members. By mid-March, health clubs return to normal. Like so many New Year's resolutions, the initial burst of resolve too often fades. What happens to all that determination? Folks generally think they've simply lost their willpower. Actually, interfering thoughts creep into their minds and steal their motivation. They start to think that they don't have the time or the money or that they can get in shape later. Such thoughts seduce them into abandoning their goals.

Thoughts about abandoning your quest to overcome anxiety may disrupt your efforts at some point. If so, the first step involves identifying the thoughts that are streaming through your mind. The next step is to fight off these counterproductive thoughts; we give you strategies for doing just that in the following section. But first, in the style of late-night talk-show host David Letterman, here are our top ten excuses for staying stuck:

- **Number 10:** Anxiety isn't really that big a problem for me. I thought it was when I bought this book, but my anxiety isn't as bad as some of the people I've been reading about. Maybe it's not that big a deal.

- **Number 9:** If I try and fail, I'll make a fool of myself. My friends and family would think I was stupid to even try.

- **Number 8:** My anxiety feels too overwhelming to tackle. I just don't know if I could handle the additional stress of even thinking about it.

- **Number 7:** I'm afraid of trying and not getting anywhere. That would make me feel even worse than if I did nothing at all. I'd feel like a failure.

- **Number 6:** Feelings can't really be controlled. You're just fooling yourself if you think otherwise. You feel the way you feel.

- **Number 5:** I'll do something about my anxiety when I feel the motivation. Right now, I don't really feel like it. I'm sure the motivation will come; I just have to wait for it.

- **Number 4:** Who would I be without my anxiety? That's just who I am. I'm an anxious person; it's just me.

- **Number 3:** I don't believe I can really change. After all, I've been this way my entire life. Books like this one don't work anyway.

- **Number 2:** I'm too busy to do anything about my anxiety. These activities look like they take time. I could never work it into my hectic schedule.

- **And the number 1 reason people stay stuck:** I'm too anxious to do anything about my anxiety. Whenever I think about confronting my anxiety, it makes me feel worse.

Look over our preceding list several times. Mull over each excuse, and circle any that seem familiar or reasonable to you. Agreeing with any of these will hinder your progress. Now, we have some ways for you to challenge these excuses, no matter how reasonable they may seem.

Deciding to Get the Show on the Road

If any of our top ten excuses for staying stuck (see the preceding section) resonate with you, then your decision to overcome anxiety is not stable. Those thoughts can sabotage your best intentions. Don't underestimate their power.

The next two sections show you a couple of strategies for helping you turn your intentions into actions.

If you start losing your motivation or your belief in your ability to do something about your anxiety, come back to this section! It can help you get back on track.

Arguing with your arguments

Consider starting a notebook for carrying out various exercises in this book. Whether you use a notebook, computer file, or paper file, divide a page into two columns. Label the left column "Excuses" and the right Column "Arguments Against My Excuses." Under "Excuses" write each of the top ten excuses (see the earlier section "Having Second Thoughts about Change") that apply to you. Then, as a way to come up with arguments against your excuses, ask yourself the following questions:

- ✔ Does my excuse presume a catastrophe is coming?

- ✔ Am I exaggerating the truth?

- ✔ Can I find any evidence that would contradict my excuse?

- ✔ Can I think of people to whom my excuse doesn't apply? And if it doesn't apply to them, why should it apply to me?

- ✔ Am I trying to predict the future with negative thinking when no one can ever know the future?

Using those questions to guide your effort, jot down the best arguments you can for picking your excuses apart. The following example of Miguel shows how he attacked one of his most stubborn excuses for not changing.

> **Miguel** suffers from anxiety and has resisted dealing with his problem for years. He lists his major excuses for not doing anything and uses the preceding questions to develop arguments against them. He develops arguments for each of his excuses. Table 4-2 shows what he came up with for what he considered his most compelling excuse.

Miguel discovered that arguing against his excuses finally gave him the courage to start making changes. You can do the same.

Table 4-2	Miguel's Excuse versus Arguments Against His Excuse	
Excuse for Staying Stuck	*Arguments Against My Excuse*	
Feelings can't really be controlled. You're just fooling yourself if you think otherwise. You feel the way you feel.	Evidence tells me I've made other changes in my life. Many people go to therapy for some reason; surely it makes them feel better or there wouldn't be a zillion therapists in the world. My best friend overcame his anxiety, so why can't I?	

Taking baby steps

If you find that the idea of dealing with your anxiety is just too much to handle, you may be struggling with excuse number 8 for staying stuck (see the earlier section "Having Second Thoughts about Change"): "My anxiety feels too overwhelming to tackle. I just don't know if I could handle the additional stress of even thinking about it." In this case, it may help if you start by putting one foot in front of the other — take baby steps.

Stop dwelling on the entire task. For example, if you thought about all the steps that you'll take over the next five years, you'd be envisioning an incredible amount of walking. Hundreds, if not thousands, of miles await you. The mere thought of all those miles could stress you out.

You may, like many folks, wake up early in the morning on some days facing huge lists of things you need to do in the coming week. Ugh. A sense of defeat sets in, and you feel like staying in bed for the rest of the day. Dread replaces enthusiasm. If, instead, you clear your mind of the entire agenda and concentrate on only the first item on the list, your distress is likely to diminish, at least a little.

In order to take baby steps, it's a good idea to write down your overall, end-point goal. For example, perhaps you eventually hope to be able to give an hour-long speech in front of a crowd without being overcome with fear, or maybe you want to be able to master your fear of heights by taking a tramway to the top of a mountain.

Sit down and chart out your ultimate goal, and then chart a goal that isn't quite so lofty to serve as a stepping stone — an intermediate goal. Then chart out the action that would be required of you to meet that goal. If your intermediate goal feels doable, you can start with it. If not, break it down further into smaller goals, even baby steps. It doesn't matter how small you make your first step. Anything that moves you just a little in the right direction can get you going and increase your confidence with one step at a time. Here's how Paula put this plan into action.

Persevering through the peaks and valleys

A group of psychologists has conducted extensive research on how people make important changes, such as quitting smoking, losing weight, and overcoming emotional difficulties. They found that change isn't a straightforward process. It includes a number of stages.

Precontemplation: In this stage, people haven't even given a thought to doing anything about their problem. They may deny having any difficulty at all.

Contemplation: People start thinking about tackling their problem. But in this stage, it feels a little out of their reach to do anything about it.

Preparation: In preparation, people develop a plan for change. They gather their resources and make resolutions.

Action: The real work begins, and the plan goes into action.

Maintenance: Now is the time to hold one's ground. People must hang tough to prevent sliding back. During this phase, one wants to develop a plan for dealing with both expected and unexpected problematic events.

Termination: The change has become habit, so much so that relapse is less likely and further work isn't particularly necessary.

These stages look like a straight line from precontemplation to termination, but what these psychologists found is that people bounce around the stages in various ways. They may go from contemplation to action without having made adequate preparation. Others may reach the maintenance stage and give up on their efforts, slipping back to the precontemplation stage.

Many successful changers bounce back and forth in these stages a number of times before finally achieving their goals. So don't get discouraged if that happens to you. Keep your goal in mind, and restart your efforts if you slip. Yep. Try, try, and try again.

Paula has a social phobia. She can't stand the idea of attending social functions. She feels that the moment that she walks into a group, all eyes focus on her, which sends her anxiety through the roof. She desperately wants to change. But the idea of attending large parties or company functions overwhelms her with terror. Look at Table 4-3 to see how Paula broke the task down into baby steps.

Table 4-3	Paula's Baby Steps to Success
Goals	*Step-by-Step Breakdown of Actions*
Ultimate goal	Going to a large party, staying the entire time, and talking with numerous people without fear.
Intermediate goal	Going to a small party, staying a little while, and talking to a couple people although feeling a little scared.
Small goal	Going to a work-related social hour, staying 30 minutes, and talking to at least one person in spite of some anxiety.
First baby step	Calling a friend and asking her to go to lunch in spite of anxiety.

Paula found that starting with a brief phone call to a friend helped get her moving. From there, she moved to the next step and continued on. Some people find that breaking tasks down into many smaller steps helps, especially for formidable goals. See Chapter 8 for more information about taking action against anxiety in graded steps.

Watching Worries Come and Go

Sometimes anxiety feels like it will never go away. Believing that you have no control over it and that stress invades your every waking moment is easy. This section helps you to realize that anxiety actually has an ebb and flow. We show you how taking a few minutes to write down your feelings each day may discharge a little of your anxiety and possibly improve your health. We also help you understand that progress, like anxiety, ebbs and flows.

Following your fears

One of the best early steps that you can take to conquer anxiety is to simply follow it every day in a couple of different ways. Why would you want to do that? After all, you already know full well that you're anxious. Watching your worries is a good idea because it starts the process of change. You discover important patterns, triggers, and insights into your anxiety.

Observing anxiety fulfills several useful functions. First, monitoring forces you to be aware of your emotions. Avoiding and running away from troubling emotions only causes them to escalate. Second, you'll see that your anxiety goes up and down throughout the day — which isn't quite as upsetting as thinking it rules every moment of your life. And you're likely to discover that recording your ratings can help you to take charge and feel more in control of what's going on inside of you. Finally, keeping track helps you see how you're progressing in your efforts to quell your distress.

Track your anxiety in a notebook for a few weeks. Notice patterns or differences in intensity. Carry your anxiety-tracking notebook with you, and try to fill it out at the same time each day. On a scale of one to ten, ten being total panic and one being complete calm, rate the level of anxiety you experience around the same time in the morning, then again in the afternoon, and later in the evening. Virginia's story shows you how tracking anxiety can be helpful.

Virginia complains to her friends that she's the most nervous person on the planet and that she's close to a nervous breakdown. Recently, her father had heart surgery and her husband lost his job. Virginia feels completely out of control and says that her anxiety never stops. When her counselor suggests that she start tracking her anxiety, she tells him,

"You've got to be kidding. I don't need to do that. I can tell you right now that I'm anxious all the time. There's no letup." He urges her to go ahead and try anyway. Table 4-4 shows what Virginia comes up with in her first week of tracking.

Table 4-4	Virginia's Day-by-Day Anxiety Levels			
Day	*Morning*	*Afternoon*	*Evening*	*Daily Average*
Sunday	4	6	8	**6**
Monday	6	7	9	**7.3**
Tuesday	5	6	6	**5.7**
Wednesday	4	5	7	**5.3**
Thursday	3	8	8	**6.3**
Friday	5	9	9	**7.7**
Saturday	3	5	5	**4.3**
Average	**4.3**	**6.6**	**7.4**	**6.1**

Virginia discovers a few things. First, she notices that her anxiety is routinely less intense in the morning. It also escalates in the afternoon and peaks in the evenings. With only one week's records, she can't discern whether her anxiety level is decreasing, increasing, or remaining stable. However, she notices feeling a little better simply because she feels like she's starting to take charge of her problem. She also realizes that some days are better than others and that her anxiety varies rather than overwhelming her all the time.

Writing about your worries

Millions of people keep a diary at some point in their lives. Some develop daily writing as a lifelong habit. Keeping a journal of life's emotionally significant events has surprising benefits:

- Journal writing appears to decrease the number of visits people make to the doctor for physical complaints.
- Writing increases the production of T cells that are beneficial to the immune system.
- Keeping a journal about emotional events improved the grades of a group of college students compared to those who wrote about trivial matters.
- Recently, unemployed workers who wrote about the trauma of losing their jobs found new employment more quickly than those who did not.

The power of positive psychology

The field of psychology focused on negative emotions for most of the 20th century. Psychologists studied depression, anxiety, schizophrenia, behavior disorders, and a slew of other maladies. Only recently has the field looked at the pluses of positive emotions, the characteristics of happy people, and the components of well-being. People who feel grateful usually say they feel happier as well.

A study reported in the *Journal of Social and Clinical Psychology* (2000, volume 19) assigned people to three groups. The first group wrote only about the hassles of everyday life. The researchers asked the second group to write about emotionally neutral events. The third group journaled about experiences that they were grateful for. All the groups performed this task merely once a week for ten weeks. At the end of the experiment, the group that wrote about gratitude exercised more, had fewer physical complaints, and felt more optimistic than those in the other two groups. That such an easy, simple task could be so beneficial is surprising.

Throwing out the rule book

Journal writing doesn't have rules. You can write about anything, anywhere, anytime. However, if you want the full benefits of writing in a journal, we encourage you to write about feelings and the emotionally important events of your life. Write about anything that troubles you during the day and/or past difficulties. Spend a little time on it.

Writing about past traumas may bring considerable relief. However, if you find that the task floods you with overwhelming grief or anxiety, you'll probably find it helpful to seek professional assistance.

Counting your blessings: An antidote for anxiety

Writing about your distressing feelings makes a great start. However, if you'd like more bang for your buck, take a few extra minutes and write about what you feel grateful for each day. Why? Because positive emotions help counteract negative emotions. Writing about your boons and blessings improves mood, increases optimism, and may benefit your health.

At first blush, you may think that you have little to be grateful for. Anxiety can so easily cloud vision. Did your mother ever urge you to clean your plate because of the "starving kids in China?" As much as we think that pushing kids to eat is a bad idea, her notion to consider those less fortunate has value. Take some time to ponder the positive events and people in your life.

- ✔ **Kindnesses:** Think about those who have extended kindness to you.
- ✔ **Education:** Obviously, you can read; that's a blessing compared to the millions in the world with no chance for an education.

✔ **Nourishment:** You probably aren't starving to death, whereas (as your mother may have noted) millions are.

✔ **Home:** Do you live in a cardboard box or do you have a roof over your head?

✔ **Pleasure:** Can you smell flowers, hear birds sing, or touch the soft fur of a pet?

Sources of possible gratitude abound — freedom, health, companionship, and so on. Everyone has a different list.

The brain tends to focus on what's wrong or threatening in our lives. Noticing and actively appreciating what's right helps counteract that tendency and will make you feel better.

Getting Help from Others

If your problems with anxiety are significantly interfering with your life, you're probably going to want to work with a mental-health professional in addition to reading this book. In the following two sections, we tell you what kind of treatment to ask for and give you a set of questions to ask a potential therapist before you begin treatment.

Seeking the right therapies

Mental-health professionals offer a wide variety of treatments. We've thoroughly studied the research on what works for anxiety disorders so you don't have to. Studies *consistently* show that two treatments stand out as the most effective for this type of problem — cognitive therapy and behavior therapy, as well as a combination of the two (known as *cognitive behavior therapy* or *CBT*):

✔ **Cognitive therapy** focuses on teaching you new ways of *thinking*. People with anxiety often have distortions in the way they perceive events, and this approach helps you correct those distortions. For example, an anxious client may be overestimating the risks involved with flying. A cognitive approach would help her discover that the risks are small enough to warrant tackling her fear. See Chapters 5, 6, and 7 for a thorough discussion about how cognitive therapy can be applied to your problems with anxiety.

✔ **Behavior therapy** operates on the premise that changing the way you *act* or *behave* changes the way you feel about the things that happen in your life. Using the previous example of the woman with a fear of flying, a behavior therapist would likely help the woman go through a series of steps related to flying such as watching movies of flying, going to the airport, and eventually booking and taking a flight. Chapter 8 reviews how to bring behavior therapy principles to bear on your anxiety.

Other therapies work for other types of problems, and some also work for anxiety, too. But nothing has been shown to beat cognitive therapy, behavior therapy, and their combination (CBT) for anxiety disorders.

Medications also play a role in the treatment of some anxiety disorders. We usually don't recommend using them as your sole strategy, however. See Chapter 9 for a discussion of the advantages and disadvantages of medication for anxiety.

Seeking the right therapist

In addition to knowing the right therapy, you need to know whom to look for. Start by making sure that the therapist you seek is licensed to provide mental-health services, whether as a counselor, psychiatrist, psychiatric nurse, psychologist, or social worker. Sources for finding one of these licensed practitioners include local professional associations (such as state psychology associations, state counselor associations, and so forth), your primary healthcare provider, your insurance company, or trusted friends and family who can recommend someone.

After you've found someone who seems to fit the bill, be sure to ask the following questions:

- ✔ What are your charges for services, and does my insurance cover them?
- ✔ What are your hours?
- ✔ How soon can you see me?
- ✔ What is your experience in treating anxiety disorders?
- ✔ Do you take a cognitive or behavioral approach in treating anxiety?
- ✔ Are you willing to collaborate with my doctor?

You should feel comfortable talking with your therapist. After a few sessions, you should feel listened to and understood and sense that your therapist has legitimate empathy and concern for your well-being. Don't hesitate to inquire about the nature of your treatment plan — that plan should make sense to you. Most therapists take a few weeks getting to know you before they formulate an entire plan. If you're uncomfortable for any reason, by all means seek a second opinion from another therapist. Research shows that how you feel about the relationship with your therapist makes a big difference in how well the therapy goes.

Part II
Battling Anxiety

The 5th Wave   By Rich Tennant

"Well, Dad, if you're feeling down, why don't you watch some TV. Let's see, there's 'Silent Killers', 'When Puppies Attack,' and 'War of the Worlds.'"

In this part . . .

We talk about one of the most effective therapies for anxiety and show you methods for tracking your anxiety-arousing thoughts, along with ways to change anxious thoughts into calmer thinking. Next you see how the very words you use to think about yourself and the world can intensify anxiety. The good news is that you can replace your worry words with more reasonable language. In so doing, your anxiety decreases.

Then we describe the agitating assumptions that underlie many anxious thoughts. You discover which agitating assumptions plague you and how you can do something about them. We also show you how to battle anxiety by changing your behavior. This part concludes with a review of medical and biological strategies for treating anxiety.

Chapter 5

Becoming a Thought Detective

*T*houghts powerfully influence your emotions. At the same time, your feelings also influence your thoughts. In order to battle anxiety, you need to be aware of both your thoughts and feelings.

The following true story from our lives illustrates how profoundly thoughts influence the way people feel.

> Some time ago, we took a cruise to reward ourselves for completing a major project. One evening, we sat on deck chairs enjoying a fabulous sunset: Brilliant red and orange clouds melted into the deep blue sea The wind picked up ever so slightly, and the ship rolled gently. We sat relaxed, quietly enjoying the scene and the cradle-like motion. We reflected that in our lifetime, we had rarely felt so at peace.

> The captain's weather announcement interrupted our tranquil state of mind. Apologizing for the inconvenience, he informed us that because of a hurricane, he would have to steer a slightly different course, and we may feel some choppy seas. Still, he assured us that the storm presented no threat.

> The breeze suddenly felt chilling. The clouds, so spectacular before, appeared ominous. The gentle roll that had relaxed us now generated nervousness. Yet nothing about the sky or the sea had changed from moments earlier.

> Our thoughts jerked us from blissful relaxation to mounting anxiety. We pulled our jacket tighter and commented that the weather looked nasty, and perhaps we'd be better off inside.

Clearly, our thoughts, or the way we interpreted the weather, greatly affected the way we felt. A state of relaxed bliss turned into nervous anxiety even though the weather itself had not changed.

In this chapter, we show you how to become aware of your feelings and thoughts as well as the events that connect them. The goal is to become a thought detective, able to uncover the thoughts that contribute to anxious feelings. We show you how to gather evidence and put your thoughts on trial. We help you see how thoughts all too easily trigger your anxiety, and we give you proven techniques for transforming your anxious thoughts into calm thoughts.

Distinguishing Thoughts from Feelings

Psychologists often query their clients to find out how they feel about recent events in their lives. Frequently, clients answer with how they *think* about the events rather than how they *feel*. Others know how they feel but are stumped when it comes to what they're thinking. In the next section, we discuss why people often end up out of touch with their feelings, thoughts, or both. Then, we discuss how to tune your thoughts and feelings.

Blocking the blues

People often have trouble identifying and labeling their feelings and emotions, especially negative ones. Actually, the difficulty makes sense for two reasons.

First, emotions often hurt. No one wants to feel profound sadness, grief, anxiety, or fear. One simple solution is to *avoid* feelings entirely, and many creative ways to avoid emotion are available. Unfortunately, most of these methods can be destructive:

- **Workaholism:** Some folks work all the time rather than think about what's disturbing them.

- **Alcoholism and drug abuse:** When people feel bad, numbing their emotions with drugs and alcohol provides a temporary, artificial emotional lift; of course, habitually doing so can lead to addiction, ill health, and sometimes, even death.

- **Denial and repression:** One strategy for not feeling is to fool yourself by pretending that nothing is wrong. Denial is often thought to be a conscious process whereas repression is done outside of people's awareness, but the result is pretty much the same.

- **Sensation seeking:** High-risk activities, such as sexual promiscuity and compulsive gambling, can all push away distress for a while.

- **Distraction:** Athletics, entertainment, hobbies, television, surfing the Internet, and many other activities can cover up bad feelings. Unlike the preceding strategies, distraction can be a good thing. It's only when distractions are used in excess to cover up and avoid feelings that they become problematic.

The price of ignoring your feelings

In *Gone with the Wind,* Scarlet O'Hara says time and again, "I'll think about that tomorrow. After all, tomorrow is another day." What a nice, easy solution to tough times — shove the issue out of the way. But we're discovering more about the costs of avoiding and repressing emotions.

According to researchers at Adelphi University and the University of Michigan, people who declare themselves as mentally healthy over the years when other evidence shows they're not have higher heart rates and blood pressure in response to stress than folks who own up to their emotional difficulties or those who truly don't have problems at the time. Studies also show that when people write about their emotions on a daily basis, their immune system improves. Amazing stuff.

The second reason that identifying, expressing, and labeling feelings is such a struggle for people is because they're taught from an early age that they "shouldn't" feel certain feelings. Parents, teachers, friends, and relatives bombard kids with "don't feel" messages. See the following examples of "don't feel" messages that you've probably heard before:

- Big boys don't cry; don't be a baby!
- You shouldn't feel that way!
- Get over it!
- It couldn't possibly hurt that bad.
- Don't be a scared chicken.
- Stop crying or I'll give you something to cry about!

That many people are described as "out of touch with their feelings" is no wonder. The problem with the habitual tendency to avoid feelings is that you don't find out how to cope with or resolve the underlying issue. Chronic avoidance creates a certain kind of low-level stress that builds over time.

Getting in touch with your feelings

Noticing your emotions can help you gain insight and discover how to cope more effectively. If you don't know what your feelings are, when they occur, and what brings them on, you can't do much about changing them.

To illustrate problems with identifying feelings, we turn to Dr. Wolfe and her patient, Jim, who is struggling with his marriage.

Dr. Wolfe: How did you feel when your wife said you were irresponsible?

Jim: I thought she was really out of line.

Dr. Wolfe: I see. But how did you *feel* about what she said?

Jim: She's at least as irresponsible as I am.

Dr. Wolfe: I suppose that's possible. But again, what were your *feelings,* your emotional reaction to what she said? Were you anxious, even angry, or upset?

Jim: Well, I couldn't believe she could accuse me of that.

Dr. Wolfe: I wonder if we should take some time to help you get in touch with your feelings?

Perhaps Jim is extremely anxious and worried that his wife will leave him, or he may be angry with her. Maybe her stinging criticism hurt him. Whatever the feeling, both Jim and Dr. Wolfe could find out plenty from knowing what emotion accompanies his upset.

This example shows that people may not always know how to describe what they're feeling. If you don't always know what you're feeling, that's okay. We realize that some people are aware of their feelings and know all too well when they're feeling the slightest amount of anxiety or worry. If you're one of those, feel free to skip or skim the rest of this section.

If you need to become more aware of your feelings, you can start immediately. Take some time right now to assess your mood. First, notice your breathing. Is it rapid and shallow or slow and deep? Check your posture. Are you relaxed or is some part of your body in an uncomfortable position. Notice all your physical sensations. Tune in to sensations of tension, queasiness, tightness, dizziness, or heaviness. No matter what you find, just sit with the sensations a while. Then ask yourself what *feeling* captures the essence of those sensations. Of course, at this moment, you may not have any strong feelings. If so, your breathing is rhythmic and your posture relaxed. Even if that's the case, notice what it feels like to be calm. At other times, notice your stronger sensations.

Feeling words describe your physical and mental reaction to events.

The following vocabulary list describes anxious feelings. The next time you can't find the right words to describe how you feel, one of these words may get you started.

Afraid	Disturbed
Agitated	Dread
Anxious	Fearful
Apprehensive	Frightened

Insecure	Self-conscious
Intimidated	Shaky
Jittery	Tense
Nervous	Terrified
Obsessed	Timid
Out of it	Uneasy
Panicked	Uptight
Scared	Worried

We're sure that we've missed a few dozen possibilities on the word list, and maybe you have a favorite way to describe your anxiety. That's fine. What we encourage you to do is to start paying attention to your feelings and bodily sensations. You may want to look over this list a number of times and ask yourself whether you've felt any of these emotions recently. Try not to make judgments about your feelings. They may be trying to tell you something.

Bad feelings only cause problems when you feel bad chronically and repeatedly in the absence of a clear threat. Anxiety and fear also have a positive function: They alert your mind and body to danger and prepare you to respond (see Chapter 3 for more on the fight-or-flight concept). For example, if King Kong knocks on your door, adrenaline floods your body and mobilizes you to either fight or run like your life depends on it, because it does! That's good for situations like that. But if you feel like King Kong is knocking on your door on a regular basis and he's not even in the neighborhood, your anxious feelings cause you more harm than good.

Whether or not King Kong is knocking at your door, identifying anxious, fearful, or worried feelings can help you deal with them far more effectively than avoiding them. When you know what's going on, you can focus on what to do about your predicament more easily than you can when you're sitting in the dark.

Getting in touch with your thoughts

Just as some people don't have much idea about what they're feeling, others have trouble knowing what they're thinking when they're anxious, worried, or stressed. Because thoughts have a powerful influence on feelings, psychologists like to ask their clients what they were thinking when they started to feel upset. Sometimes, clients describe feelings rather than thoughts. For example, Dr. Baker had the following dialogue with Susan, a client who had severe anxiety:

Dr. Baker: So when your supervisor reprimanded you, you said you felt panicked. What thoughts went through your mind?

Susan: Well, I just felt horrible. I couldn't stand it.

Dr. Baker: I know; it must have felt really awful. But I'm curious about what thoughts went through your mind. What did you say to yourself about your supervisor's comments?

Susan: I felt my heart pounding in my chest. I don't think I really had any thoughts actually.

Dr. Baker: That's possible. Sometimes our thoughts escape us for a while. But I wonder, if you think about it now, what did those comments mean to you? What did you think would happen?

Susan: I'm shaking right now just thinking about it.

As this example illustrates, people don't always know what's going on in their heads when they feel anxious. Sometimes you may not have clear, identifiable thoughts when you feel worried or stressed. That's perfectly normal.

The challenge is to find out what the stressful event *means* to you. That will tell you what your thoughts are. Consider the prior example. Susan may have felt panicked because she feared losing her job, or she may have thought the supervisor's criticism meant that she was incompetent. The boss's reprimand may have also triggered memories of her abusive father. Knowing what thoughts stand behind the feelings can help both Dr. Baker and Susan plan the next step.

Tapping your triggers

You may not always know what's going on in your mind when you feel anxious. To figure it out, you need to first identify the *situation* that preceded your upset. Zero in on what had just transpired moments before your troublesome feelings. Perhaps you

- Opened your mail and found that your credit card balance had skyrocketed
- Heard someone say something that bothered you
- Read the deficiency notice from your child's school
- Wondered why your partner was so late coming home
- Got on the scales and saw a number you didn't like
- Noticed that your chest felt tight and your heart was racing for no clear reason

On the other hand, sometimes the anxiety-triggering event hasn't even happened yet. You may be just sitting around and *wham* — an avalanche of anxiety crashes through. Other people wake up at 4 a.m. with worries marching through their minds. What's the trigger then? Well, it can be an image or a fear of all sorts of future events. See the following examples of anxiety-triggering thoughts and images:

- ✔ I'll never have enough money for retirement.
- ✔ Did I turn off the stove before I left the house?
- ✔ We'll never finish writing this book on time!
- ✔ No one is going to like my speech tomorrow.
- ✔ What if I get laid off next week?
- ✔ What if my partner leaves me?

 When you get upset or anxious, take a moment to reflect. Ask yourself what event just occurred or what thoughts or images floated into your mind just before you noticed the anxiety. Bingo! You'll see what triggered your anxious feelings. After you see how to snare your anxious thoughts in the next section, we show you how to put thoughts and feelings all together.

Snaring your anxious thoughts

If you know your feelings and the triggers for those feelings, you're ready to become a thought detective. Thoughts powerfully influence emotions. An event may serve as the trigger, but it isn't what directly leads to your anxiety. It's the *meaning* that the event holds for you, and your thoughts reflect that meaning.

For example, suppose your spouse is 45 minutes late coming home from work. You may think *anxious* thoughts:

- ✔ Maybe she's had an accident.
- ✔ She's probably having an affair.

Or you may have different thoughts that don't cause so much anxiety:

- ✔ I love having time alone with the kids.
- ✔ I like having time alone to work on house projects.
- ✔ Traffic must be really bad tonight.

Some thoughts create anxiety; others feel good; and still others don't stir up much feeling at all. Capturing your thoughts and seeing how they trigger anxiety and connect to your feelings is important. If you're not sure what thoughts are in your head when you're anxious, you can do something to find them.

 First, focus on the anxiety trigger — the event or image that seemed to set things off. Think about it for a while; don't rush it. Then ask yourself some questions about the trigger. The following list of what we call *minding-your-mind questions* can help you identify your thoughts or the meaning that the event holds for you:

✓ Specifically, what about this event do I find upsetting?

✓ What's the worst that could happen?

✓ How might this event affect my life?

✓ How might this affect the way that others see me?

✓ Does this remind me of anything in my past that bothered me?

✓ What would my parents say about this event?

✓ How might this affect the way that I see myself?

Andrew's story illustrates how the questions about a triggering event can help clarify the nature of how one's thoughts influence feelings.

> **Andrew** loves his work. He manages computer systems and designs Web pages for small businesses in his community. Andrew believes in hands-on service and often visits his clients just to see whether things are running smoothly. One Friday, Andrew pulls up to one of the law firm offices he's working for and sees three police cars parked by the front door. Andrew's heart races, and he perspires profusely at the mere sight of police. He feels terrified, but doesn't know for sure what he's thinking.

In order to capture what's going on in his head, he answers a few of the minding-your-mind questions:

✓ **Specifically, what about this event do I find upsetting?**

Something violent may be going on. I've always been afraid of violence.

✓ **How might this event affect my life?**

I could get killed.

✓ **How might this affect the way that others see me?**

Other people will think I'm a foolish coward.

✓ **How might this affect the way I see myself?**

Like the coward I've always thought I was.

Andrew merely saw three police cars in front of a law office. Can you see where his mind took this event? Although workplace violence does occur, many other interpretations of this event are actually more likely. Nevertheless, Andrew needs to know what thoughts are running through his head when he feels anxious if he's going to be able to change how he responds to events like these.

When you work with the minding-your-mind questions, use your imagination. Brainstorm, and take your time. Even though Andrew's example doesn't answer all the questions, you may find it useful to do so.

Tracking Your Thoughts, Triggers, and Feelings

Monitoring your thoughts, feelings, and whatever triggers your anxiety paves the way for change. This simple strategy helps you focus on your personal pattern of stress and worry. The very act of paying attention brings your thinking process to light. This clarification helps you gain a new perspective.

Try using a thought-therapy chart like the one in Table 5-1 to connect your thoughts, feelings, and anxiety triggers. When you monitor the triggers, include the day, time, place, people involved, and what was going on. When you record your anxious thoughts, use the minding-your-mind questions in the "Snaring your anxious thoughts" section earlier in this chapter. Finally, write down your anxious feelings and physical sensations, and rate the severity of those feelings. Use 1 to represent almost no anxiety at all and 100 to indicate the most severe anxiety imaginable (sort of like how you might feel if 100 rattlesnakes suddenly appeared slithering around your bedroom!).

To show you how to use the chart, we've filled it in with Andrew's notes that he took for a few days after starting therapy for his anxiety about violence.

Table 5-1	Thought-Therapy Chart		
Anxiety Triggers	*Anxious Thoughts*	*Feelings & Sensations*	*Rating*
Tuesday morning on the way to work I heard a police siren in the distance.	I worried that a dangerous hot pursuit was in progress behind me.	Anxious, fearful, heart racing	75
At work on Wednesday I heard a sharp crashing sound.	I jumped and thought either a gun had gone off or something horribly destructive had occurred.	Jumpy and startled	70
I had to walk through a dark parking lot on Friday evening.	I imagined being mugged by someone jumping out from behind almost every car I passed by.	Tense, rapid breathing	65

You can use this simple technique to monitor your anxious feelings, thoughts, and triggers. Simply design your own thought-therapy chart using the headings of Table 5-1. Keep track, and look for patterns. Sometimes, just becoming more aware of your feelings, thoughts, and triggers can reduce your anxiety.

If recording your thoughts, feelings, and triggers makes you more anxious, that's okay. It's common. Many other techniques in this book should help, especially the ones for challenging your thoughts in this chapter. But if the techniques in this book don't help you, consider seeking professional help.

Although monitoring may produce useful insights that reduce your anxiety a bit, you, like most people, may need a little more assistance. The next section shows you how to tackle your anxious thoughts and make them manageable.

Tackling Your Thoughts: Thought Therapy

When you've snared what your anxious thoughts are on paper, you're ready for the next steps. In fact, we have three simple strategies for tackling your anxious thoughts:

- **Going to thought court:** Taking your thoughts to court and sifting through the evidence.

- **Rethinking risk:** Recalculating the odds of your anxious thoughts coming true — most people overestimate the odds.

- **Imagining worst-case scenarios:** Reexamining your ability to cope — if, in fact, the worst does occur. Most folks underestimate their coping resources.

Tracking anxious thoughts and events is an important step in arresting anxiety. But thought therapy takes those arrested thoughts, books them, takes them to trial, and throws them into jail. We show you how in the following sections.

Weighing the evidence: Thought court

The thoughts that lead to your anxious feelings have most likely been around a long time. Most people consider their thoughts to be true. They don't question them. You may be surprised to discover that many of your thoughts don't hold up under scrutiny. If you carefully gather and weigh the evidence, you just may find that your thoughts rest on a foundation of sand.

Keep in mind that gathering evidence when you're feeling really anxious isn't always easy to do. At those times, it's hard to consider that your thoughts may be inaccurate. When that's the case, you're better off waiting until you calm down before hunting for the evidence. At other times, you may be able to find evidence right away if your anxiety isn't too out of control.

You can evaluate the validity of your thoughts by first jotting down an anxiety-arousing thought that you take from the thought-therapy chart that we describe how to create in the earlier section "Tracking Your Thoughts, Triggers, and Feelings." Then, collect evidence that either supports the likelihood of your thought being true or disputes the likelihood of your anxious thought being true. Use the following questions to come up with disputing evidence:

- ✔ Have I had thoughts like these at other times in my life? Have my dire predictions come true?

- ✔ Do I have experiences that would contradict my thoughts in any way?

- ✔ Is this situation really as awful as I'm making it out to be?

- ✔ A year from now, how much concern will I have with this issue?

- ✔ Am I thinking this will happen just because I'm feeling anxious and worried? Am I basing my conclusion mostly on my feelings or on the true evidence?

- ✔ Am I assuming something without any solid evidence for my negative thought?

Feelings are always valid in the sense that you feel what you feel, but they're not evidence for supporting anxious thoughts. For example, if you feel extremely anxious about taking a test, the anxiety is not evidence of how you will perform.

These evidence-gathering questions can help you discover evidence against your anxious or worrisome thoughts, because an anxious mind already knows the evidence that supports anxious thoughts.

To see how this works, take a look at Andrew's notes in Table 5-2. Andrew was afraid that someone would hurt him and jumped to conclusions without evidence to support those conclusions. First, Andrew filled out the evidence supporting his anxious thought, which he found easy to do. Then he used the evidence-gathering questions in this section to list the evidence against his anxious thoughts in the second column of the table.

Table 5-2	Weighing the Evidence
Anxious Thought: I think I will probably get mugged here.	
Evidence Supporting My Anxious Thoughts	**Evidence Against My Anxious Thoughts**
People do get mugged, every day in fact!	I have this thought all the time and it has never once come true. It may be possible, but not likely.

(continued)

Table 5-2 *(continued)*	
Evidence Supporting My Anxious Thoughts	*Evidence Against My Anxious Thoughts*
It's dark out here.	I've walked in the dark hundreds of times without getting mugged.
My parents always warned me about the dangers in the world.	I have no real evidence that this parking lot is dangerous; after all, it's a good neighborhood!
I feel weak and vulnerable.	Just because I feel something doesn't make it true.

After completing the task, Andrew makes a new judgment about his anxious thought. He realizes that the evidence supporting his anxious thought doesn't hold up to scrutiny. He understands that his fears exceed the actual risks involved. He decides to take a self-defense class but to let go of his constant high state of alert (what shrinks call *hypervigilance*).

Consider filling out your own chart so that you can weigh the evidence carefully. Use the same column headings and format shown in Table 5-2. Be creative and come up with as much evidence for and against your anxious thoughts as you can.

Don't forget to use the evidence-gathering questions listed earlier in this section if you need help generating ideas.

Make a decision as to whether you truly think your anxious thoughts hold water. If they don't, you just may start taking them less seriously, and your anxiety could drop a notch or two.

Although charting your anxious thoughts and weighing the evidence just once may prove to be helpful, practice magnifies the effect. Mastering any new skill always requires practice. The longer you stay at it and the more times you chart your anxious thoughts versus the real evidence, the more benefit you'll gain. Many of our clients find that charting these out regularly for three or four months alleviates a considerable amount of their negative feelings.

Rethinking risk

Another important way to challenge your anxious thoughts is to look at how you assess the likelihood that an event may occur. When you feel anxious, like many people, you may *overestimate the odds* of unwanted events actually occurring. It's easy to do. For example, when was the last time you heard a news bulletin reporting that no one got bitten by a snake that day, or that half a million airplanes took off and landed and not a single one crashed? No

wonder people overestimate disaster. Because disasters grab our attention, we focus on dramatic events rather than routine ones. That's why it's useful to think about the real, objective odds of your predicted catastrophe.

Thoughts are just thoughts. Subject them to a reality test.

When you find yourself making negative predictions about the future — such as the horrible time you'll have at a party, your odds of failing a test, or the likelihood that you'll end up in financial ruin — ask yourself the following reassessment of risk questions:

- ✔ How many times have I predicted this outcome, and how many times has it actually happened to me?
- ✔ How often does this happen to people I know?
- ✔ If someone I know made this prediction, would I agree?
- ✔ Am I assuming this will happen just because I fear that it will, or is there a reasonable chance that it will really happen?
- ✔ Would people pay me to predict the future?
- ✔ Do I have any experiences from my past that would suggest my dire prediction is unlikely to occur?

In addition to asking these questions, whenever possible, look up the statistical evidence as it relates to your fears. Of course, you can't always find statistics that help you. Nevertheless, the answers to the preceding questions will help you reassess your true risk and stop habitually making catastrophic predictions about the future.

What are the odds?

On any given day, the odds of being struck by lightning are about 1 in 250 million, and the lifetime odds of being killed by a few other means are as follows:

- ✔ By a dog: About 1 in 700,000
- ✔ By a poisonous snake, lizard, or spider: About 1 in 700,000
- ✔ In air or space transport: About 1 in 5,000
- ✔ By a firearm: About 1 in 202
- ✔ In an auto accident: About 1 in 81

Notice how the actual odds don't match very well with what people fear most. Many more people fear thunderstorms, snakes, spiders, and flying in airplanes than driving a car or being killed by a firearm. It doesn't make a lot of sense, does it? Finally, we should note that your individual odds may vary. If you regularly stand outside during thunderstorms, holding your golf clubs in the air, your chances of being struck by lightning are a little higher than average.

The following story shows how Dennis overestimates the probability of a horrible outcome.

> **Dennis** rudely grabs the pan from his wife, Linda. He snaps at her, "I'll finish browning the meat. Go ahead and set the table." His abrupt demeanor stings Linda's feelings, but she knows how anxious he gets when company comes over for dinner. Dennis tightly grips the pan over the stove, watching the color of the meat carefully. He feels irritable and anxious, "knowing" that the dinner will turn out badly. He frets that the meat is too tough and that the vegetables look soggy from overcooking. The stress is contagious, and by the time the company arrives, Linda shares his worries.

What outcome does Dennis predict? Almost every time that he and Linda entertain, Dennis believes that the food they prepare will be terrible, their guests will be horrified, and he'll be humiliated. The odds of this outcome can't be looked up in a table or a book. So how can Dennis assess the odds realistically? Naturally, he answers the reassessment of risk questions and starts to change his anxious thoughts.

In doing so, Dennis comes to realize that he and his wife have never actually ruined a dinner, although he has predicted it numerous times before. Furthermore, he tested his second prediction that his guests would feel horrified if the dinner did turn out badly. He recalled that one time he and Linda attended a barbeque where the meat was burned to the extent that it was inedible. Everyone expressed genuine sympathy and shared stories about their own cooking disasters. They ended up ordering pizza and considered it one of the more enjoyable evenings they'd spent in a long time. The hosts, far from humiliated, basked in the glow of goodwill.

Deconstructing worrisome scenarios

Even faced with the evidence of the unlikelihood of the events you fear happening, you may be thinking that bad things still do, in fact, happen. Lightning strikes. Bosses hand out bad evaluations. Airplanes crash. Some days are just "bad hair days." Ships sink. People stumble and get laughed at. Some lose their jobs. Lovers break up.

The world gives us plenty of reasons to worry. Recalculating the true odds often helps. But you may still be stuck with the what-if worry — what if your concern truly happens? First we show you how to cope with smaller, everyday worries, and then we address worst-case scenarios.

Small-potatoes scenarios

What do people worry about? Most of the time they worry about inconsequential, *small-potatoes scenarios.* In other words, outcomes that, while unpleasant, hardly qualify as life threatening. Nevertheless, these small scenarios manage to generate remarkable amounts of stress, apprehension, and worry.

Listen to what's worrying Gerald, Sammy, and Carol. Their stories illustrate common concerns that lead people to feel highly anxious.

> **Gerald** worries about many things. Mostly, he worries about committing a social blunder. Before parties, he obsesses over what to wear. Will he look too dressed up or too casual? Will he know what to say? What if he says something stupid and people laugh? As you can imagine, Gerald feels miserable at social events. When he walks into a crowd, he feels as though a spotlight has turned his way and everyone in the room is staring at him. He imagines that people not only focus on him but that they also judge him negatively.

> **Sammy** worries as much as Gerald; he just has a different set of worries. Sammy obsesses over the idea that he'll lose control and have to run away from wherever he is. If he's sitting in a classroom, he wonders whether he'll get so anxious that he'll have to leave, and of course, he assumes everyone will know why he left and think something is terribly wrong with him. If he's at a crowded shopping mall, he's afraid he'll "lose it" and start screaming and running out of control.

> **Carol** is a journalist. She feels anxiety almost every day. She feels pressure in her chest when each deadline approaches and dreads the day when she fails to get her story in on time. Making matters worse, she sometimes has writer's block and can't think of the next word to type for 15 or 20 minutes; all the while, the clock advances and the deadline nears. She's seen colleagues lose their jobs when they consistently failed to reach their deadlines, and she fears meeting the same fate one day. It's hard for Carol to stop thinking about her deadlines.

What do Gerald, Sammy, and Carol have in common? First, they all have considerable anxiety, stress, and tension. They worry almost every single day of their lives. They can't imagine the horror of dealing with the possibility of their fears coming true. But, more importantly, they worry about events that happen all the time and that people manage to cope with when they do.

Gerald, Sammy, and Carol all underestimate their own ability to cope. What if Gerald spills something at a party and people around him notice? Would Gerald fall to the floor unable to move? Would people point and laugh at him? Not likely. He'd probably blush, feel embarrassed, and clean up the mess. The party and Gerald's life would go on. Even if a few rude people laughed at Gerald, most would forget the incident and certainly wouldn't view Gerald any differently.

Sammy panics over the possibility that his feelings may overwhelm him. He worries that he'll have to run from wherever he is and look foolish in doing so. The fact that this has never happened to him doesn't stop Sammy's worrying.

Carol, on the other hand, has a bigger worry. Her worst-case scenario involves losing her job. That sounds serious. What would she do if she lost her job?

Whether you experience small- or medium-sized worries (small- or medium-potato scenarios), you can use the following *coping questions* to discover your true ability to cope. The answers to these questions help you deal with your own worst fears.

1. **Have I ever dealt with anything like this in the past?**

2. **How much will this affect my life a year from now?**

3. **Do I know people who've coped with something like this, and how did they do it?**

4. **Do I know anyone I could turn to for help or support?**

5. **Can I think of a creative new possibility that could result from this challenge?**

Carol, who worried about losing her job, turns to these questions to help her come to terms with her fears. Carol writes these answers to the coping questions:

1. **Have I ever dealt with anything like this in the past?**

   No, I've never lost a job before. This first question doesn't help me discover any better ways of coping, but it does help me see the possibility that I've been overestimating the risks of losing my job.

2. **How much will this affect my life a year from now?**

   If I did lose my job, I'd probably have some financial problems for a while, but I'm sure I could find another job.

3. **Do I know people who've coped with something like this, and how did they do it?**

   Well, my friend Janet lost her job a few months ago. Janet got unemployment checks and asked her parents for a little assistance. Now she has a new job that she really likes.

4. **Do I know anyone I could turn to for help or support?**

   I'd hate to do it, but my brother would always help me out if I really needed it.

5. **Can I think of a creative new possibility that could result from this challenge?**

When I think about it, I really sort of hate these daily deadlines at the newspaper. I do have a teaching certificate. What with the shortage of teachers right now, I could always teach high school English and have summers off. Best of all, I could use those summers to write the novel I've always dreamed about writing. Maybe I'll quit my job now and do that!

It's amazing how often asking yourself these questions can eliminate the catastrophic consequences you associate with your imagined worry scenarios. Answering these questions can help you see that you can deal with the vast majority of your worries — at least the small- to medium-sized potatoes. But how about the worst-case scenarios (the really, really big potatoes)? Could you cope with real disasters?

Worst-case scenarios

Some peoples' fears involve issues that go way beyond social embarrassment or temporary financial loss. Severe illness, death, terror, natural disasters, disfigurement, major disabilities, and loss of a loved one are worst-case scenarios. How would you possibly cope with one of these? We're not going to tell you it would be easy, because it wouldn't be.

> **Marilyn**'s mother and grandmother both died of breast cancer. She knows her odds of getting breast cancer are higher than most. Almost every day of her adult life, she worries about her health. She insists on monthly checkups, and every stomach upset, bout of fatigue, or headache becomes an imagined tumor.
>
> Her stress concerns both her family and her physician. First, her doctor helps her see that she is overestimating her risk. Unlike her mother and grandmother, Marilyn goes for yearly mammograms, and she performs regular self-exams. Not only that, she exercises regularly and eats a much healthier diet than her mother or grandmother did.

Marilyn realistically has a chance of getting breast cancer. How would she possibly cope with this worst-case scenario? You may be surprised to discover that the same questions used to deal with the small-potatoes scenarios can help you deal with the worst-case scenarios. Take a look at how Marilyn answered our five coping questions:

1. **Have I ever dealt with anything like this in the past?**

   Unfortunately, yes. I helped my mother when she was going for chemotherapy. It was horrible, but I do remember laughing with her when her hair fell out. I understand chemotherapy isn't nearly as bad as it used to be. I never felt closer to my mother than during that time. We talked out many important issues.

2. **How much will this affect my life a year from now?**

Well, if I do get breast cancer, it will have a dramatic affect on my life a year from now. I may still be in treatment or recovering from surgery.

These first two questions focus Marilyn on the possibility of getting cancer. Even though she obsesses and worries about cancer, the intensity of the anxiety has prevented her from ever contemplating how she would deal with cancer if it actually occurred. Although she certainly hates the thought of chemotherapy or surgery, after she imagines the possibility, she realizes she could probably cope with them.

The more you avoid a fear, the more terrifying it becomes.

3. **Do I know people who've coped with something like this, and how did they do it?**

   Of course, my mother died of breast cancer. But during the last three years of her life, she enjoyed each moment. She got closer to all her kids and made many new friends. It's funny, but now that I think about it, I think she was happier during that time than any other time I can remember.

4. **Do I know anyone I could turn to for help or support?**

   I know of a cancer support group in town. And my husband and sister would do anything for me.

5. **Can I think of a creative new possibility that could result from this challenge?**

   I never thought of cancer as a challenge; it was a curse. But I guess I realize now that I can choose to be anxious and worried about it or just take care of myself and live life fully. If I do get cancer, I can hopefully help others like my mother did, and I'll use the time I have in a positive way. Besides, there's a good chance that I could beat cancer, and with medical advances, those chances improve all the time. Meanwhile, I'm going to make sure that I don't wait until my final days to get close to my family.

When you have anxiety about something dreadful happening, it's important to stop avoiding the end of the story. Go there. The more you avoid contemplating the worst, the bigger the fear gets. In our work, we repeatedly find that our clients come up with coping strategies for the worst-case scenario, even the big stuff. Consider George's case.

George fears flying. He recalculates the risks of flying and realizes they're low. He says, "I know it's relatively safe and that helps a little, but it still scares me." Recently, George got a promotion. Unfortunately for George, the new position requires considerable travel. George's worst nightmare is that the plane will crash. George asks himself our coping questions and answers them as follows:

1. **Have I ever dealt with anything like this in the past?**

   No, I've obviously never been in a plane crash before.

2. **How much will this affect my life a year from now?**

   Not much, I'd be dead!

3. **Do I know people who've coped with something like this, and how did they do it?**

   No. None of my friends, relatives, or acquaintances has ever been in a plane crash.

4. **Do I know anyone I could turn to for help or support?**

   Obviously not. I mean, what could they do?

5. **Can I think of a creative new possibility that could result from this challenge?**

   How? In the few minutes I'd have on the way down, it's doubtful that many creative possibilities would occur to me.

Hmm. George didn't seem to get much out of our coping questions, did he? These questions don't do much good for a small number of worst-case scenarios. For those situations, we have the *ultimate coping questions,* followed by George's responses to these questions:

1. **What is it about this eventuality that makes you think you absolutely could not cope and could not possibly stand it?**

   Okay, I can imagine two different plane crashes. In one, the plane would explode and I probably wouldn't even know what happened. In the other, something would happen to the engine, and I'd experience several minutes of absolute terror. That's what I really fear.

2. **Is it possible that you really could deal with it?**

   Could I deal with that? I guess I never thought of that before; it seemed too scary to contemplate. If I really put myself in the plane, I'd probably be gripping the seat, maybe even screaming, but I guess it wouldn't last for long. I suppose I could stand almost anything for a short while. At least if I went down in a plane, I know my family would be well taken care of. When I really think about it, as unpleasant as it seems, I guess I could deal with it. I'd have to.

Most people fear dying to some extent — even those with strong religious convictions (which can help) rarely welcome the thought. Nevertheless, death is a universal experience. Although most people would prefer a painless, quick exit during sleep, many deaths aren't as easy.

If a particular way of dying frightens you, actively contemplating it works better than trying to block it out of your mind. If you do this, you're likely to discover that, like George, you can deal with and accept almost any eventuality.

If you find yourself getting exceptionally anxious or upset by such contemplation, professional help may be useful.

Cultivating Calm Thinking

Anxious thoughts capture your attention. They hold your reasonable mind hostage. They demand all your calmness and serenity as ransom. Thus, when you have anxious thoughts, it helps to pursue and destroy them by weighing the evidence, reassessing the odds, and reviewing your true ability to cope (see the previous sections for the how-tos).

Another option is to crowd out your anxious thoughts with calm thoughts. You can accomplish this task by using one of three techniques. You can try what we call the friend perspective; you can construct new, calm thoughts to replace your old, anxious thoughts; or you can try positive affirmations.

Considering a "friend's" perspective

Sometimes, simple strategies work wonders. This can be one of them. When your anxious thoughts hold most of your reasonable mind hostage, you still have a friend in reserve who can help you find a fresh perspective. Where? Within yourself.

Try this technique when you're all alone — alone, that is, except for your friend within. Truly imagine that a good friend is sitting across from you and talk out loud. Imagine that your friend has exactly the same problem that you do. Take your time, and really try to help your friend. Brainstorm with your friend. You don't have to come up with instant or perfect solutions. Seek out every idea you can, even if it sounds foolish at first — it just may lead you to a creative solution. This approach works because it helps you pull back from the overwhelming emotions that block good, reasonable thinking. Don't dismiss this strategy just because of its simplicity!

Juan's example demonstrates this technique in action.

>**Juan** worries about his bills. He has a charge card balance of a few thousand dollars. His car insurance comes due in a couple of weeks, and

he doesn't have the money to pay for it. When Juan contemplates his worry, he thinks that maybe he'll go broke, his car will be repossessed, and eventually, he'll lose his house. He feels he has no options and that his situation is hopeless. Juan loses sleep because of his worry. Anxiety shuts down his ability to reason and analyze his dilemma.

Now, we ask Juan to help an old friend. We tell him to imagine Richard, a friend of his, is sitting in a chair across from him. His friend is in a financial bind and needs advice on what to do. Richard fears he will lose everything if he can't come up with some money to pay his car insurance. We ask Juan to come up with some ideas for Richard.

Surprising to Juan, but not to us, he comes up with a cornucopia of good ideas. He tells Richard, "Talk to your insurance agent about making payments monthly rather than every six months. Also, you can get an advance on your credit card. Furthermore, isn't there an opportunity to do some overtime work? Talk to a credit counselor. Couldn't one of your relatives loan you a few hundred dollars? In the long run, you need to chip away at that credit-card debt and pull back a little on your spending."

Creating calm

Another way to create calm thoughts is to look at your anxious thoughts and develop a more reasonable perspective. The key with this approach is to put it on paper. Leaving it in your head doesn't do nearly as much good.

This strategy doesn't equate with mere positive thinking, because it doesn't help you create a Pollyanna alternative — that is, a thought that is unrealistically optimistic. Be sure that your reasonable perspective is something that you can at least partially believe in. In other words, your emotional side may not fully buy into your alternative view at first, but the new view should be something that a reasonable person would find believable.

Your task will be easier if you've already subjected your anxious thinking to weighing the evidence, rethinking the risk, and reevaluating your coping resources for dealing with your imagined worst-case scenarios, as we describe in earlier sections.

Table 5-3 provides some examples of anxious thoughts and their reasonable alternatives. We also provide you with a Pollyanna perspective that we *don't* think is useful.

Table 5-3	Developing a Reasonable Perspective	
Anxious Thought	*Reasonable Alternative*	*Pollyanna Perspective*
If I wear a tie and no one else does, I'll look like an idiot.	If no one else wears a tie, some people will no doubt notice. However, they probably won't make a big deal out of it. Even if a couple of people do, it really won't matter to me at all a few weeks from now.	Everyone will think I look great no matter what!
If I get a C on this exam, I'll be humiliated. I have to be at the top of my class. I couldn't stand it if I wasn't.	If I get a C, I certainly won't be happy. But I'll still have a good grade average and a good chance at a scholarship. I'll just work harder the next time. I'd love to be at the top of my class, but life will go on just fine if I fall short of that.	There's no way that I won't get an A. I must, and I shall.
If I lose my job, in a matter of weeks I'll be bankrupt.	If I lose my job, it will cause some hardship. However, odds are good I'll find another one. And my wife has offered to increase her hours to help out if I need her to.	I could never lose my job!
I'd rather walk up 20 flights of stairs than take this elevator. The thought of the doors closing terrifies me.	It's time I tackled this fear, because the odds of an elevator crash are infinitesimally small. Taking the elevator is pretty scary, but perhaps I can start by just riding up or down a couple of floors and work my way on from there.	I need to quit being such a wimp. I'm just going to jump on this thing and take it to the top!

We showed you the Pollyanna perspective because it's important not to go there. You may think the last example of the Pollyanna perspective — getting over your fear in an instant — looks great. That would be nice, we suppose, if only it worked that way. The problem with that approach is that you set yourself up for failure if you try it. Imagine someone truly terrified of elevators trying to jump on and take it to the top floor all at once. More likely than not, the person would do it that one time, feel horror, and make the fear even worse.

Be gentle with yourself; go slowly when confronting your anxious thoughts and fears.

Affirming affirmations?

The field of mental health has a long tradition of advocating that people use affirmations to improve their emotional well-being. Stuart Smalley, a character played by Al Franken on *Saturday Night Live,* used to look in the mirror and say, "I'm good enough; I'm smart enough; and doggone it, people like me." Does this approach for managing emotions really help?

Many people swear by the value of positive self-affirmations. However, a 2009 study reported in the journal *Psychological Science* suggests that positive affirmations may actually cause harm to some people. Although the doctors who conducted the study found that people with high self-esteem seem to feel better after repeating positive self-affirmations, those with low self-esteem reported actually feeling worse after doing so. This result may be due to the fact that positive self-affirmations feel unbelievable and out of contact with reality to people with really low opinions of themselves.

So, if you're tempted to use positive self-affirmations, we recommend that you make sure you design statements that feel reasonably believable to you. Good statements often include reminders to cope or calm down. Some of our favorites include:

- Relax.
- With time, I can get through this.
- I need to keep at this.
- I don't have to be perfect.
- Mistakes are not awful.
- Breathe in and out very slowly.
- Next year (or next month), this won't matter.

Repetition does help information sink in and feel like part of you. Be sure that whatever you repeat to yourself feels reasonable to you.

Chapter 6

Watching Out for Worry Words

● ●

● ●

*T*hink about the mental chatter that goes on in your mind. Do you ever exaggerate? Put yourself down? Predict horrible outcomes? For example, if your computer is acting up, do you get angry at yourself, predict that you'll never get anything done, and surmise that the day will surely be ruined? Those inner conversations can stir up a whirlwind of anxiety.

This chapter helps you discover what words contribute to your anxiety. They come in several forms and categories, and we show you how to track these words down. Then we offer strategies for finding alternative words and phrases to quell your unnecessary anxiety.

Stacking Sticks into Bonfires of Anxiety

"Sticks and stones can break my bones, but words can never hurt me." Perhaps you heard this saying as a child. Parents often try to assuage their kids' hurt feelings through this catchphrase, but it usually doesn't work because words do have power. Words can frighten, judge, and hurt.

If those words came only from other people, that would hurt enough. But the words that you use to describe yourself, your world, your actions, and your future may have an even greater impact on you than what you hear from others. The example of Jason and his wife Beverly illustrates this point. What starts out as a simple conversation between husband and wife leads to lots of anxiety and marital stress.

Jason's wife Beverly, who's a little worried about her husband's blood pressure, mentions at breakfast that it looks like he's gained a little weight. "Oh, really?" Jason queries.

"Maybe just a little bit; it's no big deal. I just worry about your health," she replies.

Over the course of the next few hours, Jason starts ruminating about what his wife said. "I'm a *pig* . . . She's *totally disgusted* with me . . . She'll *never* want to have sex with me again . . . Losing weight is *impossible* for me . . . I'm *certain* that she'll leave me; that would be *unbearable*."

By the afternoon, Jason feels intense anxiety and tension. He's so upset that he withdraws and sulks through the rest of the day. Beverly knows something's wrong and worries that Jason is losing interest in her.

What happened? First, Beverly delivered a fairly mild statement to Jason. Then, rather than ask Beverly for clarification, Jason pounded himself with a slurry of anxiety-arousing words — *pig, totally disgusted, never, impossible, certain,* and *unbearable.* Jason's mind overflowed with powerful words that grossly distorted Beverly's original intention. His inner thoughts no longer had any connection to reality.

The worry words that you use inflame anxiety easily and are rarely supported by evidence or reality. They become bad habits that people use unwittingly. However, we have good news: Like any habit, the anxiety-arousing word habit can be broken.

Worry words come in four major categories. In the upcoming sections, we go through each of them with you carefully:

- **Extremist:** Words that exaggerate or turn a minor event into a catastrophe

- **All-or-none:** Polar opposites with nothing in between

- **Judging, commanding, and labeling:** Stern evaluations and name-calling

- **Victim:** Underestimating your ability to cope

Encountering extremist words

It's amazing how selecting certain words to describe events can literally make mountains out of molehills. Extremist words grossly magnify or exaggerate troubling situations. In doing so, they aggravate negative emotions. Read about Emily, who turns a fender bender into a catastrophe.

Emily, pulling out of a tight parking spot at the grocery store, hears metal scraping metal. Her bumper dents a side panel of a late-model SUV parked next to her. Emily stomps on the brake, jams her car into park, and leaps out to inspect the damage — a 4-inch gash.

Using her cellphone, she calls her husband, Ron. Hysterical, she cries, "There's been a *horrible* accident. I *destroyed* the other car. I feel *awful;* I just *can't stand it.*" Ron attempts to calm his wife and rushes to the scene from work. When he arrives, he's not that surprised to find the damage to be quite minor. He's well aware of Emily's habit of using extreme words, but that doesn't mean Emily isn't upset. She is. Neither she nor Ron realizes how Emily's language lights the fuse for her emotional response.

Most of Emily's problematic language falls under the category of extremist words. The following list gives you a small sample of extremist words: *agonizing, appalling, awful, devastating, disastrous, horrible,* and *unbearable.*

Of course, reality can be horrible, appalling, and downright awful. It would be hard to describe the Holocaust, September 11th, famine, or a worldwide pandemic in milder terms. However, all too often, extremist words like these reshape reality. Think about how many times you or the people you know use these words to describe events that, while certainly unpleasant, can hardly be described as earth-shattering.

Life presents challenges. Loss, frustration, aggravation, and pain routinely drop in like annoying, unwelcome guests. You may try to banish them from your life, but your best efforts won't keep them from stopping by — uninvited as usual. When they arrive, you have two choices. One is to magnify them and tell yourself how *horrible, awful, unbearable,* and *intolerable* they are. But when you do that, you only manage to intensify your anxiety and distress. Your other option is to think in more realistic terms. (See the "Exorcising your extremist words" section, later in this chapter, for more on realistic options.)

Misrepresenting with all-or-none, black-or-white words

Pick up any black-and-white photograph. Look carefully, and you'll see many shades of gray that likely dominate the picture. Most photos contain very little pure black or white at all. Calling a photo black-and-white oversimplifies and fails to capture the complexity and richness of the image. Just as calling a photograph black-and-white leaves out many of the details, describing an event in black-and-white terms ignores the full range of human experience. Like a photograph, little of life is black or white.

Nevertheless, people easily slip into language that oversimplifies. Like extremist language, this all-or-nothing approach intensifies negative feelings. The following example shows how categorizing life in all-or-nothing terms can lead to upset feelings.

> **Thomas** puts his newspaper down, unable to concentrate, and tells his wife that he'd better get going. "I didn't sleep a wink last night. I've been *totally* freaked about my sales quota this month. I'll *never* make it. There's *absolutely* no way. Sales *entirely* dried up with the slower economy, but the boss has *zero* tolerance for extenuating circumstances. I'm *certain* he's going to jump my case. It would be *absolutely* impossible to find another job if he fires me."

Thomas distorts reality by declaring that he'll *never* make the sales quota. Then his anxiety escalates. In the process, he concentrates on the negative rather than searching for positive solutions. If Thomas is at a loss for additional all-or-none words, he can borrow from the following list: *all, always, ceaseless, complete, constant, everyone, forever, invariably, no one, none . . .* you get the idea.

Few things (other than death, taxes, and change) occur with absolute certainty. You may recall pleading with your parents for a later curfew. We bet you told them that *everyone* stays out later than you. If so, you did it for good reason, hoping that the word *everyone* would make a more powerful statement. Nevertheless, your parents probably saw right through your ploy. Everyone oversimplifies sometimes; our language has many words for distorting reality. (For an all-or-none antidote, see the "Disputing all-or-none" section later in this chapter.)

Running into judging words

You *must* read this book more carefully than you have been. Not only that, but you *should* have read more of it by now. And you *should* have taken the exercises more seriously. You're a *pathetic jerk. Shame* on you!

We're just kidding.

What authors in the world would take their readers to task like that? None that we can think of. That sort of criticism is abusive. People react with dismay when they witness parents humiliating their children by calling them *stupid* or *rotten.* Many would view a teacher who calls his students *fools* and describes their best effort as *awful* or *pathetic* as equally abusive. That kind of harsh judgment hardly inspires; berating crushes the will.

However, many people talk to themselves this way or even worse. Some hear a steady stream of critical commentary running through their minds. You may be your own worst critic. Many folks take the critical voice that they heard in childhood and turn it on themselves, often magnifying the critique in the process. Critical words come in three varieties, although they overlap, and sometimes a particular word can belong in more than one category:

- **Judgments:** These are harsh judgments about yourself or what you do. For example, when you make a human mistake and call it an utter failure, you're judging your actions rather than merely describing them. Words like *bad, inadequate, stupid, pathetic,* or *despicable* are judgments.

- **Commandments:** This category contains words that dictate absolute, unyielding rules about your behavior or feelings. If you tell yourself that you *should* or *must* take a particular action, you're listening to an internal drill sergeant. This punishing drill sergeant tolerates no deviation from a strict set of rules.

- **Labels:** Finally, self-critical labels put the icing on the cake. Words like *loser, pig, monster, jerk,* and *failure* come to mind as disturbing labels people sometimes put on themselves like a name tag worn at a party.

Consider Steve, who makes a minor mistake in his checkbook and launches into a self-critical tirade.

> **Steve,** balancing his checkbook, discovers that he neglected to enter a check a few days ago. Fretting and worrying about the possibility that the check he wrote will bounce, Steve thinks, "I *should* be more careful. It's *pathetic* that someone with a master's degree could do something this *stupid.* I *ought* to know better. I'm such a *jerk.* I *disgust* myself. I *must* never, ever make this kind of mistake again."

By the time he finishes his self-abuse, Steve feels more anxious and even a little depressed. His mistake leads him to make all three types of condemnations: He judges his error as stupid, he says he shouldn't have allowed it to happen, and he declares himself a jerk when it does. It's no wonder that Steve feels anxious when he works on his checkbook. Ironically, the increased anxiety makes further mistakes more likely.

See the later section "Judging the judge" for ways to replace these words with more positive language.

Turning to victim words

You may remember the story *The Little Engine That Could* by Watty Piper, about the train that needed to climb a steep hill. The author of the book wisely chose not to have the engine say, "I think I *can't;* I'll never be able to do it; this hill is impossible."

The world feels like a much scarier place when you habitually think of yourself as a victim of circumstance. Certain words can serve as a flag for that kind of thinking, such as these victimizing words: *can't, defenseless, frail, helpless, impossible, impotent, incapacitated, overwhelmed, powerless,* and *vulnerable.*

Victim words demoralize. They offer no hope. Without hope, there's little reason for positive action. When victims believe themselves defenseless, they feel vulnerable and afraid.

However, people who describe themselves as victims do enjoy a few advantages: They don't feel compelled to do much about whatever predicaments they face; people express sympathy for them; and some people offer to take care of them. Yet these advantages become self-defeating in the long run. To help yourself overcome the victim mind-set, flip to the later section "Vanquishing victim words."

Tracking Your Worry Words

You probably don't realize how often you use worry words inside your head. Because worry words contribute to stress and anxiety, performing a checkup on your use of these words is a good idea. You can start by tuning in to your *self-talk* that works like a play-by-play sports announcer in your mind. Get a small notepad and carry it with you for a few days. Listen to what you say to yourself when you feel stressed or worried. Take a few minutes to write the internal chatter down.

Now, check your internal monologue for worry words. You may discover that you use a few worry words that we haven't listed, and some words could fit into more than one category. That's okay. Just look for the relevant themes. Underline them and then put them into these general categories:

- **Extremist:** Words that exaggerate or make something seem catastrophic
- **All-or-none:** Polar opposites with nothing in between
- **Judging, commanding, and labeling:** Stern evaluations and name-calling
- **Victim:** Words that underestimate your ability to cope

In the following example, Frank discovers how prevalent his use of worry words really is:

Frank, a talented mechanic, is promoted to shop supervisor. Frank's punctuality, attention to detail, and perfectionism reflect his stellar work ethic. Unfortunately, Frank's perfectionism goes too far. He obsesses over the quality of his employees' work. He checks and rechecks everything. In order to feel like he's doing his job properly, he starts working 60 hours or more each week. His blood pressure starts to rise, and his doctor tells him that he needs to reduce his stress and anxiety. So Frank picks up a copy of *Overcoming Anxiety For Dummies* and decides to try tracking and trapping his worry words. This is what he writes; then he underlines each worry word he detects:

The workload is dreadful. It's impossible to keep up; I'm overwhelmed. But I should be able to do everything. I'm an absolute failure if I can't get the work out. Because I'm the boss, I must be responsible for all the workers. If everyone doesn't do his job, I'm totally responsible. If someone else makes a mistake, I should be on top of it. I can't stand the idea of a dissatisfied customer. When someone complains, it feels like a calamity. I feel like a loser and a jerk if I can't make things right.

Frank categorizes the worry words he discovers as follows:

- **Extremist words:** *dreadful, calamity, can't stand*
- **All-or-none words:** *totally, absolute*
- **Judging, commanding, and labeling words:** *loser, jerk, should, must, failure*
- **Victim words:** *overwhelmed, impossible*

Frank is surprised to see how many worry words pepper his mind. He vows to try and replace his extreme words with more moderate words. The next sections show you how to revise your own internal language.

Refuting and Replacing Your Worry Words

Ask yourself how you truly want to feel. Few people like feeling anxious, worried, and stressed. Who would choose those feelings? So perhaps you agree that you prefer to feel calm and serene rather than wound up.

A good way to start feeling better is to change your worry words. However, you aren't likely to stop using worry words just because we told you that they create anxiety. That's because you still may think that these words accurately describe you and/or your world. Many people go through life without questioning their self-talk, simply assuming words equate with reality.

In order to refute the accuracy of your internal chatter, consider a small change in philosophy. This shift in philosophy entails questioning the idea that thoughts, language, and words automatically capture truth. Then substitute that idea with a new one: using logic and evidence-gathering to structure your reality (Chapter 5 has more on this). At the same time, keep in mind that your goal is to experience more calm.

In the following sections, we look at each category of worry words and show you how to replace them with words that more accurately represent the situation.

Exorcising your extremist words

The vast majority of the time when people use extremist words, such as *intolerable, agonizing, horrible, awful, hopeless,* and *ghastly,* they use them to describe everyday events. When you hear yourself using those words, subject them to a logical analysis.

For example, few events in life are unbearable. After all, you've managed to get through every single difficult time in your life up to now or you wouldn't be alive and reading this book. Many circumstances feel really bad, but somehow, you deal with them. Life goes on.

When you think in extreme terms, such as *unbearable, intolerable, can't stand it, awful,* and *disastrous,* you lose hope. Your belief in your ability to manage and carry on diminishes. Consider whether your unpleasant experiences are actually described more accurately in a different way:

- ✔ Difficult but not unbearable
- ✔ Uncomfortable but not intolerable
- ✔ Disagreeable but not devastating
- ✔ Distressing but not agonizing

Remember your goal of feeling calmer. When you drop extreme language from your vocabulary, your emotions also drop. Moderate descriptors soften your reactions. Less-extreme portrayals lead you to believe in your ability to cope. Humans have a surprising reservoir of resilience. You cultivate your capacity for problem-solving and survival when you have hope.

Disputing all-or-none

People use all-or-none words, such as *never, always, absolute, forever, unceasing,* and *constant,* because they're quick and easy and they add emotional punch. But these terms have insidious downsides: They push your thinking to extremes, and your emotions join the ride. Furthermore, all-or-none words detract from coping and problem-solving.

Rarely does careful gathering of evidence support the use of all-or-none words. Many people use all-or-none words to predict the future or to describe the past. For example, "I'll *never* get promoted," or, "You *always* criticize me." Whether you're talking to yourself or someone else, these words hardly produce calmness, nor do they describe what has happened or what's likely to happen in the future. So try to stay in the present. Table 6-1 illustrates the switch between all-or-none words and calm, evidence-gathering words that keep you *in the present without distortion.*

Table 6-1	Switching to the Present
All or None	*In the Present without Distortion*
I'll *never* get promoted.	At this moment, I don't know whether I'll be promoted. However, I'll do everything that I can to see to it that it happens.
You *always* criticize me.	Right now, your criticism makes me feel bad.
I *always* panic when I'm in a crowd.	Right now, I can't know for certain whether I'll panic the next time I'm in a crowd. I may panic, and I may not. If I do, it's not the worst thing in the world, and I won't die from it.

Judging the judge

Words that judge, command, or label, such as *should, must, failure, fool, undeserving,* and *freak,* inflict unnecessary pain and shame on their recipients. You may hear these words from others or from your own critic within.

Labels and judgments describe a person as a whole, but people usually use them to describe a specific action. For example, if you make a mistake, you may say to yourself, "I can't believe that I could be such an *idiot!*" If you do, you just made a global evaluation of your entire being based on a single action. Is that useful? Clearly, it's not accurate, and most importantly, the judgment doesn't lead you to feel calm or serene.

Like the other types of worry words, commandments don't inspire motivation and improved performance. Yet people use these words for that very purpose. They think that saying "I *must* or *should*" will help them, but these words are more likely to make them feel guilty or anxious. Self-scolding merely increases guilt and anxiety, and guilt and anxiety inevitably decrease both motivation and performance.

Try replacing your judging, commanding, and labeling words with more reasonable, accurate, and supportable alternatives. Consider the following examples:

✔ **Judging:** I got a pathetic score on my ACT test. I must be stupid.

  Reasonable alternative: It wasn't the score that I wanted, but I can study more and retake it.

✔ **Commanding:** I must have a happy marriage. I should have what it takes to keep it happy.

  Reasonable alternative: Much as I'd like to have a happy marriage, I was okay before I met my wife, and I can learn to be okay again if I have to. Being happily married is just my strong preference, and I don't have complete control over the outcome — it does take two, after all.

Vanquishing victim words

Victim words, such as *powerless, helpless, vulnerable, overwhelmed,* and *defenseless,* put you in a deep hole and fill you with a sense of vulnerability and fear. They make you feel as though finding a way out is impossible and that hope remains out of reach. Yet as with other worry words, only rarely do they convey absolute truth.

Nevertheless, victim words can become what are known as self-fulfilling prophecies. If you *think* a goal is impossible, you're not likely to achieve it. If you *think* that you're powerless, you won't draw on your coping resources. As an alternative, consider the logic of your victim words. Is there anything at all that you can do to remedy or at least improve your problem?

Gather evidence for refuting victim words that appear in your self-talk. Ask yourself whether you've ever managed to cope with a similar situation before. Think about a friend, an acquaintance, or anyone at all who has successfully dealt with a burden like yours.

After you consider the logic and the evidence, ask whether victim words make you feel better, calmer, or less anxious. If not, replace those words with new ones, as in the following examples:

✔ **Victim:** I have a fatal disease, and I'm totally powerless to do anything about it.

Reasonable alternative: I have a disease that's indeed often fatal. However, I can explore every avenue from new experimental treatments to alternative treatments. If that doesn't work, I can still find meaning with the rest of my life.

✔ **Victim:** I feel overwhelmed by debt. I feel helpless and have no options other than declaring bankruptcy.

Reasonable alternative: I do have a considerable debt. However, I could go to a credit-counseling agency that specializes in renegotiating interest rates and payments. I may also be able to get a second, part-time job and chip away at the bills. If I ultimately do have to declare bankruptcy, I can slowly rebuild my credit.

Chapter 7

Busting Up Your Agitating Assumptions

. . . .

In This Chapter

▶ Understanding how some beliefs make you anxious

▶ Discovering your agitating assumptions

▶ Challenging your anxious beliefs

▶ Replacing your worry convictions

. . . .

Some people love to speak in front of crowds; others shake at the very thought of public speaking. Ever notice how people respond to criticism? Some blow it off, some get angry, and others are extremely embarrassed. While one person may become anxious about traffic, airplanes, or health, another becomes anxious about finances, and still another feels anxious only around bugs. A few people rarely become anxious at all.

This chapter explains why different people respond to the same event in extremely different ways. We show you how certain beliefs or assumptions about yourself and the world cause you to feel the way you do about what happens. These beliefs are also called *schemas*. One way to think about these schemas or beliefs is to think of them as lenses or glasses that you look through. As you know, sometimes lenses can be cloudy, dirty, smoky, cracked, distorted, rose-colored, or clear. Some schema lenses make people scared or anxious when they see their world through them. We call those *anxious schemas* or *agitating assumptions*.

We show you how certain anxious schemas generate excessive worry and anxiety. These beliefs come primarily from your life experiences — they don't mean you're defective. Of course, as discussed in Chapter 3 and elsewhere, all aspects of anxiety are also influenced by biological factors. The questionnaire in this chapter helps you discover which assumptions may agitate and create anxiety in you. We provide ways for you to challenge those anxious schemas. Replacing your agitating assumptions with *calming schemas* can reduce your anxiety.

We consider the terms *anxious schemas* and *agitating assumptions* equivalent, but we get bored easily, so we like to mix them up.

Understanding Agitating Assumptions

A *schema* is something that you presume to be correct without question. You don't think about such assumptions or schemas; rather, you take them for granted as basic truths. For example, you probably believe that fall follows summer and that someone who smiles at you is friendly and someone who scowls at you isn't. You assume without thinking that a red light means stop and a green light means go. Your assumptions provide a map for getting you through life quickly and efficiently.

And that's not necessarily a bad thing. Your schemas guide you through your days with less effort. For example, most people assume their paychecks will arrive more or less on time. That assumption allows them to plan ahead, pay bills, and avoid unnecessary worry. If people didn't make this assumption, they'd constantly check with their payroll department or boss to ensure timely delivery of their checks to the annoyance of all concerned. Unfortunately, the schema of expecting a paycheck is shattered when jobs are scarce or layoffs increase. Understandably, people with expectations of regular paychecks feel pretty anxious when their assumptions don't hold true.

Similarly, most people have assumptions (or schemas) about food. They assume that the food sold in the grocery store is safe to eat — in spite of occasional news reports about tainted food showing up in stores. On the other hand, food sold on a street corner in a third-world country might be assumed to be less safe to eat. Many tourists would avoid such food even if was actually fine. So, while people act on their schemas and assumptions, they're not always correct in doing so.

As you can see, sometimes schemas fail to provide useful information. They may even distort reality so much that they arouse considerable distress. For example, before giving a speech, you may tremble, quiver, and sweat. You may worry that you'll stumble over your words, drop your notes, or even worse, faint from fear. Even though these things have seldom happened when you've previously given speeches, you always assume that they will this time. That dread of embarrassment comes from an anxious schema.

Anxious schemas assume the worst about yourself or the world — and usually they're incorrect.

When activated, agitating assumptions cause anxiety and worry. Unfortunately, most people don't even know they have these schemas. Therefore, agitating assumptions can go unchallenged for many years, leaving them free to fuel anxiety.

Sizing Up Anxious Schemas

Perhaps you're curious as to whether you hold any anxious schemas. People usually don't even know if they have these troubling beliefs, so they don't question them. Challenging agitating assumptions has to start with knowing which ones you have. In the following sections, we identify five anxious schemas and then provide a quiz to help you determine whether you suffer from any of them.

Recognizing schemas

In our work with clients, we've found that five major anxious schemas plague them:

- **Perfectionism:** Perfectionists assume that they must do everything right or they will have failed totally, and the consequences will be devastating. They ruminate over minor details.

- **Approval:** Approval addicts assume they must win the approval of others at any cost to themselves. They can't stand criticism.

- **Vulnerability:** Those afflicted with the vulnerability assumption feel at the mercy of life's forces. They worry all the time about possible disasters.

- **Control:** Those with the control assumption feel that they can't trust or rely on anyone but themselves. They always want to be the driver — never the passenger.

- **Dependency:** Those with the dependency assumption feel they can't survive on their own and turn to others for help.

These anxious schemas have a powerful influence on the way you respond to circumstances. For example, imagine that the majority of comments you get on a performance review at work are quite positive, but one sentence describes a minor problem. Each schema causes a different reaction:

- **If you have the perfectionism schema,** you severely scold yourself for your failure. You won't even see the positive comments.

- **If you have the approval schema,** you obsess about whether your boss still likes you.

- **If you have the vulnerability schema,** you believe that you're about to lose your job, and then your house and car.

- **If you have a control schema,** you focus on how working for someone else makes you feel out of control and helpless.

- **If you have the dependency schema,** you look to others for support and help. You ask your coworkers to intervene on your behalf with the boss.

Various individuals react completely differently to the same event, depending on which assumption those individuals hold. Just imagine the reaction of someone who simultaneously holds several of these schemas. One sentence in a performance review could set off a huge emotional storm of anxiety and distress.

You may have one or more of these anxiety-creating schemas or assumptions to one degree or another. Taking the quiz in the following section helps you find out which, if any, anxious schemas you hold.

Assessing your agitating assumptions

In Table 7-1, place a check mark in the column marked "T" if a statement is true or mostly true as a description of you; conversely, place a check mark in the column marked "F" if a statement is false or mostly false as it pertains to you. Please don't mark your statement as "T" or "F" simply based on how you think you *should* be; instead, answer on the basis of how you really do act and respond to events in your life.

Table 7-1		The Anxious Schemas Quiz
T	*F*	*Perfectionism*
		If I'm not good at something, I'd rather not do it.
		When I make a mistake, I feel terrible.
		I think if something's worth doing, it's worth doing perfectly.
		I can't stand to be criticized.
		I don't want to turn my work in to anyone until it's perfect.
T	*F*	*Approval*
		I often worry about what other people think.
		I sacrifice my needs to please others.
		I hate speaking in front of a group of people.
		I need to be nice all the time or people won't like me.
		I can rarely say no to people.
T	*F*	*Vulnerability*
		I worry about things going wrong.
		I worry a great deal about my safety, health, and finances.
		Many times, I feel like a victim of circumstances.
		I worry a great deal about the future.
		I feel pretty helpless much of the time.

T	F	Control
		I hate taking orders from anyone.
		I like to keep my fingers in everything.
		I hate to leave my fate in the hands of others.
		Nothing would be worse than losing control.
		I do much better as a leader than a follower.
T	F	Dependency
		I'm nothing unless someone loves me.
		I could never be happy on my own.
		I ask advice about most things that I do.
		I need a great deal of reassurance.
		I rarely do things without other people.

Most people endorse one or more of these items as true. So don't worry too much if you find quite a few statements that apply to you. For example, who doesn't hate being embarrassed? And most people worry at least a little about the future.

So how do you know whether you have a problem with one of these assumptions? You start by looking at each assumption one at a time. If you checked one or more items as true, that raises the possibility that this assumption causes you some trouble. Just how much trouble depends on how much distress you feel.

Ask yourself what makes you feel especially anxious. Does it have to do with one or more items that you checked as true? If so, you probably struggle with that anxious schema. We cover each schema and ways to overcome it later in this chapter.

If you have a number of these agitating assumptions, don't get down on yourself! You likely developed your anxious schemas for good reasons. You should congratulate yourself for starting to figure out the problem. That's the first step toward feeling better.

Coming Down with a Case of Anxious Schemas

If you have too much anxiety, one or more agitating assumptions undoubtedly cause you problems. But it's especially important to know that you're not crazy for having agitating assumptions! People acquire these schemas in two completely understandable ways:

- When experiences in childhood prevent the development of a reasonable sense of safety, security, acceptance, or approval
- When shocking, traumatic events shatter previously held assumptions

The following sections explain in more detail how these experiences lead to anxious schemas.

Acquiring assumptions in childhood

You may have been one of the lucky ones who glided through childhood feeling loved, accepted, safe, and secure. Perhaps you lived in a home with two loving parents, a dog, a station wagon, and a white picket fence. Or maybe not. You probably didn't have a perfect childhood. Not many people do. For the most part, your parents probably did the best they could, but they were human. Perhaps they had bad tempers or ran into financial difficulties. Or possibly, they had addictions or failed to look out for your safety as well as they should have. For these and numerous other reasons, you may have acquired one or more agitating assumptions.

The following example illustrates the most common time in life for anxious schemas to develop: childhood.

> **Harold** developed his agitating assumption as a child. Harold's mother rarely gave him much approval. She harshly criticized almost everything he did. For example, his room was never quite clean enough, and his grades were never quite stellar enough. Even when he brought his mother a gift, she told him it was the wrong color or size. He felt he could do almost nothing right.
>
> Slowly but surely, Harold acquired an agitating assumption — "I must be absolutely perfect, or I will be a total failure." Being perfect is pretty hard. So you can imagine why he now feels anxious most of the time.

Notice that Harold's anxious schema about perfection didn't come about from a massive, single event. Rather, a series of criticisms and corrections built his schema of perfection up over time. Unfortunately, his schema continues to plague him as an adult.

If you have agitating assumptions, you don't question them. You believe in them wholeheartedly. Just as Harold assumes the sky is blue, he believes that he's either perfect or a complete failure. When Harold undertakes a project, he feels intense anxiety due to his morbid fear of making a mistake. Harold's agitating assumption is that of painful perfectionism, and it makes him miserable, but he doesn't know why.

Shattering your reasonable assumptions

Anxious schemas most often begin during childhood (see the preceding section), but not always. Sometimes, what seems to be a common, though unfortunate, occurrence can lead to an anxious schema. The following example illustrates how present-day life can create an agitating assumption.

> **Bill** had always assumed, like most people do, that working hard and saving his money would assure him a safe, secure financial future and retirement. He has worked at his family's auto parts and service store for 25 years. He follows his financial advisor's advice and, at the age of 50, has half of his money in the stock market. The economy takes a horrible hit and his shop lays off most of its employees. Bill reluctantly puts a substantial part of his savings into buoying the business. Then the stock market tanks and Bill sees that his hard-won gains have virtually evaporated. Eventually, the store closes its doors and Bill looks for work.

> At the age of 50, he sees that he's not likely to find something that pays what he used to get from the family business. Instead of looking at ways to develop new skills or options, he sits hopelessly watching the stock market on television for many hours every day.

> Bill, formerly confident and self-assured, feels insecure, worried, and obsessed about his financial status. He has formed a new assumption — a vulnerability schema focused on money. He worries constantly about how he'll get by financially.

Bill had a very good reason to form that assumption, and like most agitating assumptions, Bill's schema contains some truth — you can never know with certainty what the future will bring. However, as with all agitating assumptions, the problem lies in the fact that Bill underestimates his ability to adapt and cope. Therefore, he now spends his days engaged in unproductive obsessing rather than changing his goals and lifestyle while developing new skills or possibilities.

Cars: A dangerous mode of transportation?

Although many people overestimate the risks of driving, you should know that driving does involve significant dangers. The National Safety Council has compared travel on buses, planes, trains, and cars. Deaths from automobile accidents far exceed deaths from all of these other modes of transportation combined. Sounds scary, doesn't it? However, the odds of dying in your car don't look all that bad. For every 100 million miles driven, there is less than one fatality.

Perhaps you consider yourself immune from inordinate amounts of anxiety, but don't be so quick to jump to that conclusion. In fact, many people who read our books are therapists or counselors who have skills and tools that keep them on an even keel most of the time. Nonetheless, anxious schemas can pop up for anyone at any time. The following true story about Dr. Laura Smith (coauthor of this book) is a case in point.

> One evening Dr. Smith sat in the hair salon. Suddenly, a thug stormed in, demanding that everyone lie on the floor, face down, and hand over their money and jewelry. He brandished a .44 magnum pistol to emphasize his point. Not long after the incident, Dr. Smith realized that she had acquired the agitating assumption of vulnerability. She found herself worrying about safety much more than she had in the past. She began to nervously scan parking lots and jump at loud noises. When she found herself waking up from nightmares, she knew the vulnerability assumption was creating trouble and that she needed to do something about it. So she used some of the techniques described in this book, especially Chapter 8. These strategies included gradually returning to the scene of the crime, talking about the crime, and relaxation. Soon, her vulnerability schema began to fade. By the way, it's now almost ten years later and she still goes to the same hair salon.

Anxious schemas may begin when you're quite young — perhaps only 4 or 5 years old — or they may emerge much later in life. Either way, they cause problems.

Challenging Those Nasty Assumptions: Running a Cost/Benefit Analysis

After taking our quiz and finding out about anxious schemas in the previous sections, you now have a better idea about which ones may be giving you trouble. In the old days, many therapists would have told you that insight is enough. We disagree. Pretend you just took an eye test and found out that you suffer from severe nearsightedness. Wow, you have insight! But what does that change? Not much. You still walk around bumping into the furniture.

You're about to get a prescription for seeing through your problematic assumptions. It starts with a cost/benefit analysis. This analysis paves the way for making changes.

Perhaps you think your perfectionism assumption is good and appropriate. Maybe you believe that you have profited from your perfectionism and that it has helped you accomplish more in your life. If so, why in the world would you want to challenge or change it? The answer is simple. You wouldn't.

Therefore, you need to take a cold, hard look at the costs as well as any possible benefits of perfectionism. Only if the costs outweigh the benefits does it make sense to do something about your perfectionism. After looking at the examples in the next five sections, see the "Challenging your own anxious schemas" section for directions on how to conduct a cost/benefit analysis for your personal problematic anxious schemas.

Analyzing perfection

Knowing which problematic anxious schemas lurk in your mind is the first step toward change. However, just knowing isn't going to get you there. You need to feel motivated to make changes. Change takes effort, and frankly, it's downright hard to change. The story about Prudence shows you someone who has the perfection schema and how she finds the motivation to change her assumption through a cost/benefit analysis.

> **Prudence**, a successful trial attorney, works about 70 hours per week. Her closet is full of power suits; she wears her perfectionism like a badge of honor. Prudence works out to maintain her trim figure and manages to attend all the right social events. At 43 years of age, Prudence stands on top of her profession. Too busy for a family of her own, she dotes on her 9-year-old niece and gives her lavish presents on holidays.
>
> Prudence is shocked when her doctor tells her that her blood pressure has gone out of control. Her doctor wonders about the stress in her life. She says it's nothing that she can't handle. He inquires about her sleep habits, and she replies, "What sleep?"
>
> Prudence is in trouble, and she doesn't even know it. She believes that her high income is due to her relentless standards and that she can't let up in the slightest way.
>
> Prudence has little hope of changing her anxious schema of perfection if she doesn't face it head on. Her doctor suggests that she see a counselor, who tells her to run a cost/benefit analysis of her perfection assumption.

A cost/benefit analysis starts with listing every imaginable benefit of an agitating assumption. Including every benefit your imagination can possibly conjure up is important. Then, and only then, should you start thinking about the costs of the assumption. Take a look at Table 7-2 to see what Prudence sees as perfectionism's benefits.

Table 7-2	Cost/Benefit Analysis of Prudence's Perfectionism Schema: Part 1	
Benefits		*Costs*
My income is higher because of my perfectionism.		
I rarely make mistakes.		
I'm widely respected for my work.		
I always dress professionally and look good.		
Other people admire me.		
I'm a role model for my niece.		

Prudence's fondness for her perfectionism is no small wonder. Filling out the benefits in her cost/benefit analysis is easy for her, but what about the costs? Prudence will probably have to expend much more effort to complete the costs, and she may even have to ask other people for ideas. Now, review in Table 7-3 what she writes after she works at the task and consults others.

Table 7-3	Cost/Benefit Analysis of Prudence's Perfectionism Schema: Part 2
Benefits	*Costs*
My income is higher because of my perfectionism.	I don't have much time for fun.
I rarely make mistakes.	I'm anxious, and maybe that's why my blood pressure is so high.
I'm widely respected for my work.	I don't have many friends.
I always dress professionally and look good.	I spend plenty of time and money on clothes and makeup.
Other people admire me.	I get very irritable when people don't measure up.
I'm a role model for my niece.	Some people hate me for my harsh standards and expectations of them. I've lost several secretaries in the last six months.
	I hardly ever see my niece because I'm so busy.
	Sometimes I drink too much to unwind.

Benefits	Costs
	Actually, I think my focus on work has kept me from finding a meaningful relationship.
	My schema causes me to procrastinate because I can't do things perfectly. That's caused me to miss deadlines sometimes.

The cost/benefit analysis helps you to know whether you really want to challenge your agitating assumptions. You would probably agree that Prudence's example shows more costs than benefits. But wait, it isn't finished. The final step is to examine carefully whether you would lose all the benefits by changing the assumption.

For example, Prudence attributes her high income to her dedication and long work hours. Perhaps she's partly right, but would her income evaporate if she worked just a little less? Most likely, if she worked less, her income might drop a bit, but with less anxiety, she might increase her efficiency enough to make up the difference. If she were less irritable, she would be able to retain her secretarial staff and gain efficiency there too. And would Prudence actually start making more mistakes if she relaxed her standards? Research suggests that excessive anxiety decreases performance. With respect to her niece, Prudence isn't really getting the benefit that she thinks she is, because she's not around enough to serve as an effective role model. Finally, more people fear Prudence than admire her. So you see, many times the perceived benefits of an assumption evaporate upon close inspection.

Anxiety: How much is too much?

A little bit of anxiety seems to improve performance and reduce mistakes. Some anxiety channels attention and effort to the task at hand. Without anxiety, people don't take tasks seriously or prepare sufficiently. However, when perfectionism reaches extreme levels, so does anxiety, and performance drops off. Excessive anxiety interferes with the ability to recall previously learned information, and mistakes multiply. That's why people with perfection schemas often have severe test anxiety. They know the material, but their anxiety causes them to forget what they have previously learned. Their fear of imperfection causes what they fear.

Tabulating approval

Approval addicts constantly crave admiration and acceptance from others. They worry about rejection and criticism. They constantly scan people's faces for any sign of disapproval. People with this anxious schema often misinterpret the intentions of others. However, they're reluctant to give up their anxious approval schema. That's because they fear that letting go of their worry habit will result in abandonment or rejection.

> **Anne**, a graduate student in social work, has to meet each week with her advisor for supervision of her casework. She dreads those supervision sessions, always fearing her advisor's criticism. Anne does plenty for her clients; she does anything that she thinks they may need help with — spending hours of her own time, even running errands for them if they ask. Her supervisor tries to tell her to pull back from giving excessive help to her clients; he says that her bending over backwards to assist clients doesn't help her or her clients. She cries after hearing her supervisor's comments.

> However, Anne's worst fears surround the required presentations in front of graduate school classmates. Before giving talks to her classmates, she spends an abundance of time in the bathroom feeling ill. During lively discussions in her class, Anne remains quiet and almost never takes sides. Anne is addicted to approval.

> Anne walks quietly through life. People rarely criticize her. She avoids embarrassment by not taking risks. She is kind-hearted and people like her. What's wrong with that?

Well, a cost/benefit analysis of Anne's approval schema reveals that people walk all over her. It also shows that fellow students fail to appreciate how bright she is, because she rarely speaks up in class. Anne neglects her own needs and at times feels resentful when she does so much for others and they do so little to return the favor. Anne's approval addiction doesn't give her what she expects. Sure, she rarely receives criticism, but because she takes so few risks, she never gets the approval and praise that she really wants.

Reviewing vulnerability

The anxious schema of vulnerability plagues people with worries about their safety, livelihood, and security. They traverse through their worlds in a state of constant, high alert. People with this schema often receive a diagnosis of Generalized Anxiety Disorder (see Chapter 2). The following example illustrates someone with the vulnerability schema.

> **Peter,** a college graduate with a business degree, receives a promotion that requires him to move to California, but he turns it down because

he fears big cities and earthquakes. Peter watches the weather channel and listens to the news before he ventures any distance from home and avoids driving if the radio reports any chance of inclement weather. Peter's worry restricts his life. He also worries about his health and often visits his doctor, complaining of vague symptoms, such as nausea, headaches, and fatigue. Peter's doctor suggests that his worry may be causing many of his physical problems. He tells Peter to fill out a cost/benefit analysis of his vulnerability schema, which you can see in Table 7-4.

Table 7-4   Cost/Benefit Analysis of Peter's Vulnerability Schema

Benefits	Costs
I keep myself safe.	I worry all the time.
I work hard to stay healthy.	Sometimes I can't stop thinking about my health.
I stay away from harm.	I'm so concerned about getting hurt that I've never enjoyed things that other people do, such as skiing or taking trips abroad.
I am more careful than most people about saving for retirement.	I worry so much about tomorrow that I forget to enjoy today.
I don't take unnecessary risks.	My doctor tells me that my worry probably harms my health more than anything else.
	I worry so much that I make mistakes.
	My worry ruins my ability to appreciate what's important in life.

Someone as entrenched as Peter in his vulnerability schema certainly isn't going to give it up just because of his cost/benefit analysis. However, this analysis starts the ball rolling by showing him that his assumption is costing him big-time. The exercise motivates him to start thinking about doing some things differently.

Counting up control

People who have an anxious control schema only feel comfortable when they hold the reins. They fear that others won't do what's necessary to keep the world steady and safe. Giving up control makes them feel helpless. At the same time, many of those with this assumption fear losing control and embarrassing themselves if that were to happen.

> **Jeff,** the head of a division at his engineering company, likes order in his life. His employees know him as a taskmaster who micro-manages. Jeff takes pride in the fact that, although he asks for plenty, he demands more of himself than he does of his employees. He issues orders and expects immediate results. His division leads the company in productivity.
>
> You may think that Jeff has it made. It certainly sounds like his issue with control pays off handsomely. But scratch beneath the surface, and you see a different picture. Although known for productivity, his division is viewed as lacking in creativity and leads all others in requests for transfers. The real cost of Jeff's control assumption comes crashing down upon him when, at 46 years of age, he suffers his first heart attack.

Jeff has spent many years feeling stressed and anxious, but he never looks closely at the issue. Jeff's quest for control nets him the opposite of what he wanted. Ultimately, he loses control of his life and health.

If control is one of your agitating assumptions, do a cost/benefit analysis. Jeff's fate doesn't have to be yours, too.

Debating dependency

People with a dependency schema turn to others whenever the going gets tough. Or for that matter, whenever the going is pretty easy. They don't see themselves as capable. They believe they need others to help them get through almost any difficulty. Unfortunately, people with the anxious dependency schema often lose the people they depend on the most. Why? They burn them out. The next story about Daniel is typical.

> **Daniel** lived with his parents until, at 31 years of age, he married Dorothy. He met Dorothy online and, after just a few dates, decided to marry her. Dorothy seemed independent and secure, qualities that Daniel craved but lacked. At the beginning of their relationship, Dorothy was fond of Daniel's constant attention. Today, he still calls her at work three or four times every day, asking for advice about trivia and sometimes seeking reassurance that she still loves him. If she's five minutes late, he's beside himself. He often worries that she'll leave him. Dorothy's friends tell her that they aren't sure that Daniel could go to the bathroom by himself. Daniel believes that he can't survive without her. After he quits several jobs because "they're too hard," Dorothy threatens divorce. Daniel finally sees a therapist who has him conduct a cost/benefit analysis of his dependency schema, as shown in Table 7-5.

Table 7-5   Cost/Benefit Analysis of Daniel's Dependency Schema

Benefits	Costs
I get people to help me when I need it.	I never find out how to handle difficult problems, tasks, situations, and people.
Other people take care of me.	Sometimes people resent having to take care of me.
Life isn't as scary when I have someone to lean on.	My wife hates me calling her all the time.
It's not my fault when problems arise or plans don't work out.	My wife gets angry when I don't take initiative.
I'm never lonely because I always make sure that I have someone around.	I might drive my wife away if I continue to cling to her so much.
It makes life easier when someone else takes care of business.	Sometimes I'd like to take care of something, but I think I'll screw it up.
	I haven't discovered how to master very much. Sometimes I feel like a Mama's boy.

Someone like Daniel is unlikely to give up his defective dependency assumption without more work than this. However, a cost/benefit analysis can provide an initial push. Meaningful change takes time and work.

Challenging your own anxious schemas

You can run your own cost/benefit analysis. See the list of agitating assumptions in the "Sizing Up Anxious Schemas" section, earlier in this chapter. Which ones trouble you? If you haven't already taken the Anxious Schemas Quiz in Table 7-1, do so now and look at your answers. Do you tend towards perfection, seeking approval, vulnerability, control, or dependency or maybe have a combination of these schemas?

First, determine which schema applies to you; if the quiz shows that you suffer from more than one schema, select one. Then, using the format of Table 7-5, fill out all the benefits that you can think of for your anxious schema in the left-hand column. Next, fill in the costs in the right-hand column. Refer to the cost/benefit analyses that Prudence, Peter, and Daniel (see Tables 7-3, 7-4, and 7-5, respectively) filled out earlier in the chapter.

If you get stuck filling out the costs column, ask a trusted friend or partner for help. Seeking input doesn't necessarily mean that you operate on the dependency assumption or that you're overly dependent; sometimes you just need someone else's perspective to see what your anxiety is costing you.

When you've finished your cost/benefit analysis, take another look at each of the benefits. Ask yourself whether those benefits will truly disappear if you change your agitating assumption. Prudence the perfectionist believes that her income is higher because of her perfectionism, but is that really true? Many people report that they make far more mistakes when they feel under pressure. Perfectionism, if nothing else, certainly causes pressure. So, it's probably not the case that perfectionists earn more money and make fewer mistakes. As often as not, they end up not doing as well as they could because their perfectionism leads them into making more mistakes.

When you look carefully at your perceived benefits, you're likely to find, like Prudence, that the presumed benefits won't evaporate if you change your assumption.

Similarly, Anne thinks she avoids embarrassment by never speaking in class. But she finds herself even more frightened and embarrassed when she's required to present in class than if she took more risks earlier. Avoiding what she fears seems to increase her worries. So Anne receives a double dose of what she so desperately wants to avoid.

Agitating assumptions often get you the *opposite* of what you want. They cause worry and stress, and rarely give you any true benefits. If you're going to give up your assumptions, you need to replace them with a more balanced perspective.

Designing Calm, Balanced Assumptions

So, do you think you have to be perfect or that everyone has to like you all the time? Do you always need to be in charge? Do you feel that you can't manage life on your own? Or do you sometimes feel that the world is a dangerous place? These are the agitating assumptions that stir up worry, stress, and anxiety.

Another problem with these schemas is that they do contain a kernel of truth. For example, it *is* nice when people like you, and it *is* nice to be in charge sometimes. We all need to depend on others sometimes as well. That sliver of truth makes people reluctant to abandon their assumptions.

The solution is to find new, balanced schemas that hold even greater truth, but old assumptions are like habits — they're hard to break. To do so requires finding a new habit to replace the old one. It also takes plenty of practice and self-control, but it isn't that difficult. You just need a little persistence.

In the following sections, we go over each of the assumptions and help you see how to develop an alternative, more reasonable assumption to replace your old one. Try using these reasonable, balanced perspectives to talk back to your agitating assumptions when they occur. Finally, once you develop a new assumption, try acting in ways that are consistent with that new belief.

If you find that your agitating assumptions rule your life and cause you intense anxiety and misery, you may want to consult a professional psychologist or mental-health counselor. But first, start with your primary care doctor to rule out physical causes. Sometimes anxiety does have a physical base, and your primary care doctor can give you a referral after physical causes have been looked into. Should you consult a professional, you'll still find this book useful because most anxiety experts are familiar with the tools that we provide, and they'll help you implement them.

Tempering perfectionist tendencies

Perfectionists believe they have to be the best in everything they do. They feel horrible when they make mistakes, and if they're not outstanding at something, they generally refrain from trying. Fortunately, a good cost/benefit analysis can often help them see that perfectionism exacts a terrible toll.

But if not perfect, then what? Some people think it would mean going to the other extreme. Thus, if they weren't perfect, these folks assume that they would become sloths with no standards at all.

If you're worried about giving up on your perfectionism schema, we have good news for you. The alternative is not the other extreme! You may find it helpful to copy the following statements, or what we call "balanced views" on an index card. Or, you may want to think of your own alternatives. Just be sure they aim for the middle ground. Carry your card around with you as a reminder for those times when you start to get hung up on perfectionism.

- I like to do well at things, but it's silly to think that I have to be the best at everything.

- I'll never be good at everything, and sometimes it's really fun just to try something new.

- Everyone makes mistakes; I need to deal with it when I do.

The deadly secrets of perfectionism

Perfectionism pays off . . . sometimes. A little bit of perfectionism probably can improve the quality of your work, sports, and other endeavors as long as you don't let it get out of hand. How bad is it when perfectionism gets too extreme? Worse than you may think. Perfectionists often become extreme procrastinators just to avoid making mistakes. Not only that, perfectionists more often develop various types of anxiety disorders, depression, physical ailments, and eating disorders. Worst of all, it appears that adolescents who suffer from perfectionism have a higher rate of suicide.

In other words, if you currently hold the assumption that you must be perfect and do everything right or you'll fail totally, try to think in less extreme terms. A more balanced schema is that you like doing things well, but that *all humans make mistakes and so do you.* You don't want to be above the rest of us humans.

Collect evidence that refutes your perfectionist assumption. For example, think about all the people you admire, yet who make numerous mistakes over time. When they make mistakes, do you suddenly see them as defective? Doubtful. Use the same standard for yourself.

Balancing an approval addict

Approval addicts desperately want to be liked all the time. They sacrifice their own needs in order to please others. Standing up for themselves is hard because to do so would risk offending someone. When criticized, even unfairly, they tend to fall apart.

But isn't it good to want people's approval? As with all anxious schemas, it's a matter of degree. Taken too far, the approval assumption can ruin your life.

But if you quit worrying about getting people's approval, what will happen then? Will you end up isolated, rejected, and alone? Is rudeness and arrogant behavior the alternative to being nice all the time?

If you worry about giving up your approval addiction, we have an alternative. You just may want to carry these ideas in your pocket. Feel free to make up some on your own as well.

✔ What other people think matters, but it's not usually crucial.

✔ Some people won't like me no matter what I do. That's true for everyone.

✔ I need to start paying attention to my needs at least as much as other people's.

In addition, consider collecting evidence that refutes your anxious approval schema. For example, think about people whom you like and admire who manage to speak their minds and look out for their own needs. Why do you like them? It's probably not because they bow and scrape to your every whim. Besides, someone who did that would probably turn you off.

If you feel addicted to approval and assume you must have the approval of others at all times and at virtually any cost, consider a more balanced perspective. Sure, everyone likes to be liked, but realize that no matter what you do, some people won't like you some of the time. Try thinking that your needs matter and that what other people think of you does not define your worth.

Balancing vulnerability

People who hold the vulnerability schema feel unsafe and worry constantly about every conceivable mishap. They might worry about safety, health, natural disasters, or the future; they often feel like victims of life's circumstances. They feel helpless to do much about their lot. The modern world with constant news about pandemics, natural catastrophes, financial ruin, and terror probably increases everyone's sense of vulnerability. It's no wonder that anxiety rates have skyrocketed (see Chapter 1).

People with this assumption fail to understand that worry has never stopped a single catastrophe. Nor does excessive worry help you prepare for the inevitable bad luck and misfortune that occur in everyone's life.

A better, alternative assumption can keep you reasonably safe without all that worry. If you want to give up your vulnerable assumption, try carrying these ideas with you and use them like mantras, repeating them to yourself frequently:

✔ I need to take reasonable precautions but stop obsessing over safety. The amount of preparedness that I or anyone else can take action on is limited.

✔ I will go to the doctor for an annual physical, pay attention to nutrition and exercise, and follow my doctor's advice. Beyond that, worrying about my health is pointless.

✔ Some unfortunate mishaps are unforeseen and out of my control. I need to accept that bad things happen; worry is no shield.

Again, if you hold the vulnerability assumption and feel that you're at the mercy of life's dangerous forces, you may want to consider a more balanced point of view. Try thinking that no one can prevent the trials and tribulations of life, but that you can usually cope when they do occur. Collect evidence about the many unpleasant incidents that you were able to cope with in the past. For example, when you had high blood pressure, perhaps you exercised or took medication to control it, or when you lost someone whom you cared for, you grieved, but you survived.

Relaxing control

Some people always want to take charge. They can't stand taking orders. When in a group, they dominate the conversation. They always want to know everything that's going on around them in their families and at work. They don't delegate well. Some fear flying because they aren't in the cockpit.

Being a control freak is tiring and causes plenty of anxiety, too. Perhaps you have trouble with this anxious schema. Many highly successful, intelligent folks do, and this assumption isn't easy to give up. But the costs to health, well-being, and relationships are staggering.

As for all agitating assumptions, we have an alternative, balanced view that will serve you better than control ever did. Review our suggestions. And if you must take control and rewrite them, that's okay, too!

- ✔ I can usually trust other people to do what they need to do. I don't have to manage everyone, and they're likely to resent me if I do.

- ✔ Asking for help or delegating a task isn't the end of the world, and sometimes, delegating is much more efficient.

- ✔ I don't have to know every single detail of what's going on in order to feel in charge. Letting go reduces stress.

- ✔ Letting others lead can make them feel better and take a load off me.

Think of a time in your life when someone else was in charge and things turned out pretty well anyway. In other words, collect evidence about when not having control has worked out.

Diminishing dependency

People with the anxious dependency schema believe they can't make it on their own. They ask for advice when they don't really need it and seek reassurance that they're loved or that what they've done is right. The thought of not having a close relationship terrifies them. They can barely imagine trying to live life alone. You're not likely to find someone with an agitating dependency assumption eating alone at a restaurant.

Many anxious schemas ironically backfire. Excessively dependent people eventually annoy and irritate those whom they depend on. Partners of dependent people often distance themselves from the relationship after they become weary of constant clinging and helplessness.

If you battle with dependency, consider some of our alternative thoughts. Write these on an index card and keep them handy for frequent review. Feel free to embellish them or come up with some of your own.

- ✔ It's nice to have someone who loves me, but I can survive on my own and have done so in the past.
- ✔ Seeking advice can be useful; working through an issue on my own is satisfying.
- ✔ I prefer to be with other people, but I can find out how to appreciate time alone.

If you buy into the defective dependency assumption — that you can't be all right on your own and that you need help with all that you do — try thinking in a more reasonable fashion. Realize that it's nice to have someone to depend on, but that you're capable of many independent actions.

Collect evidence of your capabilities. Do you put gas in your own car? Do you manage your own checkbook? Do you get to work and back on your own? Can you remember the times that you did well without someone? Realizing that you have taken independent action successfully and remembering that you have pulled yourself through many difficult spots all on your own can boost your confidence enough to help you take more independent action in the future.

Above All: Be Kind to Yourself!

In our work with clients, we found that these anxious schemas are surprisingly common, and many successful people who don't even have a full-blown anxiety disorder tend to fall under the influence of one or more of these assumptions. Therefore, it's important that you don't beat up on yourself for "being under the influence."

The origins of your anxious schemas could be in your childhood or the result of a traumatic event. Possibly your parents peppered you with criticism and that caused you to crave approval. Perhaps you had an unfortunate accident or trauma that caused you to feel vulnerable. Maybe your parents failed to provide you with consistent care and love, leading you to feel insecure, and, as a result, you yearn for help and affection. These represent merely a few of an infinite number of explanations for why you develop agitating assumptions. The point is that you didn't ask for your problematic schemas; you came by them honestly.

You've started on the road to overcoming anxiety. Go slowly; take pleasure in the journey, and realize that change takes time and practice. Be patient with yourself.

Chapter 8

Facing Fear One Step at a Time

*W*hen life hands you lemons, make lemonade. This advice sounds a lot easier to carry out than it is. Turning a situation around for the better after a series of hurts can be tough. Shifting to another metaphor, if you fall off your horse, everyone knows that it's best to jump right back into the saddle. But getting back up isn't always so easy to do either.

This chapter explains *how* you can get back in the saddle and even make some lemonade while you're up there (sorry). We show you how to overcome your fears in manageable steps. You don't have to face them all at once, because taking small steps does the trick. This chapter provides a recipe called *exposure* for overcoming your personal anxiety problem one step at a time.

Exposure: Coming to Grips with Your Fears

No single strategy discussed in this book works more effectively in the fight against anxiety than exposure. Simply put, exposure involves putting yourself in direct contact with whatever it is that makes you anxious. Well now, that may just sound a little ridiculous to you.

After all, it probably makes you feel pretty anxious to even think about staring your fears in the face. We understand that reaction, but please realize that if you're terrified of heights, exposure doesn't ask you to lean over the edge of the Grand Canyon tomorrow. Or if you worry about having a panic attack in crowds, you don't have to sit in the stands of the next Super Bowl as your first step.

Exposure involves a systematic, gradual set of steps that you can tackle one at a time. You don't move from the first step until you master it. Only when you're comfortable with the first step do you move to the second. Each new step brings on anxiety, but not an overwhelming amount. The following sections show you how to create an exposure plan for your own fear.

If you find yourself procrastinating with the recommendations in this chapter, read Chapter 4 to build motivation and overcome obstacles to change. If you still find these ideas difficult to consider, you may want to consult a professional for help.

Don't try exposure if your anxiety is severe. You'll need professional guidance. If any step raises your anxiety to an extreme level, stop any further attempt without help. Also, don't attempt exposure if you're in the midst of a crisis or have a current problem with alcohol or substance abuse.

Getting ready by relaxing

Before you do anything else, we suggest that you practice relaxing. Consider reading Chapters 11 and 12 for a thorough review of how to do this. But for now, you can use a couple of simple, quick methods.

Why practice relaxing? Exposure makes you anxious — there's no way around that. Figuring out how to relax can help you feel more confident about dealing with that anxiety. Relaxation can help keep the inevitable anxiety within tolerable limits.

First, we suggest a breathing strategy:

1. **Inhale slowly, deeply, and fully through your nose.**

2. **Hold your breath for a slow count of six.**

3. **Slowly breathe out through your lips to a count of eight while making a slight hissing or sighing sound as you do.**

   That sound can be ever so soft.

4. **Repeat this type of breath ten times.**

Try practicing this type of breathing several times a day. See how it makes you feel. If it doesn't help you feel calmer, stop doing it. Instead, try our next suggestion, which tightens and loosens muscle groups, an abbreviation of the method discussed in Chapter 11.

If you have any physical problems, such as low back pain, recent injury, surgery, muscle spasms, or severe arthritic conditions, don't use the technique that follows. Or you can consider it, but do so gently and be sure to avoid tensing to the point of pain. Finally, even if you're in good condition, you shouldn't allow yourself to feel pain when you tighten the muscles in the ways that we suggest.

1. **Find a comfortable place to sit or lie down.**

2. **Loosen any tight clothing.**

3. **Pull your toes up toward your knees, clamp your legs together, and tighten all the muscles in your legs and buttocks.**

4. **Hold the tension for a count of eight.**

5. **Now release the tension all at once.**

6. **Allow relaxation to slowly come in and replace the tension.**

7. **Notice the relaxed feeling for a few moments.**

8. **Next, squeeze your fists, bring your hands up to your shoulders, pull in your stomach, and pull your shoulder blades back as though you're trying to make them touch. Tighten all the muscles between your waist and your neck.**

9. **Hold for eight seconds.**

10. **Repeat Steps 5–7.**

11. **Finally, tense your neck and facial muscles. Scrunch your face into a ball.**

12. **Hold the tension for eight seconds.**

13. **Repeat Steps 5–7.**

14. **Sit with the new, relaxed feelings for a few minutes.**

15. **If you still feel tense, repeat the procedure one more time.**

Most folks find that one or both of the breathing or the muscle tensing exercise techniques relax them, even if only a little. If, by any chance, these techniques fail to relax you or even make you more anxious, Chapters 11 and 12 may give you more ideas. Work through those chapters carefully.

However, even if no relaxation technique works for you, it doesn't mean that exposure won't be effective. Exposure can work on its own. Without relaxation, you simply need to proceed especially slowly and carefully.

Understanding your fears

Breaking up the exposure process into manageable steps is important. But before you can break your fears into steps, it helps to fully understand the nature of what makes you fearful. Try the following strategies:

1. **Pick one and only one of your worries.**

   For example, you might be afraid of one of the following:

   • Enclosed spaces

   • Financial ruin

   • Flying

   • Having a panic attack (a fear of a fear)

   • People

2. **Think about every conceivable aspect of your fear or worry.**

   What starts up your fear? Include all the activities that surround it. For example, if you're afraid of flying, perhaps you fear driving to the airport or packing your luggage. Or if you're afraid of dogs, you may avoid walking near them, and you probably don't visit people who have dogs. Wherever the fear starts, take some notes on it. Think about all the anticipated and feared outcomes. Include all the details, like other people's reactions and the setting.

3. **Ask yourself the following questions and jot down your answers:**

   • How does my anxiety begin?

   • What activities do I avoid?

   • What are all the things I'd have to do if I actually faced my fear head-on?

   • What other situations are affected by my fear?

   • Do I use any crutches to get through my fear? If so, what are they?

   • What bad outcomes do I anticipate if I were to encounter my fear?

Using the question-answer format, you can describe what you're afraid of. Use your imagination. Don't let embarrassment keep you from including the deepest, darkest aspects of your fears, even if you think they may sound silly to someone else.

If you find yourself getting anxious while answering the questions above, use the relaxation techniques in the preceding section to calm yourself down.

Leeann's story is a good illustration of how someone completes this exercise to enrich her understanding of her fears.

> **Leeann,** a 32-year-old pharmaceutical representative, receives a promotion, which means a large increase in salary and plenty of air travel. During her interview, Leeann doesn't mention her intense fear of flying, somehow hoping that it will just go away. Now, in three weeks she faces her first flight, and her distress prompts her to seek help.

Lucky for her, Leeann picks up a copy of *Overcoming Anxiety For Dummies*. She reads about exposure and concludes that it's the best approach for her problem. To see how Leeann completes the first task — understanding her fear and all its components — see Table 8-1.

Table 8-1	What I'm Afraid Of
Question	*Answer*
How does my anxiety begin?	The very thought of flying makes me anxious. Even driving on the same road that leads to the airport gets me worked up.
What activities do I avoid?	I've avoided vacations and trips with friends and family in order to avoid flying.
What are all the things I'd have to do if I actually faced my fear head-on?	I'd have to make a reservation. Then, I'd have to pack my luggage, drive to the airport, go through security, spend some time in the waiting area, hear my flight called, and board the plane. Then I'd take a seat and go through takeoff. Finally, I'd endure the flight.
What other situations are affected by my fear?	If I don't get over this, I'll never get my promotion at work. Not only that, I'll continue to feel embarrassed around friends and family whenever the topic comes up.
Do I use crutches to get through my fear? If so, what are they?	One time I got on an airplane and got sick to my stomach because I'd had too much to drink in order to calm my nerves.
What bad outcomes do I anticipate if I were to encounter my fear?	I fear that I'd go crazy, throw up on the passengers next to me, or start screaming, and they'd have to restrain me. Of course, the plane could crash, and then I'd die or suffer horrible burns and pain, unable to get out of the plane.

You can see that Leeann's fear of flying consists of several activities, from making a reservation to getting off the plane. Her anticipated outcomes include a range of unpleasant possibilities.

Constructing a staircase of fear

The preceding section helps you comprehend the nature of your fears. After you come to that understanding, you're ready to take your fear apart and build a staircase. Here's how to do it:

1. **Make a list of each and every single thing you'd have to do if you were to ultimately, totally face your fear.**

   See the third question in Table 8-1 for ideas.

2. **Rate each one on a scale of 0 to 100.**

   Zero represents the total absence of fear, and 100 indicates a fear that's unimaginably intense and totally debilitating.

3. **Arrange the items into a staircase beginning with the lowest-rated item at the bottom and ending with the most difficult item on the top stair.**

   This constitutes your exposure hierarchy (another term for staircase). Just making your staircase may cause you some anxiety. Again, don't worry; you will approach each step one at a time.

Figure 8-1 shows how Leeann ordered her fear staircase for flying.

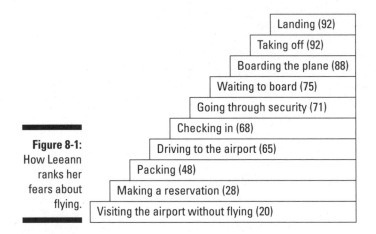

Figure 8-1:
How Leeann ranks her fears about flying.

Landing (92)
Taking off (92)
Boarding the plane (88)
Waiting to board (75)
Going through security (71)
Checking in (68)
Driving to the airport (65)
Packing (48)
Making a reservation (28)
Visiting the airport without flying (20)

Leeann's staircase contains only ten steps. You may want to break the task down into 15 or 20 steps. For example, Leeann could add an in-between step or two, such as planning her trip or parking in the airport garage.

For a phobia like Leeann's, the steps represent tasks that all directly lead to her ultimate fear. But some people have different types of anxiety. For example, someone with generalized anxiety disorder (GAD; see Chapter 2) may have a variety of fears — fear of rejection, fear of getting hurt, and worry about financial calamity. The best staircase of fear chooses one of those fears and includes everything associated with that fear.

So, now you have your staircase of fear. What do you do next? Choose between the two kinds of exposure — the kind that occurs in your imagination and the exposure that occurs in real life. In a sense, you get to pick your poison.

Imagining the worst

Many times, the best way to begin exposure is through your imagination. That's because imagining your fears usually produces less anxiety than confronting them directly. In addition, you can use your imagination when it would be impossible to re-create your real fear. For example, if you fear getting a disease, such as Hepatitis C, actually exposing yourself to the virus wouldn't be a good idea.

You may think that viewing your fears through your mind's eye won't make you anxious. However, most people find that when they picture their fears in rich detail, their bodies react. As they gradually master their fears in their minds, the fears are generally reduced accordingly when they confront the real McCoy.

Imaginary exposure follows just a few basic steps:

1. **Before you start, try getting more comfortable by using one of the brief relaxation strategies we describe earlier in this chapter.**

   See the section "Getting ready by relaxing."

2. **Choose the lowest step from your staircase of fear.**

3. **Picture yourself as though you're actually confronting your fear.**

   Leeann's was visiting the airport without any intention of flying.

4. **Imagine as many details about your fear step as you can — the sights, sounds, smells, and anything else that brings your imaginary experience to life.**

   If you have difficulty picturing the experience, see Chapter 12 for ideas on how to sharpen your mind's eye.

5. **After you have a good picture in your mind of what being exposed to your fear would be like, rate your anxiety on a scale of 0 to 100.**

6. **Keep the picture in your mind until you feel your anxiety drop significantly.**

   Waiting until your rating decreases by around half or more is best. It will come down that much as long as you stay with the imaginary exposure long enough. For example, if you experience anxiety at a level of 60, keep thinking about the exposure until it drops to around 30.

7. **Finish the session with a brief relaxation technique (see Step 1).**

8. **If the imaginary experience went easily, you may want to try the next step up in your staircase of fear, and perhaps another one after that. Continue daily practice.**

    Always start with the last step that you completed successfully (in other words, one where your anxiety level dropped by half or more).

Facing your fears (gulp)

Although we usually recommend starting exposure in the imagination, the most effective type of exposure happens in real life. The strategy works in much the same way as imaginary exposure; you break your fears down into small steps and arrange them into a staircase of fear from the least problematic to the most intensely feared. It's just that these steps all happen through action, not in your imagination as in the previous section. Now, it's time to face your fears head-on. Gulp.

1. **Start with a brief relaxation procedure, such as the ones we describe in the earlier section, "Getting ready by relaxing."**

2. **Select a fear or a group of worries with a similar theme.**

   For example, fear of rejection is a theme that involves lots of worries about criticism and evaluation by others. Similarly, anxiety about personal injury is a theme that involves a variety of fears about safety.

3. **Break the fear into a number of sequential steps, with each step being slightly more difficult than the prior step.**

4. **Take one step at a time, and keep working on each step until your anxiety drops, generally by at least 50 percent.**

   If your anxiety starts to rise to an unmanageable level, try using one of the brief relaxation techniques from Step 1.

The following hints can help you get through the exposure process:

- ✔ Enlist the help of an exposure buddy, but only if you have someone you really trust. This person can give you encouragement and support.

- ✔ If you must, back off your step just a little. Don't make a complete retreat unless you feel absolutely out of control.

- ✔ Your mind will tell you, "Stop! You can't do this. It won't work anyway." Don't listen to this chatter. Simply study your body's reactions and realize that they won't harm you.

- ✔ Find a way to reward yourself for each successful step you take. Perhaps indulge in a desired purchase or treat yourself in some other way. For example, you could put a few bucks in a shoebox each time you complete a step with a goal of rewarding yourself with a larger treat after you've made substantial progress.

- ✔ Use a little positive self-talk to help quell rising anxiety, if you need to. See Chapter 5 for ideas.

- ✔ Understand that at times, you will feel uncomfortable. View that discomfort as progress; it's part of how you overcome your fears.

- ✔ Practice, practice, practice.

- ✔ Don't forget to practice brief relaxation before and during the exposure.

- ✔ Remember to stay with each step until your anxiety drops. Realize that your body can't maintain anxiety forever. It will come down if you give it enough time.

- ✔ Don't expect an instant cure. Proceed at a reasonable pace. Keep moving forward, but don't expect to conquer your fear in a few days. Even with daily practice, exposure can take a number of months.

Remember to set realistic goals. For example, say you're afraid of spiders — so much so that you can't enter a room without an exhaustive search for hidden horrors. You don't have to perform exposure exercises to the point where you let tarantulas crawl up and down your arms. Let yourself feel satisfied with the ability to enter rooms without unnecessary checking.

Try to avoid using crutches to avoid fully exposing yourself to the steps in your staircase of fear. Some of the popular crutches that people use include the following:

- ✔ Drinking alcohol

- ✔ Taking tranquilizers, especially the benzodiazepines we discuss in Chapter 9

- ✔ Distracting themselves with rituals, song lyrics, or chants

- ✔ Holding onto something to keep from fainting

- ✔ Asking someone else to reassure you that everything will be okay if you carry out a step on your staircase

All of these crutches actually interfere with the effectiveness of exposure. But if you absolutely feel the need to use one of these crutches, use as little as you can. Sometimes a reasonable in-between step is to use lyrics or chants at first, and then make the next step in your staircase of fear the same activity without the chants.

In your later steps, it's good to drop even relaxation and self-talk as ways to completely master your fear.

Conquering All Types of Fears

Confronting your fears directly is one of the most powerful ways of overcoming them. But your exposure plan can look different, depending on the particular type of anxiety you have. This section lays out example plans for seven types of anxiety. You'll no doubt need to individualize these for dealing with your problem. However, they should help you get started.

You may want to review the descriptions of the seven major types of anxiety in detail in Chapter 2. The list that follows offers a brief synopsis of each anxiety category for which we suggest the use of real-life exposure:

- **Generalized anxiety disorder (GAD):** A chronic, long-lasting state of tension and worry.

- **Social phobia:** A fear of rejection, humiliation, or negative judgment from others.

- **Specific phobia:** An exaggerated, intense fear of some specific object, an animal, spiders, needles, or a situation, such as being high off the ground *(acrophobia)*.

- **Panic disorder:** A fear of experiencing repeated panic attacks in which you feel a variety of physical symptoms, such as lightheadedness, racing heartbeat, or nausea. You may also fear losing control, dying, or going crazy.

- **Agoraphobia:** This problem often, but not always, accompanies panic disorder. You worry about leaving home, which leaves you feeling trapped or unable to get help if you should need it. People with agoraphobia often avoid crowds, traffic, and even leaving the house.

- **Post-traumatic stress disorder:** This problem occurs after experiencing a highly threatening, traumatic event. Symptoms usually include recurrent flashbacks, a sense of re-experiencing the trauma, and avoidance of reminders of the event.

- **Obsessive-compulsive disorder:** Repetitive, unwanted thoughts jump into your mind and disturb you. It can also involve various actions or rituals that you do repeatedly as a way to prevent something bad from happening. However, these actions don't make much sense.

Waging war on worry: GAD

People with generalized anxiety disorder worry about most everything. As a result of that worry, they usually end up avoiding a variety of opportunities and other tasks of everyday life. These worries can rob their victims of pleasure and enjoyment.

Maureen's story shows you how someone with GAD tackles her worries with a staircase of fear.

> **Maureen's** friends call her a worrywart, and her children call her "the prison guard." Maureen frets constantly, but her biggest worry is the safety of her 16-year-old twin boys. Unfortunately, Maureen's worry causes her to restrict her kids' activities far more than most parents do. She doesn't allow them out of the house after dark, so they can't participate in extracurricular activities. Maureen interrogates them about every new friend. As the kids get older, they rebel. Squabbles and fights dominate dinner, but the biggest bone of contention revolves around

learning to drive. Although both are eligible to take driver's education, Maureen declares that they can't drive until they're at least 18 years old.

Maureen is surprised when the school counselor calls her to discuss her sons' concerns. He meets with her for a few sessions and helps Maureen to realize that her worries are overblown. She knows she has a problem and decides to tackle it head-on.

After helping her understand that her worries are over the top, the counselor suggests that Maureen talk to other parents at her church to get a reality check. She finds out that most parents allow their 16-year-old kids to attend supervised evening activities, to take driver's education, and even drive if they maintain good grades.

Maureen constructs her staircase of fear, stacking the steps from the least fearful to the most terrifying (see Figure 8-2). She rates the anxiety that each step causes her on a 1-to-100-point scale. Then she rates her anxiety again with repeated exposures. She doesn't go to the next step until her anxiety comes down about 50 percent.

Figure 8-2:
Maureen's staircase of fear, with the most fearful situations at the top.

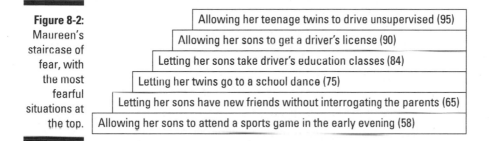

Allowing her teenage twins to drive unsupervised (95)

Allowing her sons to get a driver's license (90)

Letting her sons take driver's education classes (84)

Letting her twins go to a school dance (75)

Letting her sons have new friends without interrogating the parents (65)

Allowing her sons to attend a sports game in the early evening (58)

Although we only show six steps, Maureen's entire staircase of fear actually consists of 20 steps. She tries to make sure that each step is within five to ten anxiety points of the previous one.

If you have GAD, pick one of your various worries. Then construct your personal staircase of fear to address that particular worry.

Construct your staircase with enough steps so that the steps are small. If you find one step insurmountable, try coming up with an in-between step. If you can't do that, try taking the tough step through repeated imaginary exposures before tackling it in real life.

Fighting specific and social phobias

You fight both specific and social phobias in pretty much the same way. Take the feared situation, object, animal, or whatever, and approach it in graduated steps. Again, you construct a staircase of fear consisting of a series of small steps. Ruben's story is a good example of how the staircase of fear can help someone with a specific phobia — a fear of heights.

Ruben meets Diane through a dating Web site. They text back and forth for several weeks. Finally, they decide to meet for coffee. Several hours pass in what seems like minutes to both of them, and Ruben offers to walk Diane home.

As he holds the restaurant door open for her, her body brushes against him. Their eyes meet, and Ruben almost kisses her right there in the doorway. As they walk toward her apartment building, she asks, "Do you believe in love at first sight?" Ruben doesn't hesitate, "Yes," he answers, wrapping her in his arms. The kiss is so intense that Ruben thinks he might collapse on the spot.

"I've never done this before on a first date, but I think I'd like you to come up to my place," Diane says, as she strokes his arm. "I have a wonderful view of the entire city from my penthouse apartment."

Ruben looks up at the 25-story apartment building. His desire shrinks. "Ah, well, I've got to pick up Mom, I mean the cat at the vet," he stammers. Diane, obviously hurt and surprised, snaps, "Fine. I've really got to wash my socks."

Ruben decides to fight his phobia. He constructs a staircase of fear (see Figure 8-3) out of steps that start at the bottom and go all the way to the most fearful step at the top.

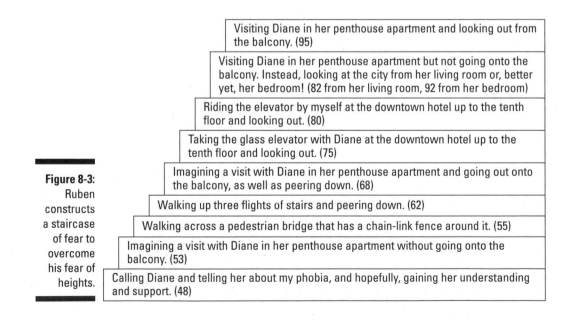

Figure 8-3:
Ruben constructs a staircase of fear to overcome his fear of heights.

Visiting Diane in her penthouse apartment and looking out from the balcony. (95)

Visiting Diane in her penthouse apartment but not going onto the balcony. Instead, looking at the city from her living room or, better yet, her bedroom! (82 from her living room, 92 from her bedroom)

Riding the elevator by myself at the downtown hotel up to the tenth floor and looking out. (80)

Taking the glass elevator with Diane at the downtown hotel up to the tenth floor and looking out. (75)

Imagining a visit with Diane in her penthouse apartment and going out onto the balcony, as well as peering down. (68)

Walking up three flights of stairs and peering down. (62)

Walking across a pedestrian bridge that has a chain-link fence around it. (55)

Imagining a visit with Diane in her penthouse apartment without going onto the balcony. (53)

Calling Diane and telling her about my phobia, and hopefully, gaining her understanding and support. (48)

Confessing his problem to Diane is a step that may appear unrelated to Ruben's fear. However, not admitting to his fear is avoidance, which only fuels fear. Including any step that's connected to your fear is good. Ruben also included steps in his staircase that required him to use his imagination to face his fear. It's fine to do that. Sometimes, imaginary steps can help you take the next behavioral step.

Imagining the real-life steps before actually doing them doesn't hurt and will likely help prepare you for the real thing.

Pushing through panic and agoraphobia

Some people have panic disorder without agoraphobia, others have both, and still others have agoraphobia without a history of panic disorder. Whether you have one or both of these problems, you can approach them in much the same way. That's because both panic attacks and agoraphobia usually have predictable triggers. Those triggers can form the basis for your staircase of fear. Tanya's story depicts how someone who has panic disorder with agoraphobia builds a staircase of fear.

> **Tanya** experiences her first panic attack shortly after the birth of her baby. Always somewhat shy, she begins to worry about something happening to herself when she takes the baby out. She fears that she might faint or lose control, leaving the baby vulnerable to harm.
>
> Her panic attacks start with a feeling of nervousness and sweaty palms, and then progress to shallow, rapid breathing, a racing heartbeat, light-headedness, and a sense of dread and doom. Trips away from the house trigger her attacks, and the more crowded the destination, the more likely she is to experience panic. By six months after her first attack, she rarely leaves the house without her husband.
>
> One day, Tanya's baby girl develops a serious fever, and she needs to take her to the emergency room. Panic overtakes her; she frantically calls her husband, but he's out on a business call. Desperate, she calls 911 to send an ambulance, which she and her husband can't afford on their limited budget.
>
> Tanya knows that she must do something about her panic disorder and its companion, agoraphobia. She constructs a staircase of fear (see Figure 8-4) out of a set of steps, starting with the least problematic and progressing to the most difficult goal.

Notice that Tanya's staircase of fear contains quite a few steps between 80 and her top item of 98. That's because she needs to make each step very gradual to have the courage to proceed. She could make the steps even smaller, if necessary.

Figure 8-4:
Tanya's
staircase of
fear focuses
on her panic
disorder
and agora-
phobia.

Taking baby by myself to the mall on Saturday afternoon, when it's most crowded. (98)

Taking the baby to the grocery store during the day, when it's only moderately crowded. (92)

Going to the mall without the baby or my husband, when it's crowded. (88)

Going to the grocery store with the baby when it first opens, when hardly anyone is there. (86)

Going to the grocery store by myself when it's only moderately crowded. (84)

Taking the baby to the pediatrician by myself. (80)

Taking the baby on three errands in one day. (74)

Taking the baby to the bank when it's crowded. (65)

Taking the baby in the car to my mother's house, 5 miles away, for the afternoon. (30)

Walking the baby around the block. (25)

You can break your staircase of fear down into as many small steps as you need to avoid feeling overwhelmed by taking any single step.

Another type of exposure that aims specifically at panic attacks involves experiencing the sensations of the attacks themselves. How do you do that? You repeatedly and intentionally bring them on through a number of strategies, as follows:

- ✔ **Running in place:** This accelerates your heartbeat, just as many panic attacks do. Run for at least three to five minutes.

- ✔ **Spinning yourself around until you feel dizzy:** Panic attacks often include sensations of dizziness and lightheadedness.

- ✔ **Breathing through a small cocktail straw:** This strategy induces sensations of not getting enough air, which also mimics panic. Try this for a good 60 seconds at a time.

- ✔ **Putting your head between your knees and rising up suddenly:** You may feel lightheaded or dizzy.

After you experience these physical sensations repeatedly, you discover that they don't harm you. You won't go crazy, have a heart attack, or lose control. Frequent, prolonged exposures tell your mind that sensations are just sensations.

Don't bring on these physical sensations if you have a serious heart condition or any other physical problem that could be exacerbated by the exercise. For example, if you have asthma or a back injury, some of these strategies are ill-advised. Check with your doctor if you have any questions or concerns.

Taking on post-traumatic stress disorder

Post-traumatic stress disorder (PTSD) often occurs following a traumatic event in a person's life. We're seeing a rise in PTSD nowadays. That's partly because of good news — due to improved medical care, we're more able to keep people alive when they encounter wars, terrorism, accidents, natural disasters, and violence. However, PTSD can haunt people for years after their traumas occur.

The vast majority of people with PTSD are best served by seeking professional help that guides them carefully through their staircase of fear. We provide a sample staircase for PTSD as an illustration, but we don't advise trying it on your own.

People can acquire PTSD by directly experiencing horrible, life-threatening events or even by witnessing such events happen to others. Amihan's story illustrates how someone can end up with PTSD from observing the aftermath of a natural disaster.

> **Amihan,** a young nurse from the Philippines, arrives in New Orleans six months before hurricane Katrina hits. She enjoys her job in the intensive care unit and makes friends with the other nurses easily. She also feels privileged to be able to send much-needed money home to her family.
>
> On the day of the hurricane, her hospital survives the wind and is initially able to function on auxiliary power. But when floodwaters fill the ground floor, the power goes out. That's when mayhem breaks loose. The temperature rapidly climbs into the high 90s, compounded by unbearable humidity.
>
> Patients stream into her unit. She sees people with exposed bones, burns covering 90 percent of their bodies, horrific injuries from projectiles launched by the hurricane's winds, and some people who were savagely attacked by other survivors. Those who are conscious either moan or scream in agony. Still others lay still, barely clinging to life. The number of patients overwhelms the staff's ability to attend to them. The stench from unwashed bodies, open wounds, burned flesh, feces, urine, and sewer water gags her. She stays on the job three days without sleep or rest.

Amihan sees a psychologist a few months later for treatment of her nightmares, isolation from others, irritability, intrusive images that bombard her mind, and her inability to return to work. She's desperately fearful that she'll be deported if she can't go back to her job. Her psychologist diagnoses her with PTSD and develops a staircase of fear. Her staircase (see Figure 8-5) has a number of gruesome images and scenes. Yet, by working through the steps, she slowly but surely regains much of her emotional well-being.

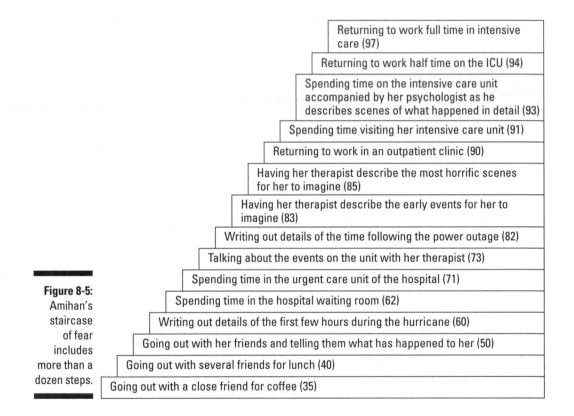

Figure 8-5:
Amihan's staircase of fear includes more than a dozen steps.

Returning to work full time in intensive care (97)

Returning to work half time on the ICU (94)

Spending time on the intensive care unit accompanied by her psychologist as he describes scenes of what happened in detail (93)

Spending time visiting her intensive care unit (91)

Returning to work in an outpatient clinic (90)

Having her therapist describe the most horrific scenes for her to imagine (85)

Having her therapist describe the early events for her to imagine (83)

Writing out details of the time following the power outage (82)

Talking about the events on the unit with her therapist (73)

Spending time in the urgent care unit of the hospital (71)

Spending time in the hospital waiting room (62)

Writing out details of the first few hours during the hurricane (60)

Going out with her friends and telling them what has happened to her (50)

Going out with several friends for lunch (40)

Going out with a close friend for coffee (35)

You should know that Figure 8-5 is a partial list of the items that Amihan dealt with. She actually went through more than 25 items, one at a time. Note that a few items involve going out with friends and don't seemingly have much to do with her trauma. That's because PTSD often causes people to avoid more than just reminders of the traumatic event itself — sometimes it includes avoiding friends and family. Treatment for severe PTSD like Amihan's often takes longer than treatment of milder anxiety disorders.

Overriding an obsessive-compulsive disorder

Obsessive-compulsive disorder (OCD) sometimes overwhelms and dominates a person's life, and the help of an experienced professional is commonly required to treat this disorder. Only attempt the strategies that we describe in this section on your own if your problems with OCD are relatively mild. Even then, you may want to enlist a friend or partner to help you. Furthermore, you may want to read *Obsessive Compulsive Disorder For Dummies* (Wiley), which we also wrote.

Chapter 2 discusses this disorder, which often starts with obsessive, unwanted thoughts that create anxiety. People with this problem then try to relieve the anxiety caused by their thoughts by performing one of a number of compulsive acts. Unfortunately, it seems that the relief obtained from the compulsive acts only fuels the vicious cycle and keeps it going.

Therefore, for obsessive-compulsive disorder, exposure is only the first step. Then you must do something even harder — prevent the compulsive, anxiety-relieving actions. This strategy is called *exposure and response prevention* (or *ERP*).

The first step, exposure, deals with the obsessional component of OCD — feared thoughts, images, and impulses. The exposure is often imaginary (see the earlier section "Imagining the worst"). This may be the only strategy you can use if your obsessions can't or shouldn't be acted out in real life, as in the following examples:

- ✔ Thoughts that tell you to violate your personal religious beliefs
- ✔ Repetitive thoughts of harm coming to a family member or loved one
- ✔ Frequent worries about burning alive in a home fire
- ✔ Unwanted thoughts about getting cancer or some other dreaded disease

Proceed as follows:

1. **List your distressing thoughts and images, and then rate each one for the amount of distress it causes.**

2. **Next, select the thought that causes the least upset, and dwell on that thought over and over, ad nauseam, until your distress drops at least 50 percent.**

   Sometimes, listening over and over to a recorded description of your obsession is useful.

> 3. **Then proceed to the next item on your list that causes a little more discomfort. Keep working your way up the list.**

This approach is quite the opposite of what people with OCD usually do with their unwanted obsessions. Normally, they try to sweep the haunting thoughts out of their minds the moment they appear, but that only succeeds ever so briefly, and it maintains the cycle.

Give imaginary exposure enough time — keep the thoughts and images in your head long enough for your anxiety to reduce at least 50 percent before moving to the next item.

If you also suffer from compulsive acts or avoidance due to obsessive thoughts, it's now time for the more difficult, second step — response prevention. Again, make a staircase or hierarchy of feared events and situations that you typically avoid: a staircase of fear. Then proceed to put yourself in each of those situations, but don't allow yourself to perform the compulsive act.

For example, if you fear contamination from dirt and grime, go to a beach, play in the sand, and build sand castles, or go out in the garden, plant flowers, and keep yourself from washing your hands. Remain in the situation until your distress drops by 50 percent. If it doesn't drop that much, stay at least 90 minutes and try not to quit until a minimum of a third of your distress goes away. Don't proceed to the next item until you conquer the one you're working on.

Although using relaxation procedures with initial exposure attempts is a good idea, you shouldn't use relaxation with exposure and response prevention for OCD as you proceed further. That's because one of the crucial lessons is that your anxiety will come down if and only if you give exposure enough time. Furthermore, some people with OCD actually start to use relaxation as a compulsive ritual itself. Thus, it's fine if you want to practice a little relaxation for anxieties not related to your OCD, but don't use it with exposure and response prevention.

Preparing for exposure and response prevention

Prior to actual exposure and response prevention, you may find it useful to alter your compulsive rituals in ways that start to disrupt and alter their influence over you. Methods for initiating this assault on compulsions include:

✔ Delay performing your ritual when you first feel the urge. For example, if you have a strong compulsion to wipe the doorknobs and the phones with Lysol, try putting it off for at least 30 minutes. The next day, try to delay acting on your urge for 45 minutes.

✔ Carry out your compulsion at a much slower pace than usual. For example, if you feel compelled to arrange items in a perfect row, go ahead and do it, but lay them out with excruciating slowness.

✔ Change your compulsion in some way. If it's a ritual, change the number of times that you do it. If it involves a sequence of checking all the door locks in the house, try doing them in a completely different order than usual.

Seeing exposure and response prevention in action

Cindy's story shows how someone with OCD begins to face her fears one step at a time.

> **Cindy** obsesses incessantly about getting ill from dirt, germs, and pesticides. Whenever she imagines that she has come into contact with any of these to the slightest degree, she feels compelled to wash her hands thoroughly, first with soap containing pumice to scrape off the dirty layer of skin, and then with antibacterial soap to kill the germs. Unfortunately, this ritual leaves her hands cracked, sore, and bleeding. When she goes out into public, she wears gloves to hide the self-inflicted damage. Not only that, she's discovering that her hand-washing consumes increasing amounts of time. Her 15-minute breaks at work are too short to complete her hand-washing ritual. Cindy finally decides to do something about her problem when her supervisor at work tells her that she must take shorter breaks. Cindy prepares for her exposure and response prevention exercise by doing the following first for a week:
>
> • She delays washing her hands for 30 minutes when she feels the urge. Later, she delays washing for 45 minutes.
>
> • She changes her washing by using a different type of soap and starting with the rubbing alcohol instead of ending with it.
>
> Cindy is surprised to find that these changes make her hand-washing urges a little less frequent, but they haven't exactly disappeared, and they continue to cause considerable distress. She needs to muster up the courage to do exposure and response prevention.
>
> First, she approaches Dolores, a trusted friend, for help. She tells Dolores about her problem and asks her to coach her through the exercises by lending support and encouragement. Then she makes a staircase of fear for her exposure and response prevention that includes touching the "dirty dozen" depicted in Figure 8-6.
>
> Dolores helps Cindy with her staircase of fear by having her start with the easiest step: touching a telephone receiver that someone else has used. She has Cindy do this a number of times and encourages her to resist the urge to wash her hands. After an hour and a half, the urge to wash drops significantly. The next day, Dolores has Cindy take on the next step.

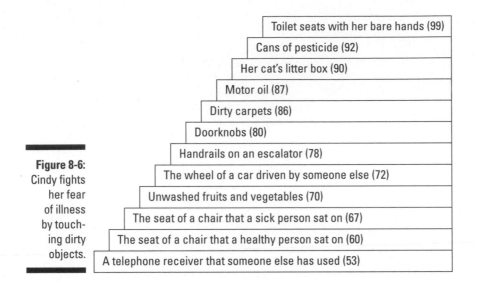

Toilet seats with her bare hands (99)

Cans of pesticide (92)

Her cat's litter box (90)

Motor oil (87)

Dirty carpets (86)

Doorknobs (80)

Handrails on an escalator (78)

The wheel of a car driven by someone else (72)

Unwashed fruits and vegetables (70)

The seat of a chair that a sick person sat on (67)

The seat of a chair that a healthy person sat on (60)

A telephone receiver that someone else has used (53)

Figure 8-6:
Cindy fights her fear of illness by touching dirty objects.

Each day they tackle one new step if Cindy succeeds the previous day. When she gets to touching the cat's litter box, Cindy balks at first. Dolores says she won't "make" Cindy do it, but she thinks it just might help her. In other words, she urges her on. The cat litter box takes many attempts. Finally, Cindy manages to touch it and stay with it. However, it takes a total of three hours of repeatedly attempting to touch and finally touching the litter box numerous times for as long as ten minutes each time for her anxiety to come down by half.

Sometimes exposure and response prevention takes a while, so set plenty of time aside. In Cindy's case, the final two items didn't require as much effort because her earlier work had seemingly cracked the compulsion enough so that it lost some of its power over her.

Upping the ante

After she gets through her staircase of fear, Cindy takes one more initiative. She tackles the toughest steps again. But this time, she asks Dolores to describe scenes of Cindy getting sick and dying a slow death from some dreaded disease because of her contamination, while Cindy is actually doing the exposure task.

We call this "upping the ante." It gives you the opportunity to practice your exposure while bombarding yourself with your worst fears. Why in the world would you want to do that? Mainly because doing so reduces the grip those

fears have on you. Of course, that's true *if and only if* you stay with the exposure, along with the dreaded outcome pictured in your mind, long enough.

If you can't do this on your own or with a friend fairly easily, please consult
a professional for help. Make sure that professional is well acquainted with
using exposure and response prevention for OCD (not everyone is).

If you get stuck on exposure and response prevention, you may want to carefully work through Chapters 5, 6, and 7. Pay particular attention to the section
on rethinking risk. Usually, those with OCD overestimate the odds of catastrophic outcomes if they halt their compulsions, and these chapters can help
you recalculate the odds.

Expecting the Impossible

Occasionally, people come to us asking for a quick fix for their anxiety problems. It's as though they think we have some magic wand we can pass over
them to make everything better. That would be so nice, but it isn't realistic.

Other folks hope that with help, they'll rid themselves of all anxiety —
another misconception. Some anxiety helps prepare you for action, warn you
of danger, and mobilize your resources (see Chapter 3). *The only people who
are completely rid of anxiety are unconscious or dead.*

Overcoming anxiety requires effort and some discomfort. We have no way
around that. No magic wand. But we know that those who undertake the challenge, make the effort, and suffer the discomfort are rewarded with reduced
anxiety and increased confidence.

Chapter 9

Considering Medications and Other Physical Treatment Options

. . . .

In This Chapter
▶ Deciding whether to take medication
▶ Knowing what medication choices are available
▶ Looking at supplements
▶ Seeing some stimulating possibilities

. . . .

The last several decades have witnessed an explosion in new knowledge about emotions, mental illness, and brain chemistry. Scientists recognize changes in the brain that accompany many psychological disorders. New and old drugs address these chemical imbalances, and using these drugs has both advantages and disadvantages.

This chapter helps you make an informed decision about whether or not to use medication for your anxiety. We give you information about the most widely prescribed drugs and some of their more common side effects. Only you, in consultation with your healthcare provider, can determine what's best for helping you. Next, we tell you about over-the-counter supplements for anxiety. More importantly, we share with you the latest information about their effectiveness and warn you about possible dangers and downsides. Finally, we alert you to some of the methods that involve stimulating the brain for those whose anxiety is severe and resistant to standard treatments.

Making Up Your Mind About Medications

Deciding whether to medicate your anxiety brings up a number of issues to consider. This decision isn't one to take lightly. You should consult with your therapist, if you have one, as well as your physician. Before you decide on medication, ask yourself what you've done to alleviate your anxiety. Have you challenged your anxious thoughts and beliefs (see Chapters 5, 6, and 7)? Have you faced your fears head-on (see Chapter 8)? And have you looked at lifestyle changes, relaxation strategies, or mindfulness techniques (see Part III)?

With a few important exceptions, which we review in this chapter, we recommend that you try various psychological approaches prior to adding medication. Why? Consider the following:

- Some research suggests that certain medications may actually interfere with the long-term effectiveness of the most successful treatments for anxiety. That's especially true of the techniques designed to confront phobias and fears directly through exposure.

- If you try psychological strategies first, you very well may discover that you don't need medication. Many of our recommended anxiety axes have the potential to cement change for the long haul as well as positively affect your entire life.

- Studies show that cognitive behavioral therapy (the type of strategies we discuss throughout this book) helps prevent relapse. Many people who take medication alone experience a quick reoccurrence of symptoms when they discontinue taking medication for any reason.

The downside of medications

You need to reflect on both sides of any important decision. Medications have an upside and a downside. The negative side of the argument includes:

- **Addiction:** Some medications can lead to physical and/or mental dependency. Getting off of those medications can be difficult, or even dangerous, if not done properly. (However, contrary to what some people think, many medications are available that do *not* have addictive potential.)

- **Long-term effects:** We don't really have good information on possible long-term effects with some of the newest medications. And some medications can lead to serious problems, such as diabetes and tremors.

- **Philosophical aversions:** Some people just feel strongly that they don't like to take medications. And that's okay, but only to a point.

- **Pregnancy and breast-feeding:** Only a few drugs are recommended for women who are pregnant or breast-feeding. The potential effects on the baby or fetus are just too risky for most situations.

- **Side effects:** Most medications have various side effects, such as gastrointestinal upset, headaches, dizziness, dry mouth, and sexual dysfunction. Working with your physician to find the right medication — a drug that alleviates your anxiety and doesn't cause you overly troublesome side effects — may take some time.

The upside of medications

Sometimes medications make good sense. In weighing the pros and cons, we suggest that you take a good look at the benefits that medications can offer:

- ✔ When serious depression accompanies anxiety, medication can some-times provide faster relief, especially when a person feels hopeless, helpless, or suicidal.

- ✔ When anxiety severely interferes with your life, medication sometimes provides relief more quickly than therapy or lifestyle changes. Such interferences include:

    - Panic attacks that occur frequently and cause expensive trips to the emergency room.

    - Anxiety that feels so severe that you stop going to work or miss out on important life events.

    - Compulsions and obsessions (see Chapter 2) that take control of your life and consume large blocks of time.

- ✔ When you've tried the recommendations in this book, consulted a quali-fied therapist, and you still suffer from excessive anxiety, medication may provide relief.

- ✔ If your physician tells you that your stress level must be controlled quickly to control your high blood pressure, that blood pressure medi-cation may, in a few cases, also reduce your stress, in addition to adding a few years to your life.

- ✔ When you experience a sudden, traumatic event, a brief regimen of the right medication may help you get through it. Traumas that happen to most people at one time or another include

    - The sudden death of a loved one

    - An unexpected accident

    - Severe illness

    - An unexpected financial disaster

    - A natural disaster, such as a hurricane or earthquake

    - Being the victim of a serious crime

    - Being the victim of terrorism

Understanding Medication Options

Today, physicians have a wide range of medications for the treatment of anxi-ety disorders. New drugs and applications appear all the time. Don't expect our list to cover every possible medication for anxiety. In addition, our review is not intended to replace professional medical advice.

If you decide to ask your doctor about medication, don't forget to discuss the following critical issues if they apply to you. Communicating with your doctor about these considerations can help prevent a bad outcome. Be sure to tell your doctor if you

- Are pregnant or plan to become pregnant
- Are breast-feeding
- Drink alcohol
- Take any other prescription drugs
- Take any over-the-counter medications
- Take herbs or supplements
- Have any serious medical conditions
- Have had any bad reactions to medications in the past
- Have any allergies
- Take birth control pills (some medications for anxiety reduce their effectiveness)

Most drugs prescribed for anxiety belong to one of the following categories. In addition to a few intriguing medication options, we discuss the following:

- Antidepressants
- Benzodiazepines (minor tranquilizers)
- Miscellaneous tranquilizers
- Beta blockers
- Atypical antipsychotics
- Mood stabilizers

You may notice that some of these categories sound a little strange. For example, antidepressants (typically used to treat depression) and beta blockers (generally prescribed for hypertension) don't sound like groups of medications for the treatment of anxiety. But we show you that they play an important role with certain types of anxiety.

Antidepressants

Antidepressant medications have been used to treat anxiety for many decades. That's interesting, because anxiety and depression often occur together. And both problems appear to have some similarity in terms of their biological underpinnings. Antidepressants increase the availability of different neurotransmitters or chemical messengers in the brain. The most frequently prescribed antidepressants increase the levels of serotonin, which helps regulate mood, anxiety, and the ability to control impulses.

Selective serotonin reuptake inhibitors (SSRIs)

Doctors prescribe SSRIs for all types of anxiety disorders (see Chapter 2 for a description of anxiety disorders). The SSRIs increase the levels of the critical neurotransmitter serotonin at the nerve synapses by inhibiting the reabsorption of serotonin into the nerve cells. You should know that SSRIs still have significant side effects, though they tend to be milder than earlier types of antidepressants and some ease with time.

Side effects from SSRIs can include sedation, stomach upset, headaches, dizziness, weight gain, insomnia, restlessness, irritability, sexual problems, unusual behaviors, and even thoughts of suicide. Talk to your prescribing professional about any and all side effects. And get help immediately if you feel suicidal.

SSRIs can interact with other drugs and, in rare cases, can cause life-threatening interactions. Be sure to tell your doctor about all medications or over-the-counter supplements you're taking.

See Table 9-1 for a listing of the popular SSRIs.

Table 9-1		Popular SSRIs
Trade Name	**Generic Name**	**Comments**
Celexa	Citalopram	Fewer side effects than many other SSRIs.
Lexapro	Escitalopram	Similar to Celexa; may work faster than other SSRIs.
Luvox	Fluvoxamine	Can be sedating; often prescribed for anxiety. Smoking and drinking reduce its effectiveness.
Paxil	Paroxetine	Sedating; weight gain common. Many have problems discontinuing use.
Prozac	Fluoxetine	Stimulating; can sometimes increase anxiety.
Zoloft	Sertraline	Stimulating; a good choice for those with heart disease.

Designer antidepressants

This class of antidepressants targets serotonin and other neurotransmitters that have various kinds of effects. Some of these neurotransmitters boost energy and alertness while others affect experiences of pleasure, motivation, and attention. Table 9-2 lists these medications alphabetically within their respective categories.

Table 9-2	Designer Antidepressants		
Category	*Trade Name*	*Generic Name*	*Comments*
Serotonin/norepi-nephrine reup-take inhibitors (SNRIs)	Cymbalta	Duloxetine	FDA-approved for treatment of major depressive disorder and generalized anxiety disorder (GAD). Also used to treat diabetic peripheral neuropathic pain and fibromyalgia.
	Effexor	Venlafaxine	FDA-approved for treatment of GAD, social anxiety, panic disorder, and major depressive disorder.
	Pristiq	Desvenlafaxine	A newer, FDA-approved SSRI for treatment of major depressive disorder, but may be prescribed for various anxiety disorders.
Serotonin-2 antagonists reup-take inhibitors (SARIs)	Desyrel	Trazadone	Used primarily as a sleep aid because sleep difficulties often accompany anxiety disorders.
	Serzone	Nefazodone	Reportedly effective for GAD and social phobias. Has the advantage of working more rapidly than most antidepressants.

Category	Trade Name	Generic Name	Comments
Noradrenergic and specific serotonergic antidepressants (NaSSAs)	Remeron	Mirtazapine	Effective for treatment of major depressive disorder, panic disorder, GAD, obsessive-compulsive disorder (OCD), and post-traumatic stress disorder (PTSD). Like Serzone, it works more rapidly than the SSRIs and causes relatively few sexual problems.
Norepinephrine reuptake inhibitor (NRI)	Welbutrin	Bupropion	Most commonly prescribed for depression or as an aid to smoking cessation; however, scattered reports indicate it may be useful for treating social anxiety and other anxiety-related problems. Paradoxically, agitation and anxiety are common side effects. Be sure to let your doctor know if you experience increased distress with this medication.

Tricyclic antidepressants

Doctors usually try to treat anxiety with the newer antidepressant medications discussed in the previous two sections. However, when those medications don't do the trick, sometimes the tricyclic antidepressants work. Tricyclic antidepressants can take anywhere from two to twelve weeks to exert maximum effectiveness.

Some people temporarily experience *increased* anxiety with tricyclic medications. In large part due to side effects that can increase anxiety and agitation, nearly 30 percent of patients discontinue taking tricyclic antidepressants.

That's why many physicians prescribe medication for anxiety disorders by starting with a low dosage and slowly increasing it as necessary. In other words, they prescribe a very low dose initially in order for your body to adjust to it with minimal side effects. They gradually increase the dosage in order to minimize negative reactions. It can take a while to reach an effective dose this way, but you'll probably find yourself able to tolerate the medication more easily.

Even with careful dosing, tricyclic medications can cause considerable side effects, including dizziness, weight gain, dry mouth, blurred vision, and constipation. Some of these effects resolve over time, but many of them persist even after several weeks. Tricyclics have lost some of their popularity to the newer SSRIs we describe earlier, because the SSRIs have fewer of these annoying side effects.

Common tricyclic medications include Tofranil, Elavil, Adapin, Pamelor, and Anafranil (prescribed especially for obsessive-compulsive disorder [OCD] and panic disorder, because it has a different mechanism of action on the brain than the other tricyclic medications).

MAO inhibitors

MAO inhibitors are the oldest type of antidepressant medication. MAO inhibitors work by allowing critical neurotransmitters to remain available in the brain to effectively regulate mood. MAO inhibitors are used infrequently because they have serious side effects.

Taking MAO inhibitors and consuming foods with tyramine can trigger a dangerous spike in blood pressure leading to stroke or death. Unfortunately, many foods, such as avocados, beer, cheese, salami, soy, wine, and tomatoes, contain tyramine.

Saving your sex life?

Many medications for the treatment of anxiety, as well as depression, interfere with arousal and the ability to achieve an orgasm. The worst offenders in this group of medications are the SSRIs. Many folks taking these medications are so pleased with their reduced anxiety that they hesitate to complain to their doctors about this side effect. Others are just too embarrassed to bring it up.

You should know that this side effect is extremely common, and your doctor has no doubt heard many patients report this problem. So go ahead and talk with your doctor — no need for embarrassment. Certain medications have a lower tendency to cause this side effect than others, so your doctor may recommend a switch. Alternatively, medications such as Viagra may be used to treat some of the sexual side effects directly. By talking to your doctor, you can explore the best options.

Nevertheless, MAO inhibitors can be effective when other antidepressants haven't worked. If your doctor prescribes one of them for you, he probably has a good reason for doing so. However, watch what you eat and ask your doctor for a complete list of foods to avoid, including those in the preceding list. MAO inhibitors include Nardil, Parnate, and Marplan.

Benzodiazepines

Better known as tranquilizers, the benzodiazepines were first introduced over 40 years ago. At first blush, these seemed like perfect medications for a host of anxiety problems. Unlike the antidepressants, they work rapidly, often reducing symptoms within 15 to 20 minutes. Not only that, they can be taken merely on an as-needed basis, when having to deal with an especially anxiety-arousing situation, such as confronting a phobia, giving a speech, or going to a job interview. The side effects tend to be less disturbing than those associated with antidepressants as well. And for 20 years or so after their introduction, they were seen as safer than barbiturates with a lower risk of overdose. They rapidly became the standard treatment for most of the anxiety disorders. They appear to work by reinforcing a substance in the brain that blocks the excitability of nerve cells. What could be better?

Well, it turns out that the benzodiazepines do have some problems. Nothing's perfect, after all. Dependency or addiction is a significant risk. As with many addictions, withdrawal from benzodiazepines can be difficult and even dangerous. Furthermore, if you stop taking them, your anxiety almost always returns. Rebound anxiety that's more severe than that experienced before taking the drug is possible upon withdrawal.

Benzodiazepines are also associated with increasing the risk of falling among the elderly. And falls among the elderly too often result in hip fractures. In addition, a recent report suggested that benzodiazepines may double the risk of getting into a motor vehicle accident.

That risk rapidly escalates when benzodiazepines are taken in combination with alcohol. In fact, benzodiazepines are particularly problematic for those who have a history of substance abuse. Those who are addicted to recreational drugs or alcohol readily become addicted to these medications and are at greater risk for combining alcohol with their medication.

Prescribing benzodiazepines to those who have suffered a recent trauma seems logical and humane. And indeed, these medications have the potential to improve sleep and reduce both arousal and anxiety. However, one study published in the *Journal of Clinical Psychopharmacology* found that the early and prolonged administration of benzodiazepines after a trauma actually appeared to increase the rate of full-blown post-traumatic stress disorder (PTSD) later. (See Chapter 2 for more information about PTSD.)

It also seems logical to assume that combining benzodiazepines with some of the various changes in behavior or thinking that can reduce anxiety (see Chapters 5, 6, 7, and 8) would make for a useful combination that could yield a better outcome than using either approach by itself. Yet studies conducted by psychologist Dr. Michael Otto at Massachusetts General Hospital have found that the risk of relapse is increased when these medications are combined with changes in thinking and behaving. In the long run, it appears that for most people, learning coping strategies to deal with their anxiety seems better than merely seeking pharmacological solutions — especially with respect to the benzodiazepines.

Nevertheless, the benzodiazepines remain one of the most popular approaches to the treatment of anxiety disorders, especially among general practitioners who have no special training in psychiatry. In part, that may be due to the low side effect profile of the drugs. And these medications can sometimes play an important role, especially for short-term, acute stress and anxiety, as well as for those for whom other medications haven't helped. We simply urge considerable caution with the use of these agents. Following are some of the most commonly prescribed benzodiazepines listed by trade name, with generic names in parentheses:

- Ativan (lorazepam)
- Centrax (prazepam)
- Klonopin (clonazepam)
- Librium (chlordiazepoxide)
- Serax (oxazepam)
- Valium (diazepam)
- Xanax (alprazolam)

Miscellaneous tranquilizers

A few miscellaneous tranquilizers are chemically unrelated to the benzodiazepines and thus appear to work rather differently.

You should know that in addition to the following list of miscellaneous tranquilizers, other types of tranquilizers are available. Furthermore, exciting new types of anti-anxiety drugs are under development, and some are undergoing clinical trials. Some of these are fast-acting, yet may have less of the undesirable side effect of addiction that has been found with the benzodiazepines.

For the time being, we list two anti-anxiety medications (with their generic names in parentheses) that your doctor might prescribe:

✔ **Buspar (buspirone):** This medication belongs to a class of chemical compounds referred to as *azaspirodecanediones* (which are actually far less intimidating than their name). Exactly how buspar works is unknown. It has been studied the most for the treatment of generalized anxiety disorder (GAD), but may have value for treating various other anxiety-related problems, such as social phobia and PTSD, among others. It may not be as useful for panic attacks as other medications. Although extensive evidence is necessary to rule out addictive potential, the current belief is that Buspar's likelihood for producing dependence is quite low.

✔ **Vistaril, also marketed as Atarax and Rezine (hydroxyzine):** This medication is an antihistamine as well as a tranquilizer. It's used to treat various kinds of anxiety and tension-related problems as well as allergic reactions, such as hives and itching. Fast-acting, this drug takes effect within 30 minutes.

Beta blockers

Because anxiety can increase blood pressure, perhaps it's not surprising that a few medications for the treatment of hypertension also reduce anxiety. Chief among these are the so-called beta blockers that block the effects of norepinephrine. Thus, they control many of the physical symptoms of anxiety, such as shaking, trembling, rapid heartbeat, and blushing. In the treatment of anxiety, their usefulness is primarily limited to specific phobias, such as social anxiety and performance anxiety. They're highly popular among professional musicians, who often use them to reduce their performance anxiety prior to an important concert or audition. Two beta blockers, Inderal and Tenormin, are most frequently prescribed for these purposes:

✔ **Inderal (propranolol):** Generally, Inderal is used for the short-term alleviation of stage fright, public speaking, test anxiety, and social anxiety. It's often given as a single dose prior to a performance.

✔ **Tenormin (atenolol):** This medication usually has fewer side effects than Inderal and is longer-acting. Tenormin is also often given as a single dose prior to a performance.

Atypical antipsychotics

Medications called *atypical antipsychotic medications* are not often prescribed for anxiety disorders. They're atypical in the sense that, unlike earlier medications, they have a lower risk of certain serious side effects, and they can be used to treat a far broader range of problems than simply *psychosis*, a disturbance in the ability to perceive reality correctly. The atypical antipsychotics target a different neurotransmitter than the SSRIs and sometimes are used in combination with SSRIs. When used to treat anxiety-related problems, these medications are usually prescribed at far lower doses than when used for psychotic disorders.

Upon seeing this category, you may have easily thought, "Hey, I'm anxious; I'm not crazy!" And, in fact, psychosis is a serious mental disorder that often involves disordered thinking, hallucinations, delusions, and other serious distortions of reality. So you may wonder why medications designed to treat psychosis have anything to do with treating anxiety. Those who merely suffer from anxiety rarely, if ever, experience the kind of substantially confused thinking that psychotics do.

These medications are primarily prescribed for people who have severe, hard-to-treat anxiety or who suffer from other mental disorders along with anxiety. They're generally not prescribed unless other forms of treatment have been unsuccessful. They have some especially distressing side effects. Possibly the most feared are known as extrapyramidal side effects (EPS), which can include a wide range of problems, such as

- ✓ Abnormal, uncontrollable, irregular muscle movements in the face, mouth, and, sometimes, other body parts
- ✓ An intense feeling of restlessness
- ✓ Muscle stiffness
- ✓ Prolonged spasms or muscle contractions
- ✓ Shuffling gait

These EPS effects appear to occur less often with the newer atypical antipsychotic medications as opposed to the older, traditional antipsychotic medications. Because the risk of EPS is relatively low, those with severe anxiety disorders for whom changes in behavior or thinking (see Chapters 5, 6, 7, and 8) or other medications haven't helped sufficiently may want to consider using these new anti-anxiety tools.

However, because the risk exists, those with relatively milder anxiety problems would probably want to avoid them.

Another disturbing side effect with many of these atypical antipsychotics is a change in metabolism that increases the risk of weight gain and can eventually lead to diabetes. As with most of the medications for anxiety, these should generally be avoided when pregnant or breast-feeding. Consult your physician for the best alternatives.

Here are four antipsychotic medications, with their generic names in parentheses. Other medications are under development.

- ✔ Risperdal (risperidone)
- ✔ Abilify (aripiprazole)
- ✔ Zyprexa (olanzapine)
- ✔ Seroquel (quetiapine)
- ✔ Geodon (ziprasivone)

Mood stabilizers

Mood stabilizers are usually prescribed for other conditions. However, when standard treatments haven't worked, doctors sometimes find them useful for treating their patients' anxiety. People who suffer mood swings like those with bipolar disorder often benefit from this particular class of drugs. Medications in this category include Depakote (valporic acid), Eskalith (lithium), Lamictal (lamotrigine), Neurontin (gabapentin), Tegretol (carbamazepine), and Topamax (topiramate).

A few intriguing medication options

The search for anti-anxiety medication options leads to a few unexpected places. The following list describes a few of these.

- ✔ **Catapres (clonidine)** is a medication usually used to treat hypertension by relaxing the blood vessels. It seems to ease some symptoms of PTSD, especially in children. Serious side effects have been reported, however.

- ✔ **D-cycloserine,** an antibiotic used as a treatment for chronic tuberculosis, appears to also help people extinguish their fears more quickly and completely when they're doing exposure types of therapy (see Chapter 8). Taking this drug while facing fears may allow people to speed up the process of unlearning the original fear, and the patient only needs to take the drug during a few therapy sessions.

- ✔ **Methylenedioxymethamphetamine (MDMA),** also known as the street drug Ecstasy, has been found to facilitate exposure treatment for people with PTSD. The studies are promising but preliminary. Ecstasy appears to have a positive effect on mood and empathy.

  During therapy, it is administered under medical supervision — we don't encourage our readers to try this at home.

🖊 **Oxytocin** is another interesting treatment for social phobia that is administered just before the client begins a session of cognitive behavioral therapy. Oxytocin, a naturally occurring hormone that is released by both men and women during orgasm, is given via nasal spray. Oxytocin won't give you an orgasm administered this way, but researchers at the University of Zurich in Switzerland have found that people with social phobia who are given a few sniffs of oxytocin feel more confident and open to therapy.

Searching for Supplements

Dietary supplements include vitamins, amino acids, minerals, enzymes, metabolites, or botanicals that reputedly enhance your health and/or your body's functions. Such supplements appear in many different forms — capsules, powders, tablets, teas, liquids, and granules. You can buy supplements from the Internet, your local drugstore, a grocery store, or a health food store. Claimed benefits of supplements include improved immune systems, enhanced sleep, stronger bones, revved-up sexual response, cancer cures, and overcoming anxiety.

People seek supplements often because they assume that they're safer than prescription drugs. That's not necessarily true. Supplements are not considered drugs in the United States and therefore are not subjected to the same level of scrutiny as most medications. Before a prescription drug can come to market, the manufacturer must conduct clinical studies to establish the safety, effectiveness, dosage, and possible harmful interactions with other medications. The U.S. Food and Drug Administration (FDA) doesn't require clinical trials to establish the safety of herbs. Instead, after a supplement makes it to market, the only way it will be removed is if enough consumers suffer serious side effects and complain to the right agencies, which can trigger an FDA investigation and possible decision to withdraw the herb from store shelves.

Another serious problem with supplements is that untrained salespeople often make recommendations for their use. Fortunately, healthcare professionals who are also interested and trained in the safe and effective use of supplements can help. By contrast, salesclerks vary widely in the usefulness of their advice. Dolores' story isn't all that unusual.

> A young, fit salesperson smiles at **Dolores** as she enters the health food store. Dolores tells him that she would like to find a natural remedy to help her calm down. She reports difficulty concentrating, poor sleep, and always feeling on edge. The young man nods and suggests a regimen of vitamins and supplements to build up her resistance to stress, improve her concentration, and ease her symptoms of anxiety.

Pulling bottles off the shelves, he tells her, "Some B vitamins to build you up; C to fight infections. Here are some amino acids — L-lysine and tyrosine — and a compound, 5-HTP. Minerals: calcium, zinc, potassium, and magnesium. Kelp nourishes. Melatonin for sleep. Oh yes, maybe some SAM-e to improve your mood. Then the herbs: hops, passionflower, valerian, lemon balm, chamomile, and kava kava. Now, take these at least an hour before you eat. Eat carbohydrates with these, not protein. And this one needs to be taken just before bed."

The bill comes to $214, and Dolores goes home feeling a bit overwhelmed. One day at work, after ingesting a dozen pills, she runs to the bathroom to throw up. A concerned friend asks her what's making her sick. Dolores tells her about all the supplements that she's taking. Her friend suggests that Dolores seek the advice of a naturopathic practitioner; she explains that these professionals attend a four-year, full-time training program and must pass a rigorous exam.

Dolores visits a naturopathic practitioner who advises her to dump the majority of her purchases in favor of a multiple vitamin and one herbal supplement. He also discusses several relaxation strategies, exercise routines, and self-help books. Within a few weeks, Dolores feels like a new person.

The example of Dolores may seem extreme. However, the supplement business is a highly profitable one. Well-intentioned salesclerks rarely have medical training.

Dolores was actually lucky compared to Hector, whose story appears next. Hector not only tries herbal supplements, but mixes them with a prescription drug and alcohol, resulting in a very dangerous scenario.

It's payday, and **Hector's** buddies invite him to hoist a few beers. "Sure," he says. "I can't stay too long, but I could use a couple of beers; it's been a tough week." Munching on spicy bar mix, Hector finishes off two beers over the course of an hour and a half. He stumbles a bit as he gets off the bar stool, and the bartender asks if he's okay. Hector reassures the bartender that he's sober. After all, he only had two beers.

Driving home, Hector drifts into the left lane for a moment but swerves back into line. Just then, he hears a car behind him honking. A few moments later, he sees police lights flashing. Puzzled, he pulls over. Hector fails a field sobriety test, but a breathalyzer test registers Hector's blood alcohol level at .03, well below the legal limit. What's going on?

Hector recently complained to his physician about feeling stressed at his job. His doctor prescribed a low dose of anti-anxiety medication and warned Hector not to take too much because it could be addictive if he wasn't careful. Hector found the medication useful, and it calmed him a bit, but the medication didn't quite do the trick. A friend recommended two herbs to try. Hector figured that would be a great, natural way to enhance the prescribed drug and that herbs certainly couldn't hurt him. To add up Hector's scorecard, he had combined two anxiety-alleviating herbs, a prescription drug, and alcohol — and was lucky that the police pulled him over. Hector could have ended up in a serious accident, harming himself or others.

Don't forget that even moderate alcohol consumption, combined with anti-anxiety agents, can intensify sedative effects to the point of substantial impairment and even death. *Be careful!*

Hunting for helpful herbs

People have used herbal remedies for thousands of years. Some of them work. In fact, a significant number of prescription medications are derived from herbs. You may want to try out an herb or two for your anxiety. We recommend that you read the literature about each herb carefully to make an informed choice before purchasing them from a reputable dealer. And always let your doctor know what herbs or supplements you're taking.

✓ **Saint John's Wort:** This plant has been used since ancient times for medicinal purposes. Studies show that it's as effective as some antidepressants for mild depression. Research on St. John's Wort is insufficient to recommend this as a treatment for anxiety. Be careful: It can intensify the effects of sun and lead to sunburn.

✓ **Kava kava:** The islanders in the South Pacific have consumed kava kava for both pleasure and healing. They have typically used it to treat a host of ailments, including obesity, syphilis, and gonorrhea. The islanders have also used it for relaxation, insomnia, and anxiety reduction. Kava kava has been used extensively in Europe for anxiety, although usage varies from area to area. Studies suggest that it does have a positive effect on anxiety, although the effect is modest. However, a few countries have banned kava kava due to its reported, but apparently rare, potential for causing liver problems.

✓ **Valerian:** Valerian is an herb native to Europe and Asia. The word comes from the Latin term meaning *well-being.* Valerian has been suggested for digestive problems, insomnia, and anxiety. Like many herbs, it's used extensively in Europe but is gaining in popularity in the United States.

Many other herbal remedies for anxiety are promoted as safe, effective methods. But beware; most of these herbs haven't been subjected to scrutiny for effectiveness or safety. We suggest that you avoid these because so many other anxiety-reducing agents and strategies work without dangerous side effects. On the other hand, we don't think that you need to be overly alarmed about drinking a little herbal tea from time to time. Most of these brews contain relatively small amounts of the active ingredients and likely pose little threat.

Viva vitamins!

Chronic stress taxes the body. The results of several studies link mood disorders to vitamin deficiencies, and especially severe deficiencies may make your anxiety worse. Therefore, some experts recommend a good multivitamin supplement.

Can vitamins and minerals cure your anxiety? That's not likely. However, they may help to keep your body in better shape for handling the stresses that come your way. Just take care not to take huge quantities. Even vitamins can produce toxic effects at megadoses.

Sifting through the slew of supplements

If you search the Internet and your local health food stores, you can probably find over a hundred supplements advertised as antidotes for anxiety. But do they work? Only a few that we know of. The following have at least garnered a smidge of evidence in support of their value as possible anxiety axes:

- ✓ **Melatonin:** Reaching a peak around midnight, this hormone helps to regulate sleep rhythms in the body. In particular, it addresses the problem of falling asleep at the right time (known as sleep onset) as opposed to the problem of awakening in the early morning and being unable to go back to sleep. Synthetic melatonin taken in the early evening, a few hours before bedtime, may alleviate this particular type of insomnia, a common problem among those who have excessive anxiety.

   Side effects such as dizziness, irritability, fatigue, headache, and low-level depression are all possible, but the long-term side effects aren't really known at this time. Avoid driving or drinking alcohol when you take melatonin.

   If you have an autoimmune disease or if you're depressed, you should probably avoid melatonin.

- ✓ **SAM-e:** Claimed to relieve the pain and stiffness of osteoarthritis and fibromyalgia, this amino acid occurs naturally in the body. It may also help treat depression and anxiety. However, research on this supplement remains limited. SAM-e appears to increase levels of serotonin and dopamine in the brain, which could theoretically alleviate anxiety.

   Possible side effects such as gastrointestinal upset, nervousness, insomnia, headache, and agitation may result, but again, little is known about the possible long-term effects.

Don't take SAM-e if you have bipolar disorder or severe depression. SAM-e may contribute to mania, which is a dangerous, euphoric state that often includes poor judgment and risky behaviors.

✔ **5-HTP:** This popular supplement is a compound that increases the levels of serotonin in the brain. Serotonin plays a critical role in regulating mood and anxiety. Some evidence also exists that 5-HTP may increase the brain's natural pain relievers, *endorphins.* Unfortunately, only limited research has been conducted on this supplement. These studies suggest that 5-HTP may reduce anxiety somewhat.

Don't take 5-HTP if you're also taking another antidepressant. Also avoid it if you have tumors or cardiovascular disease.

✔ **Omega-3 fatty acids:** Found in flax seed, avocados, soybeans, and fish, these acids have been shown to improve mood for those with depression. Evidence of their usefulness for anxiety is less robust, but there is sufficient evidence that having enough omega 3 fatty acids in the body improves cardiovascular health. So, consider taking these supplements (make sure that they're purified to eliminate toxins like mercury).

A number of alternative medicine practitioners also frequently recommend the supplement gamma-amino butyric acid (GABA). This supplement may have a mild tranquilizing effect, but little data is available to substantiate that claim.

Stimulating the Brain

People with severe cases of anxiety often try many different treatments. Unfortunately, a few cases neither resolve nor even improve with standard treatments such as psychotherapy or medication. For those people, new advances in science and technology may offer hope for improvement or even a cure to their suffering. However, you should be aware that the effectiveness of these new approaches has not yet been firmly established. They really should be considered as a last resort at this time.

Vagus nerve stimulation (VNS)

The vagus nerve sends information from the digestive system, the heart, and the lungs throughout the brain. Anxiety is usually experienced throughout these systems, with symptoms ranging from stomach upset to rapid breathing to feelings of fear to thinking that something bad might happen. VNS was developed as a treatment for people with epilepsy. A device is implanted in the chest that sends electric pulses to the vagus nerve.

Later, this treatment was found to help those with severe depression. Many of those who experienced relief from either epileptic seizures or depression also noted decreases in anxiety. Therefore, a few studies have been conducted using VNS with treatment-resistant cases of anxiety. Results are hopeful, but considerably more research is needed. For now, VNS remains an alternative only for those who have had multiple treatment failures for severe anxiety.

Although serious side effects are rare, VNS can cause pain at the site of the incision, voice hoarseness, sore throat, and facial muscle weakness.

Deep brain stimulation (DBS)

In this procedure, an electrical stimulator is surgically implanted in the chest with leads going deep into the brain. This treatment was first used to help those with Parkinson's disease, a progressive neurological disorder that effects movement. People with Parkinson's noticed an improvement in their moods when DBS was started.

Now, the FDA has approved DBS to be used with very severe, treatment-resistant OCD (see Chapter 2). This innovative treatment appears to have helped some with severe, chronic OCD.

The side effects of DBS can include bleeding of the brain, movement problems, and delirium. At this time, the treatment should only be considered in extreme cases.

Transcranial magnetic stimulation (TMS)

TMS involves inducing a magnetic field on the scalp by sending an electrical current into a coil. This treatment does not require surgical implantation, so side effects are less dangerous than those treatments that involve surgery. However, research on the successful use of this technique for those with anxiety disorders is quite sparse.

TMS has mainly been used to treat depression. Studies on TMS have been somewhat inconsistent. Because studies have varied in the strength of the magnetic field, the placement of the coil, and the duration of the treatment, it is hard to compare and contrast the results. Many more studies are needed to recommend TMS for helping people with anxiety.

Part III
Letting Go of the Battle

The 5th Wave   By Rich Tennant

"Clearly the patient's experiencing difficulty attaining the deep, final level of restful sleep."

In this part . . .

You see how to deal with anxiety more indirectly with a calm, passive approach. We show you how connections with other people, relaxation exercises, breathing techniques, good sleep habits, and proper nutrition all help quell anxious feelings.

You also discover why taking a mindful approach to anxiety is emerging as an exciting, empirically validated way to overcome anxiety. Mindfulness helps you accept the inevitable uncertainty and risk in life with calm detachment.

Chapter 10

Looking at Lifestyle

· ·

· ·

Do you lead a busy life with too much to do and too little time? Do you grab dinner from the nearest drive-through for you and the kids on the way home from soccer practice? Do you lie awake at night thinking about everything you have to do? Your frantic lifestyle probably leads to poor sleep, not enough exercise, and poor diet. You know you should be taking better care of yourself, which makes you feel stressed and anxious, compounding the problem.

In this chapter, we describe three sound strategies for calming down your life: staying connected with others, delegating, and saying "no." We also help you find the motivation for bringing exercise into your life. We show you how to get the best rest possible and what to do in the hours before bed that can help your sleep. Finally, we take a look at some tips for improving eating habits to quell anxious feelings.

Friends and Family — Can't Live with 'em, Can't Live without 'em

Some days, the people in your life provide all the love and support you could ever want. They offer to do things for you, listen to your woes, and comfort you when things go wrong. Other days, those same people make you wish you could move to a deserted island for a couple of weeks. They make unreasonable demands and lean on you excessively — complaining about problems of their own making, leaving you feeling stressed and worn out. The following three sections discuss the pros and cons of people in your life and offer suggestions on how to get the most out of your relationships.

Staying connected to others

In spite of the potential of family and friends to cause stress and aggravation, numerous studies have demonstrated that good, close relationships greatly enhance people's sense of well-being. Staying connected with people pays off in terms of substantially improved mental and physical health. Connections even appear to provide some protection against mental declines that often accompany old age.

So we highly recommend that you focus on friendship, community, and family bonds. Here are a few ideas for doing so:

- Make sure you make face-to-face contact with your friends — don't just e-mail and text them.

- Have family meals together whenever possible — it doesn't have to be any fancier than ordering pizza.

- Volunteer at a nearby Humane Society, hospital, or school.

- Call a friend you haven't talked with in a while.

- Take walks in your neighborhood and introduce yourself to people you encounter.

- Offer to help your family members with a garage sale or some other project.

You get the idea. Staying connected doesn't have to take lots of time or cost money, but it does take effort. That effort pays off not only for you but also for your friends, family, and community.

People with social anxiety may find these activities difficult. If that's the case for you, work on your social anxiety first as described in Chapters 5 through 9.

One connection involves you and at least one other person. So when you reach out to someone else, you may be doing them just as much good as you're doing yourself.

What's that? You say you don't have time to connect with friends and family members? We've got solutions for that problem in the next two sections.

Delegating for extra time

Many people with anxiety feel they must always take responsibility for their job, the care of their family, and their home. Unless they have a hand in everything, they worry that things may not get done. And if someone else takes over a task, they fear that the result will fall short of their standards.

However, if life has become overwhelming and too stressed, learning to delegate may be your only choice. Pushing yourself too hard can put you at risk for illness, bad moods, and increased anxiety. And delegating a few things usually works out much better than you think it will.

Here are a few possibilities for your delegating list:

- ✔ Take the risk of letting your partner do some laundry and cooking.
- ✔ Hire a cleaning service to come in once a month (more often if you can afford it).
- ✔ Spend a Sunday afternoon preparing large quantities of a few meals that can be frozen and consumed over the next week and much later.
- ✔ Enlist the family to spend one hour a week in a frantic, joint cleaning effort.
- ✔ Hire a monthly lawn service.
- ✔ Use online banking and bill paying — it saves more time than you think!
- ✔ Read *Organizing For Dummies* by Eileen Roth and Elizabeth Miles (Wiley).

We realize a few of these ideas cost money. Not always as much as you may think, but still, they do cost something. Partly, it's a matter of how high money stacks up on your priority list. Balance money against time for the things that you value.

Nevertheless, not all families can consider such options. You may notice that not all these options entail financial burden. Get creative. Ask your friends, co-workers, and family for ideas on how to delegate. It could change your life.

Come up with two tasks that you could delegate to someone else. They don't need to cost money — just relieve one or more of your burdens in a way that saves you time.

Just saying "no"

We have one more idea. Say "no." If you're anxious, you may have trouble standing up for your rights. Anxiety often prevents people from expressing their feelings and needs. When that happens, resentment joins anxiety and leads to frustration and anger. Furthermore, if you can't say "no," other people can purposefully or inadvertently take advantage of you. You no longer own your time and your life.

First, notice the situations in which you find yourself agreeing when you don't really want to. Does it happen mostly at work, with family, with friends, or with strangers? When people ask you to do something, try the following:

- ✔ **Validate the person's request or desire.** For example, if someone asks you if you'd mind dropping off something at the post office on your way home from work, say, "I understand that it would be more convenient for you if I dropped that off." This will give you more time to consider whether you really want to do it.

- ✔ **After you make up your mind to say "no," look the person who's making the request in the eye.** You don't need to rush your response.

- ✔ **Give a brief explanation, especially if it's a friend or family member.** However, remember that you really don't owe anyone an explanation for turning down their request; it's merely polite. You can say that you'd like to help out, but it just isn't possible, or you can simply state that you really would rather not.

- ✔ **Be clear that you can't or won't do what you've been asked.** It's a fundamental human right to say "no."

When you say "no" to bosses or family members, they may be temporarily unhappy with you. If you find yourself overreacting to their displeasure, it may be due to an agitating assumption or anxious schema. See Chapter 7 for more information.

Ready . . . Exorcise!

Please excuse our pun: We're not advising that you attempt to exorcise demons or perform hocus-pocus, but like a good housecleaning, exercise can clear out the cobwebs and cast out the cloudy thinking and inertia that may accompany anxiety.

Exercise reduces anxiety. The harder and longer that you go at it — whether you're swimming, jogging, walking, working in the yard or on your home, playing racquetball or tennis, or even walking up the stairs — the less anxious you'll be. Exercise instills a newfound sense of confidence while blowing away anxiety's cloud. With enough exercise, you'll feel your attitude changing from negative to positive.

Some people with anxiety get a little driven and compulsive. Don't take our advice on exercise and go overboard! Yes, the more, the better, but only to a point. If your exercise starts taking time from other important activities, you may be overdoing it.

Exercise reduces anxiety in several ways:

- ✔ It helps to rid your body of the excess adrenaline that increases anxiety and arousal.

- ✔ It increases your body's production of *endorphins* — substances that reduce pain and create a mild, natural sense of well-being.

- ✔ It helps to release muscle tension and frustrations.

Of course, everyone has felt that they should exercise more. Most people realize that exercise has some sort of health benefits, but not everyone knows how extensive these benefits can be. Researchers have found that exercise decreases anxiety, bad cholesterol, blood pressure, depression, and chronic pain. It also decreases risks of various diseases, such as heart disease and some cancers. Finally, exercise improves your immune system, balance, flexibility, mental sharpness, and sense of well-being.

Wow! With such extensive positive effects on anxiety, health, and well-being, why isn't everyone exercising? Millions of people do. Unfortunately, millions do not. The reasons are both simple and complex. For the most part, people hit a brick wall when it comes to finding the motivation to exercise and especially to sustain it. They complain about not having the time and being too embarrassed, too old, too fat, and too tired to exercise. But if our list of benefits appeals to you, the next section, "Don't wait for willpower — Just do it!" may help you muster the motivation. And then, because we know what you're going to think next — "I don't have time to exercise!" — we provide a list of excuse-busting ways to fit your workout into your schedule.

Before beginning an exercise program, you should check with your doctor. This is especially true if you're over 40, overweight, or have any known health problems. Your doctor can tell you about any cautions, limitations, or restrictions that you should consider. Also, if, after brief exercise, you experience chest pain, extreme shortness of breath, nausea, or dizziness, consult your physician immediately.

Don't wait for willpower — Just do it!

Have you ever thought that you just don't have the willpower to undertake an exercise program? You may be surprised to discover that we don't believe in willpower. That's right. *Willpower* is merely a word, an idea; it's not real.

Your brain doesn't have a special structure that contains so-called willpower. It's not something that you have a set quantity of and that you can't do anything about. The reason people believe that they don't have willpower is merely because they don't do what they think they should. But reasons other than willpower account for the lack of effort: namely, distorted thinking and a failure to include sufficient rewards. Therefore, dealing with distorted thoughts and designing rewards works better than waiting for willpower.

Distorted thinking

Your mind may tell you things like, "I just don't have the time," "I'm too tired," "It isn't worth the effort," or, "I'll look stupid compared to the other people who are in better shape than me."

If you're waiting for motivation to come knocking at your door, you could be in for a long wait. Not many people wake up with a burst of new enthusiasm for starting an exercise program. Like the Nike commercials say, "Just do it." That's because motivation frequently follows action; if you think otherwise, you're putting the cart before the horse.

Lack of reward

Another problem that accounts for lack of motivation comes about when you fail to set up a plan for rewarding new efforts. You may believe that exercise will cost you something in terms of leisure time, rest, or more profitable work. In some ways, this is true. That's why you need to set up a plan for reinforcing your efforts.

Psychologists have known for decades that people usually do more of what they find rewarding and less of what they find unpleasant whenever they can. That fact may sound like a no-brainer to you. Nevertheless, ignoring the importance of rewards is easy when trying to get started on an exercise program.

Set up your own personal reward system for exercising. For example, give yourself ten points for each time that you exercise for 30 minutes or more. After you accumulate 100 points, indulge yourself with a treat — buying a new outfit, going out for dinner at a nice restaurant, planning a special weekend, or setting aside a whole day to spend on your favorite hobby. Over time, as exercise becomes a little more pleasant (which it will!), up the ante — require 200 points before you treat yourself.

Eventually, you'll find that exercise becomes rewarding in its own right, and you won't need to reward yourself as a means of instilling the necessary motivation. As the pain of an out-of-shape body lessens and endurance increases, you'll discover other rewards from exercise as well:

- ✔ It can be a great time to think about solutions to problems.
- ✔ You can plan out the day or week while you exercise.
- ✔ Some people report increased creative thoughts during exercise.
- ✔ You may get a great feeling from the sense of accomplishment.

Because exercise often doesn't feel good in the beginning, setting up a self-reward system sometimes helps a great deal; later, other rewards will likely kick in.

Working in your workout

Today, people work longer hours than ever before, so it's tempting to think that the day doesn't hold enough time for exercise. However, it's all a matter of priorities; you won't find the time unless you plan for it.

That's right; you have to scrutinize your schedule seriously and work exercise into your life. Perhaps your job offers flex time, whereby you can choose to come in an hour later and stay later two or three times a week to have time to exercise in the morning, or perhaps you can exercise twice on the weekends and find just one time after work during the week. And it isn't all that difficult to add a little to your regular exercise periods. For example:

- ✔ **Park at a distance:** Park your car about a 20-minute brisk walk away from your place of work once or twice a week.

- ✔ **Take the stairs:** If you often take the elevator up five or six floors to work, try a brisk walk up the stairs several times a day instead.

- ✔ **Exercise during your breaks:** If you get a couple of 10- or 15-minute breaks at work, try going for a brisk walk rather than standing around the water cooler. Two or three 10-minute periods of exercise do you the same amount of good as that one 20- or 30-minute period does.

How about exercise and panic?

Some people fear that exercise could set off panic attacks. In part, that's because exercise produces a few bodily symptoms, such as increased heart rate, that are similar to the symptoms of panic attacks, and those with a panic disorder sometimes respond to such symptoms with panic. However, if you go at exercise gradually, it can serve as a graded exposure task, as we discuss in Chapter 8. In other words, it can be an effective treatment approach for panic.

Although the actual risk is somewhat controversial, exercise can cause a buildup of lactic acid, which does seem to trigger panic attacks in a few people. However, over the long run, exercise also improves your body's ability to rid itself of lactic acid. Therefore, again, we recommend that if you fear having panic attacks as a result of exercise, simply go slowly. If you find it absolutely intolerable, stop exercising for a while or use other strategies in this book for reducing your panic attack frequency before going back to exercise.

The ABCs of Getting Your Zs

People generally need about eight hours of sleep per night. Seniors may need a little less sleep, but this idea remains controversial among scientists. Besides, the real gauge as to whether you're getting enough sleep is how you feel during the daytime, not the exact number of hours you get. In any case, anxiety frequently disrupts sleep, and a lack of sleep can increase your anxiety.

Many people have trouble falling asleep at night. As if falling asleep isn't hard enough, many people wake up before they want to, driven into high alert as anxious thoughts race through their consciousness.

The tendency toward an early-morning awakening with an inability to get back to sleep can be a sign of depression as well as anxiety. If your appetite changes, your energy decreases, your mood swings into low gear, your ability to concentrate diminishes, and you've lost interest in activities that you once found pleasurable, you may be clinically depressed. You should check with a mental-health practitioner or a physician to find out.

More goes into sleeping than just lying down and shutting your eyes. Factors that affect your sleep include the activities you do before you go to bed, your sleeping environment, and knowing what to do when sleep is elusive. We address these topics in the following sections.

Creating a sleep haven

Your sleep environment matters. Of course, some rare birds can sleep almost anywhere — on the couch, in a chair, on the floor, in the car, or even at their desk at work. On the other hand, most folks require the comfort of a bed and the right conditions. Sleep experts report that for a restful sleep, you should sleep in a room that's

- ✔ **Dark:** You have a clock in your brain that tells you when it's time to sleep. Darkness helps set the clock by causing the brain to release melatonin, a hormone that helps to induce sleep. Consider putting up curtains that block out most of the sun if you find yourself awakened by the early morning light or you need to sleep during the day. Some people even wear masks to keep light out.

- ✔ **Cool:** People sleep better in a cool room. If you feel cold, adding blankets is usually preferable to turning up the thermostat.

- ✔ **Quiet:** If you live near a busy street or have loud neighbors, consider getting a fan or white noise generator to block out nuisance noises. The worst kind of noise is intermittent and unpredictable. If the noise is disturbing, the various kinds of sporadic noise that can be blocked out by a simple floor fan may amaze you.

✔ **Complete with a comfortable bed:** Mattresses matter. If you sleep with someone else or a dog, make sure that everyone has enough room.

In other words, make your bedroom a retreat that looks inviting and cozy. Spoil yourself with high-thread-count sheets and pillowcases. You may want to try aromatherapy (see Chapter 12). No one knows for sure whether it works, but many people claim that the fragrance of lavender helps them sleep.

Following a few relaxing routines

Sleep revitalizes your physical and mental resources. Studies show that sleep deprivation causes people to drive as if they were under the influence of drugs or alcohol. Physicians without sufficient sleep make more errors. Sleep deprivation makes you irritable, crabby, anxious, and despondent.

Thus, you need to schedule a reasonable amount of time for sleep — at least seven or eight hours. Don't burn the candle at both ends. We don't care how much work you have on your plate; depriving yourself of sleep only makes you less productive and less pleasant to be around.

So first and foremost, allow sufficient time for sleep. But that's not enough if you have trouble with sleep, so we suggest that you look at the ideas in the subsections that follow to improve the quality of your sleep.

Whenever possible, go to bed at close to the same time every night. Many people like to stay up late on weekends, and that's fine if you're not having sleep problems, but if you are, we recommend sticking to the same schedule you follow on weeknights. You need a regular routine to prepare your mind for bed.

Associating sleep with your bed

One of the most important principles of sleep is to teach your brain to associate sleep with your bed. That means that when you get into bed, don't bring work along with you. Some people find that reading before bed relaxes them, and others like to watch a little TV before bed. That's fine if these activities work for you, but avoid doing them in bed.

If you go to bed and lie there for more than 20 or 30 minutes unable to fall asleep, get up. Again, the point is to train your brain to link your bed to sleep. You can train your brain to dislike getting up by taking on some unpleasant (though fairly passive, even boring) chore while you're awake. If you do this a number of times, your brain will find it easier to start feeling drowsy when you're in bed.

Winding down before hitting the hay

Some people find that taking a warm bath with fragrant oils or bath salts about an hour before hitting the hay is soothing. You may discover that soaking in a scented bath in a dimly lit bathroom while listening to relaxing music before going to bed is just the right ticket to solid slumber. Other people find the relaxation techniques we discuss in Chapters 11 and 12 quite helpful. Studies show that relaxation can improve sleep.

You need to wind down with passive activities before you turn in for the night. Therefore, don't do heavy exercise within a few hours of going to sleep. Almost any stimulating activity can interfere with sleep, even mental exertion. For example, we discovered, somewhat to our dismay, that if we work on writing an article or a book after 9 p.m., our brains continue to spin out thoughts and ideas well after bedtime. So we've changed our routine, and we don't write late in the evening.

Watching what you eat and drink

Obviously, you don't want to load up on caffeinated drinks within a couple of hours before going to bed. Don't forget that many sources other than coffee — colas, certain teas, chocolate, and certain pain relievers — contain caffeine. Of course, some people seem rather impervious to the effects of caffeine while others are better off not consuming any after lunch. Even if you haven't been bothered by caffeine in the past, you can develop sensitivity to it as you age. Consider caffeine's effects on you if you're having trouble sleeping.

Nicotine also revs up the body. Try to avoid smoking just prior to bed. Obviously, it's preferable to quit smoking entirely, but if you haven't been able to stop yet, at least watch how much you smoke before bedtime.

Alcohol relaxes the body and should be a great way of aiding sleep, but it isn't. That's because alcohol disrupts your sleep cycles. You don't get as much of the important REM sleep, and you may find yourself waking up early in the morning. However, some people find that drinking a glass or two of wine in the evening is relaxing. That's fine, but watch the amount.

Heavy meals prior to bed aren't such a great idea either; many people find that eating too much before bed causes mild discomfort. In addition, you may want to avoid highly spiced and/or fatty foods prior to bed. However, going to bed hungry is also a bad idea; the key is balance.

So what should you eat or drink before bed? Herbal teas, such as chamomile or valerian, have many advocates. We don't have much data on how well they work, but herbal teas are unlikely to interfere with sleep, and they're pleasant to drink. Some evidence supports eating a small carbohydrate snack before bedtime to help induce sleep.

Mellowing medication

Many people try treating their sleep problems with over-the-counter medications, many of which contain antihistamines that do help, but they can lead to drowsiness the next day. Occasional use of these medications is relatively safe for most. Herbal formulas, such as melatonin or valerian, may also help.

If your sleep problems are chronic, you should consult your doctor. A medication that you're already taking could possibly be interfering with your sleep. Your doctor may prescribe medication to help induce sleep. Many sleep medications become less effective over time, and some carry the risk of addiction. These potentially addictive medications are only used for a short period of time. On the other hand, a few sleep medications work as sleep aids for a longer time without leading to addiction. Talk about your sleep problem with your doctor for more information and help.

What to do when sleep just won't come

If you've been practicing the suggestions in the previous sections and still haven't resolved your sleep problems, we have a few more suggestions. Becky's story illustrates some of the problematic thoughts people have that keep them awake. Then we tell you what to do about them.

> As the clock chimes the hour, **Becky** sighs, realizing that it's 2 a.m. and she has yet to fall asleep. She turns over and tries to be still so that she doesn't wake her husband. She thinks, "With everything I have to do tomorrow, if I don't sleep, I'll be a wreck. I hate not sleeping." She gets out of bed, goes into the bathroom, finds the bottle of melatonin, and pops three into her mouth. She's been taking them routinely for months, and they just don't seem to have the same effect that they did before.
>
> She goes back to bed, tries to settle down, and worries about the bags under her eyes and what people will think. Her itchy, dry skin starts to crawl. She can't stand the feeling of lying in bed for an eternity without sleeping.

In Becky's mind, her lack of sleep turns into a catastrophe, and her pondering actually makes it far more difficult for her to fall asleep.

When you can't sleep, try to make the problem seem less catastrophic by

- **Reminding yourself that every single time that you failed to sleep in the past, somehow you got through the next day in spite of your lack of sleep the night before.** It may not have been wonderful, but you did it.

- **Realizing that occasional sleep loss happens to everyone.** Excessive worry can only aggravate the problem.

- **Getting up and distracting yourself with something else to do.** This stops your mind from magnifying the problem and can also prevent you from associating your bed with not sleeping.

- **Concentrating solely on your breathing.** See Chapters 11 and 13 for ideas on breathing, mindfulness, and staying in the present moment as opposed to focusing on thoughts about the negative effects of your sleeplessness.

Many people try taking daytime naps when they consistently fail to sleep at night. It sounds like a great solution, but unfortunately, it only compounds the problem. Frequent or prolonged naps disrupt your body's natural clock. If you must nap, make it a short power nap — no longer than 20 minutes.

Of course, a few unusual folks find that they can nap for just three or four minutes whenever they want during the day; they wake up refreshed and sleep well at night. If that's you, go ahead and nap. Most people simply can't do that.

Designing Calm Diets

Uncomfortable emotions cause some people to eat too much, others to seek so-called comfort food (full of fat and sugar), and still others to lose their appetites. Unfortunately, emotional eating only works for the very short run — perhaps a few minutes to an hour or so. In the long run, bad dieting habits increase distress either from weight gain or the negative impact on your body due to spikes in blood sugar levels or irregularity. So we recommend that you follow a few simple, well-known principles of good eating to stabilize both your body and mind.

Enjoying small, frequent portions

Portion sizes have expanded almost as dramatically as people's waistlines over the past century. Your great grandmother's china appears doll-sized by today's standards. In fact, some antique dealers report having trouble convincing customers that grandma's dinner plates really are dinner plates and not for bread or salad.

By and large, most people simply eat too much at one time today. Here are a few ways to control portions:

- ✔ **Use smaller plates:** This creates an optical illusion, and you think you're eating more food than you really are.

- ✔ **Eat slowly:** This gives your stomach time to tell your brain that you're full and should stop eating.

- ✔ **Fill your plate once, and put away the leftovers before you start eating:** This removes the temptation to go back for seconds.

- ✔ **When you're at a restaurant, split a meal with a friend or box up half of it before you start eating:** Restaurant portions are typically twice the size they should be for one meal. Eating only half of the meal provides the right amount of calories.

In other words, plan out what you want to eat and slow down your eating. Prepare several small, healthy snacks for dealing with cravings during the day.

Following nutritional common sense

For many people, the feeling of anxiety is similar to hunger. When stressed, a bowl of ice cream or some French fries with lots of ketchup sounds yummy, and those foods can momentarily boost moods. That's because they contain loads of simple carbohydrates. The body turns those carbs into sugar and burns it up like rocket fuel — really fast. That fast burn then leads to a rapid drop in blood sugar levels often leading to a plunging mood, irritability, and a return of sugar cravings.

Replacing those simple carbohydrates with food containing complex carbs and fiber maintains more stable blood sugar levels and a more stable mood. Complex carbs are found in unprocessed foods, fruits, vegetables, whole grains, and legumes.

Check out the Web site for the U.S. Department of Agriculture at www.mypyramid.gov. Go there to find personalized eating plans, weight-loss information, and recommended nutritional guidelines.

Chapter 11

Relaxation: The Five-Minute Solution

"**I** don't have time to relax. My life is far too hectic. I barely see my friends as it is now. I can't remember the last time I took a whole weekend off. I even neglect my own family. By the time the dinner dishes are put away, I can't think about anything else — I just collapse in front of the television or waste hours in front of my computer screen."

Does this sound like you or someone you care about? When contemplating making changes in their lives, people complain about having too little time more than anything else — including no time for relaxation.

We asked a wise yogi master how long he practices every day, fully expecting to hear the discouraging answer, "An hour or two." Imagine our surprise when he told us, "Five minutes." That's all he needs. He went on to explain that he usually takes more time, but he only commits to five minutes out of each day.

We listened to our teacher, and we now ask a mere five minutes of ourselves daily. Five minutes of relaxation a day has changed our lives. Everyone can find five minutes. And if you relax for five minutes, it may stretch into 10 or 20. But if it doesn't, that's okay. Relaxation will slowly infiltrate your life without you even knowing it, and when anxiety hits, you'll have a valuable tool for calming the storm within.

The relaxation procedures we give you in this chapter fall into three major categories: breathing techniques, ways to relax the body, and a few sensory experiences. Some of these can take a little longer at first to gain full mastery over, but they can all be done in five minutes when you get the hang of them. The key is daily practice. Like every other skill, the more you do it, the easier and faster it gets.

Blowing Anxiety Away

You've practiced breathing more than anything else in your life. In waking moments, you don't even think about breathing. Yet, of all biological functions, breathing is critical to life. You can go days or weeks without food and a couple of days without water but only minutes without breathing. You need oxygen to purify the bloodstream, burn up waste products, and rejuvenate the body and mind. If you don't get enough oxygen, your thinking becomes sluggish, your blood pressure rises, and your heart rate increases. You also get dizzy, shaky, and depressed, and eventually you lose consciousness and die.

Many people react to stress with rapid, shallow breathing that throws off the desired ratio of oxygen to carbon dioxide in the blood. This phenomenon is called *hyperventilation,* and it causes a variety of distressing symptoms:

- Blurred vision
- Disorientation
- Jitteriness
- Loss of consciousness
- Muscle cramps
- Rapid pulse
- Tingling sensations in the extremities or face

Anxiety and relaxation make for strange bedfellows

Have you ever known two people who couldn't be in the same room at the same time? If they show up at the same party, trouble is bound to brew. They're like oil and water — they just don't mix.

Anxiety and relaxation are a little like that. Think about it. How can you be anxious at the same time that you're relaxed? Not an easy accomplishment. Psychologists have a term for this phenomenon: *reciprocal inhibition*. Many psychologists believe that the techniques described in this chapter work because relaxation inhibits anxiety, and vice versa. Training yourself diligently in the use of relaxation skills should help you inhibit your anxiety.

Hyperventilation frequently accompanies panic attacks as well as chronic anxiety. The symptoms of over-breathing feel like symptoms of anxiety, and people with anxiety disorders may hyperventilate. Therefore, finding out how to breathe properly is considered an effective tool for managing anxiety.

Discovering your natural breathing pattern

When you came into the world, unless you had a physical problem with your lungs, you probably breathed just fine. Look at most babies. Unless they're in distress from hunger or pain, they need no instruction in how to breathe or relax. Their little tummies rise and fall with each breath in a rhythmic, natural way. The stresses of everyday life, however, have since meddled with your inborn, natural breathing response.

Under stress, people usually breathe shallow and fast, or, sometimes, they don't breathe at all. Some people hold their breath when they feel stressed and aren't even aware that they're doing it. Try noticing your breathing when you feel stressed, and see whether you're a breath-holder or a rapid, shallow breather.

You can also check out how you breathe when you're not stressed:

1. **Lie down on your back.**

2. **Put one hand on your stomach and the other on your chest.**

3. **Notice the movements of your hands as you breathe.**

   If you're breathing correctly, the hand on your stomach rises as you inhale and lowers as you exhale. The hand on your chest doesn't move so much, and to the extent that it does, it should do so in tandem with the other hand.

The odds are that if you have a problem with anxiety, your breathing could use a tuneup. That's especially so if you have trouble with panic attacks. Breathing practice can start you on the way to feeling calmer.

Breathing like a baby

Abdominal breathing involves breathing with your *diaphragm* — the muscle that lies between your abdominal cavity and your lung cavity. Try this exercise to start breathing slowly and deeply, like a baby again. You may want to lie down, or you can do this while sitting as long as you have a large, comfortable chair that you can stretch out in. Follow these steps:

1. **Check out your body for tension. Notice whether certain muscles feel tight, your breathing is shallow and rapid, you're clenching your teeth, or you have other distressing feelings.**

Rate your tension on a 1-to-10-point scale, with 1 representing complete relaxation and 10 meaning total tension.

2. **Place a hand on your stomach.**

3. **Breathe in slowly through your nose, to a slow count of four, and fill the lower part of your lungs.**

   You're doing this correctly if your hand rises from your abdomen.

4. **Pause and hold your breath for a moment.**

5. **Exhale slowly, to a slow count of six.**

   Imagine your entire body is deflating like a balloon, and let it go limp.

   If you find this hard to do at first, exhale to a count of four. Later, you'll find that slowing down to a count of six is easier.

6. **Pause briefly again.**

7. **Inhale the same way you did in Step 3, slowly through your nose to a slow count of four.**

   Check to see that your hand rises from your abdomen. Your chest should move only slightly and in tandem with your stomach.

8. **Pause and hold your breath briefly.**

9. **Exhale as you did in Step 5, to a slow count of six.**

10. **Continue breathing in and out in this fashion for five minutes.**

11. **Check out your body again for tension, and rate that tension on a scale of 1 to 10.**

We recommend that you do this abdominal breathing exercise at least once a day for five minutes, ten days in a row. For that matter, it isn't difficult to do this four or five times each day — your gains will pile up more quickly. You can do this breathing just about anywhere, anytime. You'll find it relaxing, and it won't add stress to your day by taking away valuable time. After you do that, try noticing your breathing at various times during your regular routine. You'll quickly see whether you're breathing through the diaphragm or the upper chest like so many people do. Allow your diaphragm to take charge of your breathing. Slowly but surely, abdominal breathing can become a new habit that decreases your stress.

Consider keeping a record of your tension levels before and after this exercise. Over time you're likely to see concrete evidence that it works.

Whenever you feel anxiety or panic coming on, try using abdominal breathing. You may head it off at the pass. On the other hand, anxiety, and especially panic, may rise to a level that makes these exercises more difficult. If that happens to you, try the panic-breathing technique that we explain in the next section.

The benefits of controlled breathing

Just in case you think that breathing better sounds like a rather unimaginative, simple way of reducing anxiety, you may want to consider its healthy effects. Studies show that training in breathing can contribute to the reduction of panic attacks within a matter of a few weeks. Other studies have indicated that controlled breathing can slightly reduce blood pressure, improve the heart's rhythm, reduce certain types of epileptic seizures, sharpen mental performance, increase blood circulation, quell worry, and possibly even improve the outcome of cardiac rehabilitation efforts following a heart attack. Not a bad list of benefits for such a simple skill.

Using panic breathing in high-stress situations

Now and then, you need a faster, more powerful technique to relax. Perhaps you went to the mall and felt trapped, or maybe you were on your way to a job interview and felt overwhelmed. Whatever the situation, when stress hits you unexpectedly, try our panic-breathing technique:

1. **Inhale deeply and slowly through your nose.**

2. **Hold your breath for a slow count of six.**

3. **Slowly breathe out through your lips to a count of eight, making a slight hissing sound as you do.**

    That sound can be so soft that only you can hear it. You don't have to worry about anyone around you thinking that you're crazy.

4. **Repeat this type of breath five or ten times.**

You may think that panic breathing is difficult to do when stress strikes suddenly. We won't deny it takes some practice. The key is the slight hissing sound, which gives you a much easier way to slow down your breath.

If panic breathing doesn't help, and you feel like you may be having a full-blown panic attack that won't go away, try breathing in and out of a paper bag with the opening wrapped around your mouth. Breathing this way rebalances the ratio of oxygen to carbon dioxide and should cut the panic attack short. When you breathe too rapidly, your body accumulates an excess of oxygen, although it feels like you have too little of it. Breathing in the bag brings the level of carbon dioxide up to normal.

Don't start carrying a paper bag with you everywhere you go. You need to learn to cope with the fact that sometimes, panic attacks just happen and that you'll live through them if they do.

Relaxing Your Whole Body

Some of you may find that breathing techniques quell your anxiety quickly. Others may require a technique that directly aims at total body relaxation. Relaxing your body takes some time and practice, but it's worth it.

Over a half century ago, Dr. Edmund Jacobsen, a Chicago physician, developed what has come to be the most widely used relaxation technique in the United States, *progressive muscle relaxation.* You can find a wide variety of similar techniques, all described as progressive muscle relaxation, in various books and journals. Each of them may use different muscle groups or proceed in a different order, but they all do essentially the same thing.

Progressive muscle relaxation involves going through various muscle groups in the body and tensing each one for a little while, followed by a quick letting go of the tension. You then attend to the sensation of release, noticing how the limp muscles feel in contrast to their previous tense state.

Knowing what to expect

You'll find it useful to look for the right place to do your progressive muscle relaxation. You probably don't have a soundproof room, but find the quietest place that you can. Consider turning the phones to silent mode. Choose some comfortable clothing, or at least loosen any clothing you're wearing that's tight and constricting. You don't need shoes, belts, or anything uncomfortable.

Realize that when you begin tensing each muscle group, you shouldn't overexert; don't tighten using more than about two-thirds of all your effort. When you tense, hold it for six to ten seconds and notice how the tension feels. Then let go of the tension all at the same time, as though a string holding the muscle up were cut loose.

After you release the muscle, focus on the relaxed feeling and allow it to deepen for 10 or 15 seconds. If you don't achieve a desired state of relaxation for that muscle group, you can do the procedure one or two more times if you want.

You should know that you can't *make* relaxation happen. You *allow* it to happen. Perfectionists struggle with this idea. Don't force it, and rid your mind of the idea that you *must* do this exercise *perfectly.*

When you tighten one muscle group, try to keep all the other muscles in your body relaxed. Doing this takes a little practice, but you can figure out how to tense one body area at a time. Keep your face especially relaxed when you're tensing any area other than your face. Yoga instructors often say, "Soften your eyes." We're not exactly sure what that means, but it seems to help.

Occasionally, relaxation training makes people feel surprisingly uncomfortable. If this happens to you, stop. If it continues to occur with repeated practice, you may want to seek professional help. Also, don't tighten any body part that hurts. Avoid tightening any area that has suffered injury or has given you trouble, such as a lower back.

Discovering the progressive muscle technique

After you've read through the tips in the preceding section, you're ready to start. Sit down in your chosen place and get comfortable.

1. **Take a deep breath, hold, imagine, and let the tension go.**

   Pulling the air into your abdomen, breathe deeply. Hold your breath for three or four seconds, and then slowly let the air out. Imagine your whole body is a balloon losing air as you exhale, and let tension go out with the air. Take three more such breaths and feel your entire body getting more limp with each one.

2. **Squeeze your hands tight and then relax.**

   Squeeze your fingers into a fist. Feel the tension and hold it for six to ten seconds. Then, all at once, release your hands and let them go limp. Allow the tension in your hands to flow out. Let the relaxation deepen for 10 to 15 seconds.

3. **Tighten your arms and then relax.**

   Bring your lower arms up almost to your shoulders and tighten the muscles. Make sure you tense the muscles on the inside and outside of both the upper and lower arms. If you're not sure you're doing that, use one hand to do a tension check on the other arm. Hold the tension a little while, and then drop your arms as though you cut a string holding them up. Let the tension flow out and the relaxation flow in.

4. **Raise up your shoulders, tighten, and then relax.**

   Raise your shoulders up as though you were a turtle trying to get into its shell. Hold the tension and then let your shoulders drop. Feel the relaxation deepen for 10 to 15 seconds.

5. **Tighten and relax the muscles in your upper back.**

   Pull your shoulders back and bring your shoulder blades closer together. Hold that tension a little while . . . then let it go.

6. **Scrunch up your entire face, and then relax.**

   Squeeze your forehead down, bring your jaws together, tighten your eyes and eyebrows, and contract your tongue and lips. Let the tension grow and hold it . . . then relax and let go.

7. **Tighten and relax your neck in the back of your head.**

   Gently pull your head back toward your back and feel the muscles tighten in the back of your neck. If you feel any pain, ease up to avoid hurting your neck. Notice the tension and hold it, then let go and relax. Feel the relaxation deepening.

8. **Contract the front neck muscles and then loosen.**

   Gently move your chin toward your chest. Tighten your neck muscles, let the tension increase, and maintain it; then relax. Feel the tension melting away like candle wax.

9. **Tighten the muscles in your stomach and chest and maintain the tension. Then let it go.**

10. **Arch your back, hang on to the contraction, and then relax.**

    Be gentle with your lower back. Tighten these muscles by arching your lower back, pressing it back against the chair, or tensing the muscles any way you want. Gently increase and maintain the tension, but don't overdo it. Now, relax and allow the waves to roll in.

11. **Contract and relax your buttocks muscles.**

    Tighten your buttocks so as to gently lift yourself up in your chair. Hold the tension. Then let the tension melt and the relaxation grow.

12. **Squeeze and relax your thigh muscles.**

    Tighten and hold these muscles. Then relax and feel the tension draining out; let the calm deepen and spread.

13. **Contract and relax your calves.**

    Tighten the muscles in your calves by pulling your toes toward your face. Take care: If you're prone to muscle cramps, don't overdo it. Hold the tension . . . then let go. Let the tension drain into the floor.

14. **Gently curl your toes, maintain the tension, and then relax.**

15. **Take a little time to tour your entire body.**

    Notice whether you feel better than when you began. If you find areas of tension, allow the relaxed areas around them to come in and replace them. If that doesn't work, repeat the procedure for the tense area.

16. **Spend a few minutes enjoying the relaxed feelings.**

    Let relaxation spread and penetrate every muscle fiber in your body. Notice any sensations you have. Whatever you feel, allow it to happen. When you're ready, you can open your eyes and go on with your day, perhaps feeling like you just returned from a brief vacation.

Some people like to make a recording of the progressive muscle relaxation instructions to facilitate their efforts. If you do, be sure to make your recording in a slow, calming voice.

Extolling the virtues of progressive muscle relaxation

Many people believe that for a remedy to be truly effective, it must take plenty of work and possibly feel a little painful — the no pain, no gain philosophy. As you can see, progressive muscle relaxation isn't especially arduous, and it actually feels good, so can it really do anything for you? Well, for starters, progressive relaxation training is usually a component of most successful treatment programs for anxiety.

However, studies also show that progressive muscle relaxation can effectively reduce various types of chronic pain, such as the pain associated with ulcerative colitis, cancer, and headaches. It also works to reduce insomnia. A study published in the December 2001 issue of the *Journal of Clinical Psychology* found that in addition to inducing greater relaxation, progressive muscle relaxation also led to increased mental quiet and joy. Other studies have suggested that it may improve the functioning of your immune system. We aren't suggesting that progressive muscle relaxation cures cancer, and it won't whisk away all your pain or eradicate all your anxiety. However, many studies clearly show that it exerts benefits across a surprisingly wide range of problems. We recommend that you give it a try.

In the beginning, take a little longer than five minutes to go through the steps of progressive muscle relaxation. Taking 20 or 30 minutes several times at first usually works better. However, the more you practice, the more quickly you'll find that you can slide into serenity. Shorten the procedure as you progress. For example, you can tense all the muscles in your lower body at once, followed by all your upper body muscles. At other times, you may want to simply tense and relax a few body areas that carry most of your tension. Most often, that involves the neck, shoulder, and back muscles. Some folks discover that they can relax in a single minute after they become proficient.

Applying Relaxation in Tense Situations

Discovering how to relax using breathing techniques or progressive muscle relaxation may help you reduce your anxiety. But if you just do these activities when you're lying around in bed or spending a quiet day at home, you miss the opportunity to challenge your fears with a powerful tool. *Applied relaxation* means taking the techniques that you've practiced and putting them to work when you're under the most stress.

The key to success lies in the mastery of the technique in nonstressful settings before taking the next step. For example, maybe you've practiced the progressive relaxation technique many times, and you can tighten and loosen your muscles, achieving a state of relaxation in just a few minutes.

Now that you've mastered the technique in a nonstressful setting, think of a particular situation that frightens you, such as public speaking. For example, say you've scheduled a speaking engagement for a large event with an audience of several hundred people. Before your speech, you practice your favorite relaxation technique. You try to maintain that state as you walk up to give your speech, but you panic anyway. What happened? You tried to take on too much all at once.

Applied relaxation works best if you break the tasks into more manageable steps. For example, you could practice relaxation while thinking about giving your talk. Then you could practice relaxation just before giving your talk to a small audience rather than a large group. Continue your practice in small, graduated steps.

Relaxing through Your Senses

Your path to finding relaxation may lead you through a variety of experiences. We can't possibly know which direction will work best for you. You have to experiment with various approaches to discover your own relaxation remedy. In this section, we ask that you allow your senses to soothe you.

Sounds to soothe the savage beast

Ever since people have populated the planet, they've turned to music for comfort. From primitive drums to symphony orchestras, sound elicits emotions — love, excitement, fear — and even relaxation. An entire profession of music therapists has capitalized on the power of music. Music therapists work in hospitals, schools, and nursing homes using sounds to soothe.

But you don't need to be a music therapist to make use of music's power. You probably already know what type of music calms you. Perhaps you love classical music or jazz. You may not have thought of trying out a CD of ocean waves, babbling brooks, whispering wind, or other sounds of nature. Many people find those sounds quite relaxing.

Visit any well-supplied music store or Web site and you'll find an extensive array of possibilities. Experiment with new sounds. Many of these recordings boast of containing specially mixed music for optimal relaxation.

Buyer beware! Don't buy just any recording that promises relaxation. Unfortunately, some of these products are rather inferior. Either get recommendations or listen to a sample.

Only the nose knows for sure

Ever walk through a mall and smell freshly baked cinnamon rolls? Perhaps you were tempted to buy one just because of the aroma. We suspect that the smell of the delicacies is no accident; rather, we think that the bakers must pump the air up and out from around their ovens into the entire mall ventilation system, knowing the powerful effects of aroma.

In addition to making you hungry, the cinnamon roll scent may also elicit pleasant emotions and memories. Perhaps it takes you back to Sunday mornings when your mother baked fresh rolls or to a pleasant café. If so, the aroma automatically brings back memories — no effort required on your part.

A huge perfume industry uses the power of aromas to attract and seduce. Manufacturers of deodorants, lotions, powders, hair sprays, and air fresheners do the same, and you can explore the ability of aroma to calm your jangled nerves.

Aromatherapy makes use of essential oils, which are natural substances extracted from plants. These substances ostensibly affect both physical and emotional health. We can't vouch for these claims, because good studies on their effects are lacking. However, the theory behind aromatherapy isn't entirely wacky, because our bodies have nerves that transmit messages from the nose into the parts of the brain that control mood, memories, and appetite.

If you're physically sick, please consult a qualified doctor, because aromatherapy isn't likely to cure you. No one knows whether aromatherapy promotes good health. Also, don't use these substances if you're pregnant.

However, if you want to experiment with various aromas to see if any of them help you relax, go for it. Preliminary studies have suggested that certain aromas may alleviate anxiety and decrease nicotine withdrawal symptoms and headaches.

Consider the following aromatherapy scent suggestions, but be sure to shop around because prices can vary substantially. A trusted local health-food store may be a good place to start.

- ✔ Chamomile
- ✔ Eucalyptus
- ✔ Lavender
- ✔ Neroli (citrus aurantium)

These essential oils may help relieve anxiety and combat sleeplessness. Besides, they smell pretty good, so put a few drops in your warm bath or on your pillow. Have a good sleep.

Massaging away stress

About 15 times a day, one of our dogs sticks his nose under one of our arms to indicate that he's overdue for a rubdown. Dogs unabashedly beg for touching, petting, and rubbing. Our dogs are pretty good at getting it, too.

People need to be touched, too. It's great to be hugged and stroked by the people we care about. However, one wonderful way to satisfy the need to be touched and relax at the same time is through a professional massage. If you've never indulged, consider treating yourself to a massage. In years past, only the elite sought massage therapy. Today, people flock to massage therapists to reduce stress, to manage pain, and to just plain feel good.

Another way of getting a massage is to sit in a whirlpool for five minutes. This can be relaxing because, in addition to the massage that you get from the force of the water jets, the feel of the warm water that's forced into the whirlpool and the sound of the water rushing around also has a calming effect. Although some homes have whirlpools built into their bathtubs, most health spas and YMCAs/YWCAs also have whirlpools that patrons can enjoy for a small fee in addition to the cost of a basic membership.

Everybody needs touching

In the 1940s, many European babies ended up in orphanages. A shocking number of these orphans failed to grow or interact with others, and some appeared to wilt away and die for no discernible reason. They had sufficient food, clothing, and shelter. A physician named Dr. Rene Spitz investigated and found that their failure to thrive appeared to be due to a lack of human touch. In other words, the caregivers provided nutrients but not contact.

This early finding has been supported by numerous studies conducted by psychologist Tiffany Field and her colleagues. One of these studies found that premature infants who were given regular massages gained more weight than those who merely received standard medical care. Other studies by this research group have included normal babies, as well as infants born with HIV or cocaine addiction, and young children with diabetes, eating disorders, and asthma. Babies and children who receive a massage regularly have lower amounts of stress hormones and lower levels of anxiety than those who don't. Other benefits that were identified include pain reduction, increased attentiveness, and enhanced immune function. If it's this good for babies, we figure that it's pretty good for you, too. Indulge!

Chapter 12

Creating Calm in Your Imagination

*P*eople who have a vivid imagination (perhaps this describes you) can think themselves into all kinds of anxious situations. Just give them a moment to play with an idea, and they're off on another anxiety trip.

But the good news is that you can backtrack and rewind your mind to a calmer place. One way to do that is through *guided imagery*. Guided imagery creates a calm place by using your imagination to put yourself into a state of relaxation and peace. Your mind takes you to a pleasant, beautiful, serene time or space. The best images incorporate all your senses. When visualizing them, you see, hear, smell, feel, and possibly taste them. For example, you might imagine hearing birds, smelling flowers, feeling a slight breeze, and enjoying the taste of chocolate in the middle of a beautiful meadow.

Some people find that breathing exercises or progressive relaxation don't get them sufficiently relaxed. In those cases, guided imagery is often a good alternative. The following example demonstrates the usefulness of guided imagery.

Tense thoughts fill **Shauna's** every waking moment. From the time that she springs out of bed in the morning to the last gripping thought before restless sleep mercifully overtakes her, Shauna thinks. She replays every anxious moment at her job and dwells on each imagined error that she's made during the day, turning it over and over in her mind. She visualizes every flaw in her makeup, dress, and complexion. Images of incompetence, inadequacy, and unattractiveness flood her mind's eye.

To reduce the stress and anxiety that saturate the scenes in her mind, she decides to seek the services of a counselor. The counselor teaches her several breathing techniques, but Shauna can't hold back the avalanche of anxious images. She tries progressive muscle relaxation, massage, and then music and aromatherapy to no avail. Finally, her counselor has an insight. "Shauna thinks in pictures; she needs guided imagery!"

In Shauna's case, her day-to-day images were full of anxiety-arousing situations. When she tried other relaxation techniques, they failed because anxious images still filled her mind. With guided imagery, however, the richness of the peaceful experience pushed aside all other concerns.

In this chapter, we show you how to improve your imagination. Then we give you several scripts to play with in your mind. Feel free to revise them any way you want. Finally, you can customize your own special mental images.

Letting Your Imagination Roam

Some people, thinking of themselves as rather unimaginative, struggle to create pictures in their minds. These people generally feel uncomfortable with their drawing skills and have a hard time recalling the details of events they've witnessed. Perhaps you're one of them. If so, using your imagination to relax and reduce your anxiety may not be the approach for you.

On the other hand, it just might. Guided imagery encompasses more than the visual sense; it includes smell, taste, touch, and sound. We can help you sharpen your ability to use all these senses.

We encourage you to give these exercises a shot, but all people have different strengths and weaknesses, and you may find that one or more of these exercises just don't work for you. If you discover that guided imagery isn't for you, that's okay. For example, some folks have problems with hearing, sight, or smell that could impede their ability to use certain techniques based on those senses. Not to worry — this book discusses many other ways to relax.

We don't want to make you more anxious by telling you these exercises must be done in a certain order or frequency. Try them out as you wish. Our editor found herself surprisingly relaxed at work after reading about these techniques! But watch out; don't fall asleep on the job.

Just before doing each series of numbered steps for the guided imagery exercises in this chapter, do the following:

1. **Find a comfortable place to sit or lie down.**

2. **Make sure that you loosen any tight garments and shoes.**

3. **Close your eyes and take a few slow, deep breaths.**

Imagining touch

Imagery exercises work best if they incorporate more than one sense. Imagining bodily sensations enhances the overall experience of relaxing, guided imagery. Take the following steps to see how this works:

1. **Imagine an oversized, sunken bathtub.**

2. **Picture yourself turning the faucet on and feeling the water coming out.**

   You can feel that the water is cold and wet as it pours over your hand. Gradually, the temperature increases until it reaches your perfect range.

3. **The tub fills, and you mentally see yourself pouring bath oil in and mixing it around.**

   You can feel how silky the water becomes.

4. **You imagine putting your foot in the water.**

   The water feels just a bit too hot at first, but you find that the warm temperature soothes you after lowering your body into the bathtub.

5. **You lay back and luxuriate in the slick, smooth, warm water.**

   You can feel it envelop you as the warmth loosens your muscles.

Were you able to feel the sensations: the wetness and the silky warmth? If not, don't despair. You can improve your awareness by spending just five minutes a day actively participating in a real experience and then committing that experience to your memory.

Try one or more of the following exercises each day for five days straight. You can experiment with other exercises, too. Just be sure to focus on touch.

- ✔ **Hold your hands under different temperatures of water.** Notice how they feel. Better yet, fill the basin and submerge your hands to conserve water.

- ✔ **Rub oil on the back of your hand and wrist.** Notice how the oil feels.

- ✔ **Take a warm bath and notice the sensations of wetness, warmth, and silkiness.** Focus on all your bodily sensations.

- ✔ **Put a washcloth in hot water, wring it out, and press it to your forehead.** Notice the warmth and the texture of the cloth.

- ✔ **Sit in front of the fireplace and notice where the heat hits your body.** Experience the warmth.

After participating in one of the preceding exercises, wait one minute. Then try to conjure up what the sensations felt like in your mind. The following day, do the exercise, wait five minutes, and then recall the sensations. Each day, make the length of time between the actual experience and your recollection of the experience a little longer.

Recalling sounds

You don't have to be a musician to appreciate music or to re-create it in your mind. Guided imagery often asks you to create the sounds of nature in your mind to enhance relaxation. Taking the following steps, try imagining what an ocean beach sounds like:

1. **Imagine that you're lying on a beach.**

   You can hear the ocean waves rolling in one after the other. In and out. The soft roar soothes and relaxes. In and out.

2. **In your mind, you hear each wave rolling in and coming to a crescendo as it breaks gently onto the beach.**

   A brief moment of quiet follows as the next wave prepares to roll in. A few seagulls cry out as they fly overhead.

Were you able to hear the ocean and the gulls? You can improve your ability to re-create sounds in your mind by actively experiencing the real McCoy beforehand.

Try some of the following exercises for just five minutes a day for five days. You may think of some other ways to practice listening to sounds with your mind's eye, too.

- ✓ **Listen to a short passage from a favorite song.** Play it several times and listen to each note. Tune in and concentrate.

- ✓ **Sit in a chair in your living room and listen.** Turn off the phones, stereos, and anything else cranking out noise. Closing your eyes and listening carefully, notice every sound that you hear — perhaps the traffic outside, a dog barking, a little wind, or the house creaking.

- ✓ **Listen to the sound of yourself eating an apple, a celery stick, or a carrot.** Not only is it good for you, but you'll also hear interesting sounds. Eat slowly and hear each crunch. Notice the initial sharp sound of biting and the more muted chewing.

Following your experience, wait one minute. Then reproduce the sounds in your mind. Hear them again. Don't worry if you can't do it. With practice, you're likely to get better. Increase the wait between the actual experience and your recollection a little each day.

Remembering tastes

Which foods do you associate with comfort and relaxation? Many people think of chicken soup or herbal tea. One of us spreads peanut butter on toast when really stressed, and the other occasionally indulges in ice cream — especially chocolate and caramel swirls threaded through rich vanilla. Are you salivating yet? If not, try playing out this imaginary scene:

1. **Imagine an exquisite chocolate truffle.**

   You're not sure what's inside, but you look forward to finding out.

2. **In your mind, you bring the truffle to your lips and slowly bite off a corner of the truffle.**

   The rich, sweet chocolate coats your tongue.

3. **Imagine taking another bite and detecting a creamy, fruity center.**

   You've never tasted anything so rich and delectable yet not overpowering. The sweet but slightly tangy cherry flavor fills your body with satisfaction.

Could you taste the truffle in your imagination? Perhaps you found it easier than the smell. Either way, you can improve your ability to recall tastes with practice. Try one or more of these exercises:

- ✔ **Bake some fresh, iced brownies.** Okay, you can pick some up from a bakery if you must. First, taste the brownie with the tip of your tongue. Hold it in your mouth and move it to different spots on your tongue. Then chew it and notice the icing and the cake flavors mixing together.

- ✔ **Open and heat up a can of your favorite soup.** Pour a little into a cup or bowl. Put a small spoonful into your mouth. Be sure it's not too hot. Notice how the soup tastes on every part of your tongue.

You can do this taste-focusing activity with any food that you want. The key is to take some time and focus. Savor the flavors and pay attention to the nuances — sweet, sour, bitter, or salty. Again, try to call the tastes to mind after about a minute. Then stretch out the period between the actual experience and the recall a little longer each time you practice.

Conjuring up smells

Our dogs have a far better sense of smell than we do. They seem to know exactly which bush on their walking route needs re-marking. We're pretty sure that they know exactly which rival dog did what to which bush. Perhaps the fact that we can't smell as well as they can is a good thing.

But smell has a powerful influence on people as well. Certain smells alert us to danger, such as the smell of smoke or spoiling food. Other smells inevitably conjure up pleasant memories and feelings, such as the aroma of your favorite baked delight or the perfumed scent of a loved one. See whether this description brings a smell wafting into your mind:

1. **Imagine that you're sleeping on a screened porch in a country cottage nestled in the forest.**

   You've been aware of a slow, steady rainfall through the night. When you awaken, the sun is shining.

2. **In your mind, you can smell the sweet aroma of freshly cleaned air, crisp and cool.**

   The earthy smell of the forest floor washed by nature reaches your awareness.

3. **You stretch and breathe deeply.**

   You detect the musty odor of fallen leaves. A pleasant, refreshing feeling engulfs you.

How did this scene smell in your mind? Smell is a primitive sense and may not be as easy to consciously produce with your imagination. That may be because a description of smell is more difficult to put into words. However, with practice, you're likely to improve.

Try a few of these activities to help you develop your imagination's sense of smell:

- ✔ **Make a cup of hot chocolate.** Before drinking it, spend a minute taking in the aroma. Focus on the smell as you take each sip.

- ✔ **Bake dinner rolls.** Don't worry; you can buy the ready-made kind that you pop out onto a cookie sheet. Sit in the kitchen while they bake. Open the oven door a couple of times to intensify the experience.

- ✔ **Visit a department store, go to the perfume counter, and test several different scents.** Try to describe the differences.

Now try to remember what smell you experienced a minute later. Take a little longer each day before trying to recall the odors.

Painting pictures in your mind

Many of our clients report that scenes of anticipated disasters and doom invade their imagination. These scenes cause them more anxiety than actual disastrous events usually do. Visual imagery can fuel your anxiety, or you can enlist your visual imagination to help you drown the fires of anxiety. Try painting this picture in your mind:

1. **Imagine that you're at a mountain resort in late spring.**

2. **In your mind, you spent the day trekking through a forest. Now, you're relaxing on the deck of your cabin overlooking a valley lake ringed by mountain peaks.**

   The water on the lake is still; the dark blue surface reflects surprisingly clear images of the trees and mountains. The sun sinks behind a mountain peak, painting the clouds above in brilliant hues of red, orange, and pink. The mountains remain capped with snow from the winter. Dark green fir trees stand proudly above a carpet of pine cones and needles.

How did this scene look in your mind? If you practice sharpening your visual imagery, you'll become an expert eyewitness. Wherever you are, take one minute to inspect the view in front of you. It doesn't matter what that is. Scrutinize the image from every angle. Notice colors, textures, shapes, proportions, and positions. Then close your eyes. Try to recollect the images in your mind. Focus on every detail. You can practice this anywhere and anytime. It just takes a few minutes. Each day, delay your imagery retrieval a little longer after turning away from the scene that you just studied.

Mindfulness: Finding peace in the present

Our sense-sharpening exercises actually form part of a more powerful approach to overcoming anxiety — *mindfulness,* which we discuss in greater depth in Chapter 13. A technique that has been used for several thousands of years in both the secular and religious settings of the Far East, mindfulness involves immersing yourself in the present with full awareness. When you fully attend to your immediate surroundings, catastrophic predictions about the future fade and anxiety drops.

Mindfulness has only recently found its way into Western psychology. However, in the past few years, researchers have discovered that training in mindfulness can substantially supplement other approaches to anxiety reduction. We recommend that you work on sharpening your awareness of your experiences, and then read Chapter 13 to discover more.

Full Sensory Imaging

The best and most effective guided imagery incorporates multiple senses — not necessarily every one, every time, but for the most part, the more the better. If you aren't as adept at using one or two senses, try to focus on using your more-developed senses. We have a couple of imaginary scenes in the upcoming sections for you to try that use most of your senses to recall an experience.

If you like our scenes, use them. Perhaps you'll want to make a recording of one or both of them. If you do, feel free to modify the scene in any way that helps you to imagine it more vividly or feel more at peace. At a time when you're feeling relaxed, make an audio recording of yourself reading the following sections. Then listen to the recording at a later time to help you relax. Perhaps you can play a recording of ocean sounds in the background as you read and record the "Relaxing at the beach" exercise. Similarly, you may play a recording of forest sounds as you tape yourself reading "A forest fantasy." Commercial recordings are also available.

Relaxing at the beach

Let this scene transport you to a quiet beach where your cares can melt away.

1. **Imagine that you're walking barefoot through a sandy beach on a warm, sunny day.**

   The sand feels warm between your toes. Reaching the ocean shore and feeling the cool, refreshing water lap over your feet, you smell the crisp, salty air and take a deep breath; calmness comes over you.

2. **You walk farther and reach an area where rocks jut out into the surf.**

   A wave crashes onto the rocks and sends a fine mist high into the air; small droplets spray on your face and feel delightfully refreshing.

3. **Seagulls glide effortlessly high above and then dive, skimming the surface of the water.**

   They look like acrobats of the sky, gracefully soaring in and out of sight. The surf and the seagulls orchestrate a soothing soundtrack. A wooden Adirondack chair beckons you farther down the beach.

4. **You stroll over to the chair and stretch out on it when you get there.**

   The wood warmed by the sun is smooth against your skin.

5. **Magically, a frosted glass of your favorite beverage appears on a small side table.**

6. **Sipping and feeling the cold liquid fill your mouth and slide down your throat, you feel refreshed and satisfied, serene and content.**

7. **You take a look out at the horizon and see a couple of sailboats floating lazily in the distance.**

   You feel the warm sun bathe your skin; at the same time, a gentle breeze cools your skin to a perfect balance. You've never felt so relaxed in your life.

8. **You lie back and close your eyes.**

   You can feel all the muscles in your body let go. You feel sleepy but alert at the same time. Nature's beauty fills you with awe, melting your worries away.

A forest fantasy

Sometimes a walk in the woods, even an imaginary one, can do wonders for your body, mind, and spirit.

1. **Imagine that you're walking through pine trees and brush.**

   The sap of the trees gives off a sweet, pungent aroma. You hear the branches rustle in the breeze. Sunlight filters through the branches of the trees, making shadows dance across the ground.

2. **Your feet can feel the spring in the path covered with years of fallen leaves.**

   You hear a brook babbling in the distance.

3. **You reach into your backpack, take out a container of cold water, and sip.**

   As you sip, you feel at peace and start to relax. You hear birds overhead.

4. **As you proceed, the trees begin to thin.**

   You reach a stream with clear water flowing swiftly over and around the small rocks in its bed.

5. **You bend down to touch the water; it's cold, clean, and pure.**

6. **You splash a bit of the brisk water over your face and feel cleansed.**

   Just ahead, you notice a grassy meadow, filled with wildflowers. The flowers' fragrance gently fills the air with sweetness.

7. **You reach a grassy, soft spot and sit down.**

   From here, you can see for many miles in the distance. The air is pure and clean. The sun feels warm on your skin. The sky is a brilliant blue backdrop to a few white, billowy clouds.

8. **Sleepiness overtakes you and you lie down.**

   You can feel your entire body relaxing. Your everyday concerns seem trivial. All that matters is the moment. You cherish the experience of connection to the earth.

Customizing Your Own Images

You may want to create your own imaginary journey. It can be somewhere that you've been before or somewhere you've never seen. Try a few out to see how they work for you. Many people use guided imagery to help them go to sleep. Others use these images to help them relax before a stressful event, such as taking a test. We have a few helpful hints for designing your own guided imagery for relaxation:

- The most important hint is to enjoy yourself.
- Be creative; let your mind go wild, coming up with any scene that might feel good to you.
- Use multiple senses.
- Add descriptive details. Consider using a thesaurus for rich adjectives.
- Make your scene long enough that it lasts a little while. It takes some time for your body to relax.
- Consider playing soothing music or sounds in the background as you make the recording.
- Be sure to include relaxing suggestions, such as "I'm feeling calmer," "My worries are melting away," or "My body feels loose and relaxed."
- Realize that there's no right or wrong way to design an image. Don't judge your scene.

If creating your own imaginary journey doesn't work for you, don't sweat it. You can find many other ways to relax.

Imagining a positive outcome

Athletes commonly use images to reduce their performance anxiety. In addition, many of them create images of success. For example, a gymnast may envision himself making a perfect dismount off the balance beam over and over. Or a runner may see herself pushing through pain, stretching her legs out for a first-place finish again and again. Various studies indicate that imagery can give an athlete an extra boost.

Another way to use imagery is to face your fears in a less stressful way than meeting them head-on in real life. You do this by repeatedly imagining yourself conquering your fears. We tell you more about exactly how to do this in Chapter 8.

Chapter 13

Mindful Acceptance

In This Chapter

▶ Accepting the struggle of life

▶ Giving up ego to make life easier

▶ Focusing on the present

▶ Practicing mindfulness

▶ Cultivating your spirituality

*H*as your car ever been stuck on a muddy road? What happens if you gun the accelerator harder when the wheels start to spin? They spin even harder, the mud flies everywhere, and the rut gets deeper. Anxiety can be like that: The harder you try to break free, the tighter it seems to grip.

In this chapter, we explain how to use *acceptance* as one way to get out of your anxiety trap. Threads of what we call *mindful* acceptance show up throughout this book. We weave the threads together to form a tapestry. We show how acceptance helps you stop spinning your wheels so you can calmly consider productive alternatives. We discuss how too much concern with ego and self-esteem can make seeing the way out difficult, and we explain how living in the present provides a roadway to a more balanced life. Finally, we give you some thoughts about the possible role of spirituality in finding serenity.

When you find yourself stuck in the rut of anxiety, don't slam down on the accelerator. Sit back, let the wheels settle a bit, rock back into the rut, and then gently push forward. Eventually, you'll discover a rhythm of going forward, then rocking back, and your efforts will lead you to solid ground.

Accepting Anxiety? Hey, That's a Switch!

So why is it that after showing you how to get rid of your anxiety, we tell you to mindfully accept it? Have *we* lost our minds? Isn't this book supposed to be about *overcoming* anxiety?

Well, yes, of course we want you to overcome your anxiety. But the paradox of anxiety is that the more you feel you must rid yourself of it, the more anxious you feel. The more your anxiety disturbs you, the more it ensnares you.

Imagine going to a carnival or birthday party where someone gives you a Chinese handcuff — a little, decorative, woven straw tube. You put both index fingers into the tube. Then you try to extract your fingers. The tube closes tightly around your fingers. The harder you pull, the tighter the handcuffs squeeze; a way out doesn't seem to exist. So you pull even harder. Eventually, you realize that the only way out is to quit trying.

Anxiety mimics the squeezing of Chinese handcuffs. The more you struggle, the more trapped you feel. Insisting that your anxiety go away this second is a surefire way to increase it! Instead, sit back and think about your anxiety. We describe how in the following sections.

Taking a calm, dispassionate view

Anthropologists study the behavior and culture of human beings. They make their observations objectively from a dispassionate, scientific perspective. We want you to view your anxiety like an anthropologist — coolly detached.

Wait for the next time that you feel anxious. Study your anxiety and prepare a report that conveys what anxiety feels like in your body, how it affects your thoughts, and what it does to your actions. Don't judge the anxiety — just observe it. Then, being as objective as possible, answer the following questions in your report:

- Where in my body do I feel tension? In my shoulders, back, jaw, hands, or neck? Study it, and describe how the tension feels.

- Are my hands sweating?

- Is my heart racing? If so, how fast?

- Do I feel tightness in my chest or throat?

- Do I feel dizzy? Study the dizziness and describe it.

- What am I thinking? Am I . . .

    - Making negative predictions about the future?

    - Making a mountain out of a molehill?

    - Turning an unpleasant event into a catastrophe?

    - Upset about something that's outside of my control?

> ✔ What is my anxiety telling me to do?
>
>   • To avoid doing something that I want to do?
>
>   • That I need to be perfect?
>
>   • That I have to cover up my anxiety?

Mel's story that follows provides a good example of how your powers of observation may help you get a handle on your anxious feelings.

> **Mel,** a 38-year-old hospital administrator, experienced his first panic attack three years ago. Since then, his attacks have increased in frequency and intensity, and he's even started to miss work on days when he feared having to lead staff meetings.
>
> Now, he works with a therapist to decrease his panic. The therapist notices that Mel's perfectionism drives him to demand instant improvement. He reads everything he's assigned and tries to do every task perfectly. The therapist, realizing that Mel needs to slow down and back up, gives him an assignment to pretend that he's an anthropologist on a mission and to write a report about his anxiety. Mel completes the assignment as follows:
>
> I started noticing a little shortness of breath. I thought: It's starting again! Then my heart began to race. I noticed it was beating fast and I wondered how long it would last. Then I noticed that my hands were sweating. I felt nauseous. I didn't want to go to work. I could almost hear the anxiety telling me that I would feel much better if I stayed home because if I went to work, I'd have to talk to a room full of upset surgeons. I have to tell them about the new billing procedures. They're not going to like it. They'll probably rip me to shreds. What an interesting image. I've never really been ripped into shreds, but my image is amazing! If I get too anxious, my words will turn into nonsense, and I'll look like a total fool. This is interesting, too. I'm making incredibly negative predictions about the future. It's funny — as I say that, I feel just a tiny bit less anxious.

Mel discovered that letting go and merely observing his anxiety helped. Rather than attack his anxious feelings and thoughts, he watched and pondered his experience by really trying to emulate the sense of scientific curiosity of anthropologists.

Tolerating uncertainty

Anxious people usually detest uncertainty. If only they could control everything around them, they might not worry so much, and that's probably true: If you could control everything, you wouldn't have much cause for worry, would you?

The rather obvious flaw in this approach lies in the fact that life consists of constant uncertainty and a degree of chaos. In fact, a basic law of physics states that, even in so-called hard sciences, absolute certainty is nonexistent. Accidents and unforeseen events happen.

For example, you don't know the day and time that your car will break down on the way to work. You can't predict the stock market, although many people try. Bad things happen to good people all the time. Even if you spent every moment of your waking life trying to prevent illness, financial difficulties, and loss of loved ones, you couldn't do it.

Not only is the task of preventing calamities impossible, you can easily ruin most of your present moments if you try. Think about it. If you check your car's engine before leaving for work each day, if you scrimp and save every possible penny for retirement, if you never eat ice cream because of the fat content, if you overprotect your children because you worry that they'll get into trouble, if you wash your hands every time you touch a doorknob, if you never take a risk, then what will your life be like? Probably not much fun.

Worry doesn't change what will happen. Some people think that if they worry enough, bad things won't occur. Because bad things don't happen to them on most of those worry days, they feel like their worrying has paid off. But worry by itself has never in the history of humans prevented anything from happening. Not once.

Find out how to embrace uncertainty, which can make life both interesting and exciting. Discover how to appreciate adversity as well as a little suffering. Without some suffering and adversity, you fail to value the good moments.

When you find yourself feeling anxious, ask yourself whether your worry is an attempt to control the unpredictable. For example, many people worry about their retirement funds in the stock market. They watch how their stocks are doing every single day. They scan the newspaper for financial information that may possibly help them know when to sell at just the right moment. Yet, as the past few years have shown, there are no guarantees in the stock market.

Let go of your need to predict and control. Of course, take reasonable precautions regarding your health, family, finances, and well-being, but when worry about the future invades the present enjoyment of your life, it has gone too far. Appreciate uncertainty and live well today.

Being patient with yourself

When you think about patience, what comes to mind? Calm, acceptance, and tolerance. When you become anxious, try to be patient and kind with yourself and say to yourself,

✔ Okay, I'm feeling anxious. That's my experience.

✔ Like other feelings, anxiety comes and goes.

✔ Let me be present with my anxiety.

In the example of Jeanine that follows, Jeanine's contrasting reactions, first with impatience and then with patience, provide an illustration of how you, too, can turn your impatience into patience.

> **Jeanine** begins to feel anxious during the morning commute. She leaves home at 7:15 a.m. and usually can count on being to work on time at 8 a.m. Frequently, she arrives about five minutes early, but once a month or so, traffic backs up, and she's a few minutes late. This morning appears to be one of those.
>
> **The impatient Jeanine:** Traffic is at a standstill, and anxiety churns in Jeanine's stomach and builds. Sweating and clutching the steering wheel, she begins tracking the ways that she can change lanes and get through a bit faster. She hates starting her day out like this. She can't stand the anxiety and tries to get rid of it, but she fails. She visualizes her boss noticing her tardiness and the others at her office looking up at her. Anxiety turns to anger as she criticizes herself for not leaving earlier.
>
> **The patient Jeanine:** Traffic is at a standstill, and anxiety churns in Jeanine's stomach. Clutching the steering wheel, she fights the urge to change lanes. She notices and accepts the anxiety in her body, thinking, "I may be late, but most every morning, I am on time or early. My boss and co-workers know that. I can feel my anxiety, but that's my experience. How interesting. I'll arrive a few minutes late this morning, and that's okay."

In the second scenario, the anxiety dissipates because Jeanine allows herself to feel it without judgment or intolerance. She connects to her present situation with patience.

Like everything else, making patience a habit takes practice. You build your tolerance for patience over time. Like building muscles by lifting weights, you can build the patience muscles in your mind a little at a time.

Letting Go of Ego

Everyone wants to have high self-esteem. Bookstores and libraries display hundreds of books about how to pump up your self-esteem. You may think that having high self-esteem would decrease your anxiety. It seems logical anyway.

However, self-esteem doesn't work that way. In fact, overly positive self-esteem causes more anxiety, as well as a host of other ills. Similarly, most positive human characteristics and qualities turn into negatives when they reach extreme levels. For example, courage, generosity, diligence, and trust are all wonderful traits. But excessive courage can make a person reckless, excessive generosity can make a person an easy mark for the dishonest, excessive focus on work can leave insufficient room for pleasure, and excessive trust can turn someone into a dupe. Perhaps our upcoming description of self-esteem as similar to a balloon may help you understand the shocking dangers of too much investment in ego and self-esteem.

Inflating and deflating the self-esteem balloon

We think of self-esteem like a balloon. Too little self-esteem is like an empty balloon. It has no air; it's flat, deflated, and can't float. Therefore, a deflated balloon isn't especially fun or useful. If your self-esteem is quite low, you probably spend time judging yourself harshly and negatively. Your energy probably suffers, and you may feel quite anxious about your perceived deficiencies.

Too much ego or self-esteem, however, is like a balloon that's tightly stretched and so full of air that it's about to explode. One tiny scrape, and the balloon bursts. People with too much self-esteem worry constantly about those scrapes. Any threat to their self-esteem causes considerable anxiety and sometimes anger. You can't do much in life without running into at least some threat to your ego. If your self-esteem balloon is too full of itself, those threats can appear especially ominous.

On the other hand, a balloon with just the right amount of air is pretty tough to break. It can bounce around easily, joyfully, and playfully. The balloon with the right amount of air doesn't worry so much about crashing or bursting.

In a sense, both the deflated balloon and the one close to the bursting point worry plenty about their own state: their condition, worth, and vulnerability. The key to having just the right amount of ego — air in the balloon — is to have *less* concern with yourself (along with more concern for others) and less worry about how you stack up against others.

When you can accept both your positive and negative qualities without being overly concerned for either, you'll have the right amount of air in your ego balloon, but that isn't always so easy to do. It takes a solid focus on learning, striving, and working hard — though not to excess.

The seductive power of positive thinking

In the 1950s, self-help gurus began a movement by encouraging everyone to pump up their self-esteem. Before 1950, less than a hundred articles were written on the topic of self-esteem in professional journals; however, in the past ten years alone, more than 8,000 such articles have appeared in social science journals. In addition, literally thousands of self-help books have promoted the unquestioned value of nurturing self-esteem. The self-esteem movement now permeates parenting magazines, school curriculums, and bookshelves. It seduced a generation of parents, teachers, and mental-health workers into believing that the best thing that they could do for kids was to pump up their self-esteem.

So has more than a half-century of promoting self-esteem (also known as *ego*) paid off?

Hardly. Today, school achievement lags significantly behind where it was in 1960. School grades, however, are up. School violence is much higher than 50 years ago, and the rates of depression and anxiety among today's youth are higher than ever.

Why? An incredible number of recent research studies show a strong link between the over-abundant focus on the self and violence, poor school achievement, and emotional problems of all sorts. Deflated self-esteem also appears to be bad for you, but studies suggest that an overly inflated self-esteem is even worse. The answer appears to lie in having less focus on the almighty self.

Appreciating your imperfections

All too often, anxious people feel that they must be perfect in order for others to like and accept them. No wonder they feel anxious. Nobody's perfect, and no one ever will be. Take the case of Kelly.

> **Kelly** is perhaps as close to perfect as you can find. Kelly always wears exactly the right fashionable clothes, the right colors, and her accessories always match. She takes classes in interior design so her house has just the right look. She exercises four times a week and eats only healthy foods. Her makeup, which she applies with great care, appears flawless. She always knows just what to say, never stumbling over a single word or swearing. She always exhibits kindness and has a positive outlook.

Would you like to have a beer with Kelly? Does she seem like someone you'd like to hang out at a pool with on a summer weekend? Would you feel easy and natural around Kelly? Frankly, we'd probably pass on the idea of having her as one of our best friends.

Think about one of your good friends with whom you like to spend time, someone you enjoy and value, and someone you've known for a while. Picture that person in your mind and recall some of the good times that you've spent together. Let yourself enjoy those images. Think about how much you appreciate this person and how your life has been enriched by the relationship.

Realize that you've always known about your friend's negative qualities and imperfections, yet you've continued to appreciate your friend. Perhaps you even find some of the flaws amusing or interesting. Maybe they give your friend color. Thinking about the flaws isn't likely to change your opinion or feelings, either.

Try applying the same perspective to yourself. Appreciate your little flaws, foibles, and quirks. They make you interesting and unique. Be a friend to yourself. Notice your gifts and your imperfections. Figure out how to acknowledge it all as one package. Don't disown your flaws.

Try this exercise we call "Appreciating Flawed Friends." You'll likely notice that you accept your friend, good and bad, positive or negative.

1. **In the notebook or file you have for exercises, make two columns. Think of a good friend.**

2. **In the first column, write down a couple of the friend's positive qualities.**

3. **In the second column, describe a couple of negative qualities or imperfections that your friend has.**

Following this exercise, realize that your friends probably have a similar picture of you. The following example shows you how this particular exercise works for Curtis.

> **Curtis** fills in the "Appreciating Flawed Friends" exercise in Table 13-1 while thinking about his buddy Jack. In the respective columns, he writes about Jack's positive qualities and imperfections.

Curtis accepts Jack, flaws and all. There's no one that Curtis would rather spend time with, and Jack is the first person he would turn to in a crisis. Can Curtis accept himself like he does Jack? That's the task at hand.

If your friend filled out the same form on you, no doubt she would write about both wonderful qualities and some less-than-wonderful traits. And yet, your friend wouldn't suddenly give up the friendship because of your imperfections. Of course not; nobody's perfect. If we all gave up on our imperfect friends, we would have no friends at all.

Self-forgiveness is difficult. Perhaps even more difficult is finding out how to drop defensive barriers in response to criticism from others. Figure out how to listen to criticism. Consider the fact that it may at least have an element of truth. Appreciate that portion of truth.

Try acknowledging any sliver of truth that criticism contains. Perhaps it's true *sometimes*. Perhaps the criticism is partially applicable. Instead of putting up barriers to communication and problem solving, admitting to some flaws brings people closer.

Table 13-1	Appreciating Flawed Friends
Positive Qualities	*Negative Qualities and Imperfections*
Jack is one of the funniest guys I know.	Sometimes Jack talks too much.
He's always there for me.	Even though he's smart, sometimes Jack makes stupid decisions, especially about money.
Jack will help me anytime I need it, no matter what.	Jack's a little overweight, and sometimes he drinks a little too much.
I like going to sporting events with him.	He doesn't always listen to me.
I like the fact that Jack is really smart.	Jack has terrible taste in clothes.

Connecting with the Here and Now

In some ways, language represents the peak of evolutionary development. Language makes us human, gives us art, allows us to express complex ideas, and provides us with the tools for creating solutions to problems. At the same time, language lays the foundation for much of our emotional distress. How can that be?

You may think that dogs don't get anxious, but they do. However, they only feel anxiety when they're in direct contact with experiences that cause them pain or discomfort. For example, dogs rarely enjoy going to the vet. More than a few dog owners have had to drag their dogs through the veterinarian's door by pulling on the leash with all their might.

However, humans do what dogs would never do. Humans wake up dreading the events of the day that lies ahead. Dogs don't wake up at 3 a.m. and think, "Oh no! Is today the day that I have to go to the vet? What will happen to me there?"

And dogs have few regrets. Oh sure, sometimes dogs look pretty guilty when caught chewing on their master's shoe. But one kind word and a pat on the head, and they've forgotten all about it. Some anxious people still remember the thank-you note that they forgot to write to Aunt Betty six years ago.

Generally speaking, dogs seem much happier than most of us humans. Unless a dog has been horribly abused, he usually carries on with contentment, joy, and, of course, quite a bit of sleeping. By contrast, humans worry a lot; they obsess over imagined horrors down the road, and they dwell on their past mistakes.

When you bring possible future catastrophes as well as past regrets into the present, you're essentially using language to disconnect you from real-life experience. Doing so can absolutely ruin your *present moments* — the time that you actually *live* your entire life! Consider the following example of Reggie, who dreaded the amount of work that he believed he had to finish within five days.

> **Reggie,** a criminal defense attorney, has a solo practice. An important trial is coming up in five days. The amount of work in front of him almost chokes him with fear. Of course, he agonizes over the possibility of putting on a less-than-stellar performance, but most of all, he is concerned about the heavy preparation of papers, briefs, depositions, and petitions that must be completed, and soon. He knows that he'll be working from dawn to dusk with barely enough time to breathe.
>
> The funny thing about it, though, is that after the ordeal was over, he realized that most of those five days turned out to be fairly enjoyable. He worried over the possibility of not completing his tasks, which had nothing to do with any of the actual work that he performed. Most of that felt pretty good. Not a single, individual moment felt *horrible* by itself.

Few present moments truly feel unbearable. It's simply our ability to ruin the present with thoughts about the future or past that disturbs us.

The next time you obsess over future or past events, tasks, or outcomes, consider trying the following:

- ✔ Stay focused on each moment as it comes to you.

- ✔ Spend a few minutes noticing all the sensations in your body at the moment — touch, smell, sights, and sounds.

- ✔ When thoughts about the tasks ahead enter your mind, simply acknowledge the presence of those thoughts and move your attention back to the present.

- ✔ If thoughts about past failures or regrets enter your mind, notice the presence of those thoughts and move your attention back to the present.

- ✔ Remind yourself that *thoughts* don't reflect reality and experience; they're only *thoughts.*

> ✔ When you notice disturbing thoughts about the future or the past, try just observing them, notice how interesting it is that your mind spins out thoughts like these, and return to the present moment.

The following sections contain specific exercises you can use to keep your mind focused on the present moment. We also offer some pointers on how to slow down and enjoy mealtimes and walks.

Making contact with the present

At this very moment, consider coming into direct contact with experience. This is something many people have rarely done. Have no expectations about what this exercise is *supposed* to do. Just study what happens.

If judgments enter your mind as you're doing the following exercise, observe how your mind spins these out like a reflex. Make no judgments about these thoughts or yourself. Go back to focusing on the entire array of present-moment sensations.

1. **Notice how this book feels in your hands.**

   Feel the smooth cover and the edges of the pages. Or feel the buttons and surface of your e-book reader!

2. **Notice how your body feels and notice your position, whether you're sitting, standing in a subway, riding a bus, or lying in bed.**

   Feel the sensations in your skin as it makes contact with the chair, the bed, the floor if you're standing, and so on.

3. **Feel the muscles in your legs, back, hands, and arms as you hold this book.**

4. **Notice your breathing.**

   Feel the air go in and out of your nostrils.

5. **Notice any smells, whether pleasant or unpleasant.**

   Think about how you could write a report about these smells.

6. **Listen to any sounds around you. Imagine how you would describe these sounds to a friend.**

   If you hear loud, obnoxious sounds, try *not* to judge them. Instead of thinking about how jarring they sound, study the nuances in the sounds.

Now, notice how you feel at the end of this exercise. Did you experience the sensations fully? What happened to your anxiety? Many people report that they feel little, if any, anxiety during this experience. Others say their anxiety escalates.

If your anxiety increases during your first few attempts to connect with present-moment experience, don't worry. It happens for various reasons. Increased anxiety doesn't mean that you're doing something wrong. More than likely, it can be attributed to one or more of the following:

✔ You may have little experience connecting to the present. Therefore, it feels strange.

✔ Anxious thoughts may interrupt you frequently. If so, more practice may help to reduce their potency.

✔ You may be facing such an overwhelming stressor right now that putting this strategy into effect is unrealistic. If so, you may want to try other strategies in the book first.

Whatever the case, we recommend practicing frequent connection with present-moment experiences.

Most anxiety and distress come from thoughts about the future or the past, not what's happening at this moment.

Putting worries about the future to rest

Most people tell us that at least 90 percent of what they worry about never happens. Of those worrisome events that do occur, less than 10 percent are as bad as they anticipated. That's an overabundance of worry and ruined present moments just to anticipate a few unpleasant occurrences.

Here's a way you can quit listening to that occasional stream of worries about future events.

1. **Think about how many times you've made negative forecasts in the past about some pending event.**

2. **Then ask yourself how often those forecasts have proven true.**

   If you're not sure, keep a log of your negative predictions and see what percentage pans out.

3. **Of those forecasts that do come true, how often is it as bad as you anticipated?**

   If you're not sure how often, keep a log for a while.

Taking these predictions seriously is rather like listening to a weather reporter on the television who tells you that blizzards, severe cold, and ice storms are forecasted for every day. So you dutifully don a heavy coat, gloves, and boots. Just one problem nags you, however. Ninety percent of the time, the reporter is absolutely wrong, and the weather is sunny and warm. When the reporter gets it almost right, rarely are conditions as bad as described. Perhaps it's time to stop listening to the weather reporter in your head. You can't turn the station off, but you can at least take the reports less seriously!

Mindfully meditating

Above and beyond reducing anxiety, mindful acceptance can improve the quality of your life. When you're anxious, so much of your mental energy focuses on negative sensations, thoughts, and images that you miss many of life's simple pleasures, like eating and taking a leisurely walk.

Mindful eating

How many times have you eaten a meal and barely tasted it? Of course, if it tastes like microwaved cardboard, perhaps that's a good thing. However, most of the foods that we eat taste pretty good. What a shame to miss out on the full experience.

Choose a time to practice mindful eating. Be sure it's not a ten-minute lunch. But it doesn't require hours, either. Worrisome thoughts may sometimes distract you. That's fine and normal. However, try merely noticing them. Rather than judge those thoughts or yourself, return your focus to your eating when you can. Follow these steps:

1. **Slow down and focus before taking a bite.**

2. **Look at your food.**

   Notice how it's displayed on your plate or bowl. Observe the food's colors, textures, and shapes.

3. **Take time to smell the aroma.**

   Put a small portion on your fork or spoon. Before you take a bite, hold it briefly under your nose.

4. **Briefly put the food on your lips and then on the tip of your tongue.**

5. **Put the food in your mouth, but don't bite down for a moment or two.**

6. **Chew very slowly.**

   Notice how the taste and texture change with each bite, and how the food tastes on different parts of your tongue.

7. **Swallow the bite and notice how it feels sliding down your throat.**

8. **Follow this procedure throughout your meal.**

9. **Stay seated at the table with your meal for at least 20 minutes.**

   If you finish eating before the 20 minutes are up, continue sitting until the full 20 minutes have elapsed, and notice your surroundings and the sensations in your body.

Consider making mindful eating a regular part of your life. You'll feel calmer, enjoy your food more, and possibly even lose a little weight. Many weight-loss programs suggest slowing down your eating. However, this approach does more — it enables you to fully experience your food. When your mind totally focuses on the present pleasure of eating, anxiety fades away.

Mindful walking

Look around at people walking to their various destinations. So often they rush about like hamsters on an exercise wheel, not even aware of their surroundings. Rushing people, unlike hamsters, don't enjoy the exercise — instead, their minds fill with anxious anticipations and worries. It's a small wonder that we have an epidemic of high blood pressure these days.

We have an alternative for you to consider: mindful walking. You've probably tried taking a walk sometime when you felt especially stressed. It probably helped. However, mindful walking can help you more.

Practice the following meditation while walking for five minutes, five days in a row. Then consider whether you want to make it a regular part of your life.

If troubling thoughts intrude, simply notice them. Watch them like clouds floating overhead. Don't judge them. When you can, bring yourself back to the present.

Proceed with your walk as follows:

1. **Pause before you start.**

2. **Notice the feeling of air going in and out of your nose and lungs. Breathe quietly for five breaths.**

3. **Begin walking.**

4. **Notice the sensations in your leg muscles — your ankles, calves, and thighs.**

   Spend a minute or two focusing only on these muscles and how they feel.

5. **Now, feel the bottom of your feet as they strike the ground.**

   Try to notice how the heel hits first, then the foot rolls, and then you push off with the ball of your foot and toes. Concentrate on the bottom of your feet for a minute or two.

6. **Now, focus on the rhythm of your walking.**

   Feel the pace of your legs and the swing of your arms. Stay with the rhythm for a minute or two and enjoy it.

7. **Feel the air flowing into your nose and lungs. Feel yourself exhaling the air. Take notice of the rhythm of your breathing.**

   Focus on nothing else for a minute or two.

8. **Continue to take heed of your feet, muscles, rhythm, and breathing, shifting your attention from one to the other as you like.**

Enthusiasts extol the virtues of mindful walking. They claim it helps them reduce stress and become more serene. You can experiment with mindful walking in various ways. For example, try focusing on sights and sounds or focus on smells as you encounter them. Play with this strategy and develop your own approach. There's no right or wrong way to be mindful.

Accepting Mindfulness into Your Life

Some people read about mindfulness and worry about the time it can consume. They say that it sounds like living life in slow motion and complain that nothing would ever get done if they tried living that way. As much as we think that living a little slower isn't a bad idea for many people, mindful acceptance doesn't require significant chunks of time.

More than time, mindfulness entails a shift in philosophy that decreases the focus on ego, pride, and control, while emphasizing accepting the present with all its gifts and challenges. Being mindful requires humility because it acknowledges the uncertainty that's inherent within life.

Making mindful acceptance a habit doesn't happen overnight. With practice, allow it to evolve slowly into your life. Accept that you won't always stay in the present. Don't judge your attempts to live mindfully. When you see yourself living in the guilt-ridden past or anxious future, gently remind yourself to come back to the present.

Savoring Spirituality

Accepting anxiety involves a variety of related attitudes, such as being nonjudgmental, tolerating uncertainty, letting go of the need for absolute control, and being patient. Realize that acceptance isn't the same as resignation or total surrender.

Acceptance means appreciating that you, as well as all humans, have strengths and limitations. Many people find that the process of acquiring acceptance leads them to a greater sense of spirituality — a feeling that the purpose of life transcends one's own self-concerns. *The Serenity Prayer* captures this spirit of acceptance nicely:

> *God, grant me the serenity*
> *to accept the things I cannot change,*
> *the courage to change the things I can;*
> *and the wisdom to know the difference.*
>
> *Living one day at a time;*
> *enjoying one moment at a time;*
> *accepting hardship as the pathway to peace.*
> *Taking, as He did, this sinful world as it is,*
> *not as I would have it.*
> *Trusting that He will make all things right*
> *if I surrender to His Will;*
> *that I may be reasonably happy in this life,*
> *and supremely happy with Him forever in the next.*
>
> — Reinhold Niebuhr, 1926

Part IV
Zeroing in on Specific Worries

The 5th Wave   By Rich Tennant

Oh sure, the ocean went back out—THIS TIME.

In this part . . .

*1*n this edition, we bring you a new section devoted to many of the concerns that have emerged as major worries in the modern world. We tell you how to deal with career and financial stresses and show you how to prepare for and deal with natural calamities ranging from tsunamis to earthquakes and fires.

We review the growing problem of worldwide pandemics and show you how to inventory your own personal health risks and design a plan for maximizing your long-term health.

Finally, we show you how to evaluate risks associated with all types of violence, such as crime, terrorism, and accidents. More important, we discuss how to avoid unnecessary risks as well as how to deal with them in the event that they happen to you.

Chapter 14

Facing a Career Crisis and Financial Woes

---

*P*eople worry about money — a lot. They obsess over their 401(k) accounts, savings, salaries, home values, and promotions. More basic needs underlie these concerns — worries about job loss, foreclosures, and the ability to meet essential life needs such as food, clothing, healthcare, and shelter. Although people are generally more important than money, everyone needs a certain amount of income for survival.

In this chapter, we tackle money concerns head-on. We do so with a keen awareness of the seriousness of financial worries. In other words, we don't take a glib, *don't worry, be happy* approach to these issues. And we don't claim to be financial experts; after all, we're psychologists. So this chapter is not a prescription for getting rich fast and retiring early. It's a guide to what steps you can take to better handle your anxiety and worry over your career and financial challenges.

First, we take a hard-nosed look at job worries. Then we help you make a realistic appraisal of what you have and don't have. We also guide you through an exercise that explores your true needs as separate from your mere desires and wishes. Finally, we ask you to commit to a new, long-term financial strategy designed to minimize your financial worries.

Meeting Job Worries Head-On

If you worry about losing your job, you're in good company. Like it or not, economic recessions occur every so many years and often result in millions of people losing their jobs. And one can ever know for certain which careers will become the most vulnerable in the next recession. Thus, at one time, working for a major car manufacturer was seen as one of the most secure jobs you could have. Technology has produced huge numbers of jobs in some areas while wiping out or depleting opportunities for many jobs such as travel agents, telephone operators, and bank tellers.

As we write this book, about 1 out of 10 Americans have lost their jobs, and many more are grossly underemployed. For most of those who've held on to jobs, salary increases have stalled, and opportunities for advancement have vanished, at least for the short run. If you're faced with possible job loss, anxiety is a perfectly understandable emotion. Of course you worry! This section gives you a few tools for dealing with these worries.

Shoring up your resume

One way to decrease your worries about jobs is to maximize your market-ability. Even if you're currently working, it's a good idea to have a world-class resume. Various Web sites and search engines like Google contain sample resumes and tips for writing them. Or consider reading *Resumes For Dummies* by Joyce Kennedy (Wiley). If you're out of work, check the book out from your local library.

Keeping your resume up-to-date sounds simple, right? But it's not necessarily so. Many people find resume-writing highly anxiety-arousing. And when people have anxiety, they tend to avoid what makes them anxious. So, if you're like many people, you may find yourself procrastinating or avoiding the task.

We have some suggestions:

- ✔ Get help. If you've lost your job, state unemployment offices and local community colleges offer training on writing resumes. You can also find sample resumes on the Internet, at the library, or at a bookstore.

- ✔ Break the task into small steps. For example, vow to write out your educational background during the first session. The next day, write out your job descriptions.

- ✔ Show your resume to a few friends or colleagues for feedback. Or, if you're working with an employment agency, someone there can likely give you pointers.

- ✔ Know that avoiding this task will likely increase your anxiety rather than make you feel better. The only way to get through that anxiety is to face your fear by going right at it and tackling the task in spite of your anxiety.

Employers often spend no more than ten seconds reviewing each individual resume. Make sure yours is short, visually appealing, and highlights your best strengths. You can't afford to have any misspellings or grammatical errors. Use quality paper.

If your resume review reveals a lack of skills, you may want to consider acquiring new skills, either on your own or through a local training facility, community college, or university. See the "Considering careers with stability" section later in the chapter for fields that generally offer steady employment.

Finding flexibility in your career view

Whether you lose a job because of layoffs, can't find a job in your own field, or simply choose to leave a job, a psychological trait known as flexibility can improve your ability to handle the challenge of change. Flexible people adapt to new situations. When stuck, they look for alternatives. They take action to improve their situation.

So why is flexibility so important for handling job worries? According to the U.S. Department of Labor, an average worker holds 10.8 jobs between the ages of 18 and 42. Obviously, there's a wide range — some people never have more than 1 or 2 jobs and others have 20. The message is that very few people stay with one company for a lifetime of work. In addition, many people switch careers — some by choice (like after obtaining additional training) and others by accident (such as losing a job in one field and taking a job in another field).

Inflexible people often become angry when faced with job frustrations. Instead of acting, they react with anger at how unfair life has been for them. Inflexible people stick to old choices, don't take advantage of new opportunities, and seem stubborn and stuck.

To improve *physical* flexibility, you start with small stretches and gradually bend more. If a move is painful, you back down. You try to achieve balance by stretching both the right and left sides of your body. Gradually, your flexibility improves.

Mental flexibility involves the same principles — gradual steps, balance, and backing off when painful. Mental flexibility involves being able to see reality from different perspectives. For example, in a job interview, a person with mental flexibility would try to put himself in the shoes of the person doing the interview. Or in negotiations, a flexible person would take the time to consider the perspectives of all involved.

Mental flexibility accepts change as inevitable and expected. Such flexibility requires openness to new experiences and the understanding that most of the time, truth is unknowable. Finally, flexible people understand that in order to learn, they must listen.

Armed with a more flexible attitude, you can handle the stress and anxiety of job loss and other changes by considering all your options and alternatives. This attitude may enable you to see possibilities you wouldn't see otherwise. And your efforts will more likely result in success.

When writing your resume (see the preceding section), use flexible thinking. Look at your past jobs and consider what skills, attributes, and characteristics you brought to the table above and beyond those that are obvious from your job titles — highlight these skills on your resume. And when you interview, mention the connection between the skills you've acquired and how you can use them to advantage in your new company, instead of focusing on the past.

Considering careers with stability

You'll worry less if your career path stands on a concrete foundation rather than one made of sand. If you're underemployed or unemployed, consider updating your skills or changing your career path to one that has more stability. Get more training and education. If figuring out how to pay for classes is a concern, most postsecondary schools have student loans, grants, or other ways to help pay for their programs.

It's never too late to go back to school. Consider taking one class at a time. Also look into online courses from accredited schools. These classes can be especially convenient for some people.

Think about how many years you have left to work. Wouldn't you prefer to be doing something you like? Here are a few areas considered to be *relatively* stable in these unstable times:

- ✔ **Healthcare:** Almost all areas of healthcare will see growth over the next few decades. In addition to professionals like nurses, doctors, pharmacists, physical therapists, and dentists, others, such as home healthcare workers, medical technologists, and healthcare case managers, will be in greater demand.

- ✔ **Education:** As the baby boomers retire from teaching, the education system will see many openings. Areas of need continue to exist in math, science, and bilingual education. College instructors and professors will also be needed in greater numbers.

✔ **Law enforcement and security:** Needs for police officers, correction officers, and security personnel are likely to increase in years to come. Many of those working in this field are slated for retirement in the coming decade or so.

✔ **Green jobs:** Assuming you've heard or read a news report in the last few years, you know that there has been a cry for increasing energy independence and minimizing the harmful impact humans have on the environment. Thus, this emphasis will call for a vast pool of workers trained in areas such as engineering, chemistry, physics, hydrology, and ecology, as well as technological expertise in almost every imaginable type of alternative energy. These jobs will be available for both those with advanced degrees and those with manufacturing and technical skills. Many community colleges offer training in these emerging industries.

No career path comes with a guarantee of stability. Accept that what's stable at one time could become less so later. Remember, you need to be flexible.

Traditionally used by school guidance and vocational counselors, the *Occupational Outlook Handbook* is available for free at www.bls.gov/oco/. It contains a comprehensive listing of jobs, educational requirements, job conditions, and salaries. The U.S. Bureau of Labor Statistics updates this book frequently. Also check out the Dictionary of Occupational Titles available at www.occupationalinfo.org for more ideas. Use it to broaden your list of possibilities. Again, be flexible!

Keeping the right focus

Anxiety, fear, and dread can easily overwhelm you if you let them. When faced with the possibility of job or income loss, people fill their minds with images of living on the streets or dying of hunger. Such a scenario is indeed awful, and it occasionally happens. But you can do much to prevent this outcome, and it occurs a very small fraction of the time compared to the amount of time that people spend dwelling on this worry.

If you worry about losing your job or you find yourself unemployed, you have a new job. That new job is to cut your expenses to the bone (we give you some guidance on making these cuts in the "Tallying up your financial balance sheet" section later in the chapter). Cutting expenses helps you even if you haven't yet lost your job, because it helps you hold out longer if you do lose your income. After you've reduced the amount of money you're spending, your next step is to maximize your ability to find a new job (more on that in the "Knowing your personal assets and liabilities" section).

Other strategies, such as applying for unemployment, getting help from families, and applying for food stamps, should all be considered. But go to your state unemployment office for the nuts and bolts of that kind of advice. From a psychological perspective, we suggest the following:

- Focus on the present, taking one day at a time.
- Take care of your physical body by eating right and exercising to help your mind.
- Stay connected with friends and family — support helps!
- Consider going to a support group for job seekers — find one through the Internet or your local newspaper.
- Realize that negative predictions and worrying about possible future calamities never prevented a single catastrophe.

Taking Stock of Your Resources

Personal resources include financial and psychological assets and liabilities. *Assets* are the money or skills that you have that are of great value; *liabilities* are the money you owe or the skills that you need to gain. Both play a critical role in your adjustment to setbacks and stress. The following sections outline some of the things that can help maximize your assets and minimize your liabilities.

Tallying up your financial balance sheet

Most lenders such as mortgage companies, banks, or car dealers require customers to fill out loan applications. A standard loan application includes a description of the purpose of the loan and information about the borrowers. The application often asks about money coming in each month as well as monthly expenses. Applicants are also asked to list all their assets and liabilities. A net worth is calculated by subtracting the liabilities from the assets.

You don't have to apply for a loan to organize your assets. We suggest that you review your income, expenses, assets, and liabilities whether or not you want to borrow money. That way you can see just what you have now. Make a list for each of the four categories; the result is called your *balance sheet*.

When you think about your assets, include everything — grandma's silver, coin collections, and other prized possessions. You may not want to sell them, but you always know you could if things got really bad.

After you know your income, expenses, assets, and liabilities, take a moment to think about them. Can you find ways to improve your balance sheet? We suggest that you carefully review your expenses. All too often, people make the mistake of assuming they *need* far more than they really do. Ponder the answer to these questions:

- ✔ How could I entertain myself without 150 TV stations?
- ✔ How many outfits do I really wear regularly, and how few could I get by on?
- ✔ Can I cut out unnecessary coffee, lunches, and dinners out?
- ✔ Could I look just fine in clothes from a thrift store?
- ✔ How can I cut my use of the car by walking, biking, or using public transportation?
- ✔ How much could I save by checking books out of the library instead of purchasing them?
- ✔ How can I cut my energy use and save money?
- ✔ Can I stop spending money to impress other people?

Multiple research studies have found what most people have trouble believing: Your income has a very small relationship to how happy you are. Many people find that once they start cutting expenses, they're amazed at how much they can save without sacrificing their emotional well-being. In fact, they often report feeling less stressed. Some even say that the saving process feels like fun when they get going.

Knowing your personal assets and liabilities

Although you want to assess your financial strengths first when facing the possibility of a job loss, it's also helpful to analyze your personal strengths and attributes. Start by asking yourself the following questions:

- ✔ Am I willing to learn new skills?
- ✔ Do I get along well with other people?
- ✔ Am I persistent?
- ✔ Do I get to work on time?
- ✔ Do I finish projects on time?

✔ Do I accept feedback and criticism without becoming defensive?

✔ Am I a good team player?

✔ Do I refrain from unnecessary gossiping?

✔ Do I keep my personal life separate from my professional life?

✔ Am I self-motivated?

✔ Am I good at keeping my cool under stress?

✔ Am I creative, and can I think outside the box?

In an interview, be prepared to talk about any of the preceding questions that you feel you can answer affirmatively; these represent your assets. Any of the questions that you feel don't apply to you may represent areas for personal development. Look for ways to improve in those areas to turn your liabilities into assets.

After writing out your answers to the preceding list of questions, write down as many of your personal strengths as you can think of. Consider including examples from previous jobs that illustrate these strengths. Then list your weaker areas. The result gives you a sense of your job-related, psychological net worth.

Committing to a New Game Plan

You can reduce the amount of energy you spend worrying about jobs and money if you commit yourself to making some changes. In addition to the ideas in the previous sections, we suggest you develop a game plan for your money and your career. We recommend that you consider both short- and long-term goals. Earlier sections prepare you for what's next — where the rubber meets the road.

Setting short-term goals

You'll never get where you want to go unless you have a map. Lots of people go through their entire lives without ever thinking about what they want to accomplish. Look at your money and career, and ponder what you really want to achieve in the next couple of years.

Considering short-term career goals

Take a vocational interest inventory at your local community college. Write down the job skills that you already possess. Brainstorm job possibilities that can make use of your personal strengths and interests. Make a list of these job possibilities and, assuming you've updated your resume, prepare to market yourself.

Prior to putting in applications, we recommend that you practice interviewing with your friends or a vocational counselor or therapist. Practice until your anxiety comes down — and it will if you practice enough.

When you've got a polished resume and you're ready to face an interviewer, you need to find a job. Don't just rely on sending out resumes to jobs listed in your local paper or on the Internet. In addition to those sources, consider

- ✔ Looking in the phone book for companies that you can imagine putting your skills to use. Making cold calls can be surprisingly effective.

- ✔ Calling people you used to work or go to school with — in other words, networking.

- ✔ Asking family and friends — more networking.

- ✔ Looking at jobs working for the government.

- ✔ Working for a temporary agency — these jobs often become permanent.

Getting your money plans started

Money flows like water. If you stop spending it in one area, it flows around that area just to be spent somewhere else. The only way to save it is to channel your money carefully into a reservoir or holding tank. Yes, we're talking about saving.

Because this isn't an investment book, we're not going to suggest specific types of investments. Rather, the purpose of this book is to help you understand and deal with anxiety. So if you're anxious about money, you'll have less anxiety if you have more money saved. And it doesn't matter much where you put it — money adds up even in a savings account with zero percent interest.

So start now. Begin with what you have and build slowly. Continually increase your contributions to your savings as soon as you can. You may just surprise yourself.

Planning for the long haul

Not too many years ago, people worked for the same company for a lifetime and looked forward to a retirement of fishing and golf. More often than not, nowadays that dream is just that — a dream that won't ever find fulfillment, at least as it was originally envisioned. Many jobs have evaporated, a surprising number of pension plans have gone belly up, and many IRA and 401(k) types of accounts have shriveled.

Is this state of affairs a cause for despair and hopelessness? We don't think so. Sure, you're right to feel concerned and maybe even disappointed that you may not be able to retire when you want or live the retirement lifestyle that you once expected. But the trait of flexibility we talk about earlier in this chapter applies here too. You should know that research reported in the *Journal of Occupational Health Psychology* in 2009 actually found that people who work part time instead of completely retiring are healthier both physically and mentally. This finding held up even when controlling for variables like age, education, and wealth.

So consider that the goal of complete retirement may not even be especially good for you! You don't have to make as much as you did prior to semi-retiring or work as many hours. That's because part-time work can go a long way toward stretching whatever retirement account dollars you already have. Consider looking for an encore career that gives you more satisfaction and meaning than just money. Or try something brand new that comes with less stress but connects you with people. It's a whole lot easier to go to work if you're having fun. At this time in your life, your job doesn't need to build your ego or impress other people.

Finally, try to realize that a certain amount of uncertainty is certain! In other words, life and investments will always take unexpected twists and turns. You can't avoid setbacks, but you can recover. In the long haul, markets, economies, and people inevitably rise and fall.

Chapter 15

Keeping Steady When the World Is Shaking

*P*erhaps you think that you're a rational person. If so, you probably believe that the fears that make you the most anxious are the things that pose the greatest risk to you — after all, that would be the most rational perspective, wouldn't it? But that's not how the mind works. People focus and dwell on worries that grab their attention, not those that are most likely to happen.

News media, inadvertently or otherwise, often exacerbate the problem. When natural disasters hit, news helicopters take off like a flock of geese startled by a shotgun blast. Television screens fill with images of horror, pain, suffering, and death. Reporters seemingly thrive on interviews with grief-stricken victims and run their tales of woe repeatedly for days at a time. No wonder many people spend lots of time worrying about natural disasters.

On the other hand, perhaps you have a variety of anxieties and worries, but natural disasters aren't something that bother you. If so, you can feel free to skip this chapter — unless you're just curious about the subject.

In this chapter, we help you sort through such fears and worries. We help you see that you may be spending lots of time on issues of low risk and/or things you really can't do anything about. We also discuss how to look at your personal risks. Sometimes, worrying about natural disasters is realistic if you live in certain high-risk areas. In those cases, we suggest ways to manage such risks from a practical as well as emotional standpoint. We conclude with ideas about what you can do to cope actively rather than passively by working to improve the world and the lives of others when they encounter natural disasters.

Assessing Your Risks

Because images of natural disasters vividly stream from television screens within minutes of their occurrence, keeping a realistic perspective on how much risk they really pose to you is often difficult. In the next couple of sections, we briefly review the types of natural disasters in the world and the frequency with which they occur. We also help you understand your true risks for encountering a natural disaster.

Looking at the likelihood of dying from a natural disaster

You've certainly heard the eternal question about when a tree falls in a forest — if no one is there to hear it, does it make a sound? Natural disasters are sort of like that tree. Are calamitous events truly calamitous if no one is around when they occur? Maybe not.

However, plenty of disasters hurt people — often in significant numbers — when they occur. Disasters can also lead to financial, environmental, and emotional distress or loss. The following list represents some of the most common natural disasters that people worry about:

- ✔ **Avalanches** are sudden snow slides that break loose and pummel or bury anything in their path. They kill about 150 people per year. Most avalanches occur after a winter storm. The risk of dying in an avalanche can be put in perspective by knowing that the world population now stands at about 6.8 billion and counting.

- ✔ **Earthquakes** occur thousands of times every day. The vast majority of these quakes are minor and unnoticeable on the earth's surface. From time to time, however, earthquakes unleash a powerful explosion of pent-up energy sending huge, destructive seismic waves across a broad area. On average, about 10,000 people die in earthquakes each year. Most die in collapsed buildings, but earthquake-triggered landslides, fires, and floods also claim lives.

- ✔ **Fires,** whether in forests, houses, or buildings, kill more people than most natural disasters. The U.S. Fire Administration claims that the United States' rate of fire deaths is among the highest in the industrialized world. Nonetheless, the risk of dying from fire in the United States is somewhere around 15 in one million.

- ✔ **Floods** occur when large volumes of water submerge land, houses, buildings, and people. They often result from extreme weather such as hurricanes or torrential downpours. Floods also occur when dams and other barriers break. The overall risk of dying from floods has declined due to improved warning systems and knowledge about where they're likely to occur. According to the Civil Society Coalition on Climate Change, your overall risk of dying from floods stands at around one in a million each year. However, floods sometimes kill more than 100,000 people in a single incident. And many more people lose their possessions and property to floods.

✔ **Hurricanes** emerge from some tropical storms and generate wind speeds of 75 to over 150 miles an hour. Most of those who die from hurricanes die from flooding (see the preceding item in this list).

Have we got you worried? Consider that this list pales in comparison to all the possible natural disasters. Perhaps you can't readily think of other disasters, but Wikipedia lists these (among others!):

✔ Asteroids

✔ Blizzards & extreme cold

✔ Falling junk from outer space

✔ Gamma ray bursts (massive electromagnetic explosions in galaxies that have even been speculated as having the potential to someday cause mass extinctions on earth!)

✔ Hailstorms

✔ Heat waves

✔ Lightning

✔ Limnic eruptions (a huge eruption of carbon dioxide from deep lakes that can suffocate livestock and people in the area)

✔ Tornados

✔ Tsunamis

✔ Volcanic eruptions

You get the idea. Possibilities abound. But your overall risk of death from any particular natural disaster is far lower than death by your own hand or accidental death — both of which *most* people worry much less about than natural disasters. On the other hand, your risk of death from natural disasters may be far greater than most people's. We tell you how to determine that risk next.

Tabulating your personal risks

The lists in the preceding section include the most common natural disasters (and obviously a number that aren't so common). But you probably don't have to worry too much about them happening to you unless you live in an area plagued by them. However, you never know when something may erupt.

So make a list of your personal risk factors. Do you live, work, travel, or play in areas that may be subject to a natural disaster?

For example, people who live in certain areas of California choose the wonderful weather over the risk of living in earthquake, fire, and mudslide risk zones. And if you go helicopter skiing frequently, you darn well better know about what triggers avalanches. So a given individual may have a much greater risk of being harmed or killed by natural disasters than the average person. If that risk applies to you, you want to take extra precautions.

If you don't know your risks, try using a search engine on the Internet to find out. After all, you don't want to live in denial anymore than you want to obsess about risks that are greater in your mind than in reality.

For example, we live in landlocked New Mexico and usually don't even think about natural disasters. Every once in a while, a weather system in the Pacific causes it to rain like crazy here, and we get a few flooded streets and arroyos (you might call them drainage ditches). In some areas of the state, forest fires present some risk. In addition, if you look out our home's window, you can see some dusty old volcanoes that were active about 3,000 years ago. We don't worry too much about those either.

But just to make sure, we entered "New Mexico and volcanoes" into our browser, and, much to our surprise, we found out that our state is known as the "volcano state." Furthermore, we sit on a large continental rift and live on top of large veins of hot lava. The time frame listed for another eruption was listed as "geologically soon." Oh no! What should we do? Read on.

Preparing a Plan for Realistic Worries

You can never prepare for every imaginable crisis. Rather, it's important to assess which risks have a *realistic* chance of happening. Then prepare for those in proportion to the risks they pose, as best you can.

Probably the most important piece of advice we can give you is this: During times of crisis, listen to public service announcements and directives — and follow them. In addition, we suggest you ponder the following questions in advance of any calamity:

- ✔ Have I become educated about the specific risks in my area?
- ✔ If I live in a place in which natural disasters occur, have I made reasonable preparations?
- ✔ Do I know the emergency evacuation route for my area?
- ✔ If a disaster appears imminent, do I have a full tank of gas?

- ✔ Do I have supplies on hand, such as flashlights, warm clothing, extra batteries, at least a three-day stockpile of food and water, and a battery-powered radio?

- ✔ Do I have a first-aid kit?

- ✔ Do I have a plan if an emergency occurs?

- ✔ Do I have an emergency stash of cash?

- ✔ Do I have my important documents saved in a safety deposit box or fire-proof safe?

- ✔ Do I know how to use a fire extinguisher, and do I have a fully charged extinguisher?

- ✔ Do I know how to shut off utilities in the event of a disaster?

- ✔ Do I know what I would take with me in case I need to evacuate?

- ✔ Do I have a plan in place to communicate with my family?

- ✔ Do I have a way to protect my pets?

After you've gone through the list of questions, take any actions that seem necessary and reasonable. Then stop worrying; you've done all you can do.

Note the first question on our list is: *Have I become educated about the specific risks in my area?* So we searched the Internet to find out what to do in case of a volcano eruption. Well, the first idea is to get out of the way. If we do happen to be stuck in the house, we should close the doors, windows, and block the chimneys to keep ash out. If we go outside to watch, we should hold a damp cloth over our mouths to help us breathe. Also, we learned that hot lava and ash are heavy and should be brushed off of our roof if much lands on it. On the other hand, sometimes volcanoes blow out chunks of lava the size of a house, so sweeping it off may be difficult. Dang.

Nevertheless, we're not planning to spend a whole lot of time on preparing for this eventuality, nor do we figure on worrying a lot about it. But after writing this chapter, we did realize it wouldn't be a bad idea to check on the state of our fire extinguisher in case any of that lava lands on our backyard or house.

No matter how well you prepare, you can't prevent all calamities. Make *reasonable* efforts and get on with your life. You can never eliminate all uncertainty from life.

Nonetheless, if you find yourself still worrying after having done all you realistically should to plan for disasters, read the next section.

Finding the silver lining in adversity

Unexpected things happen even if you take precautions. The following account of a couple on a honeymoon illustrates an unexpected encounter with a natural disaster.

Sandy and **Brice** leave for their tropical honeymoon in November, carefully avoiding the peak of hurricane season. The newlyweds are exhausted from the wedding and look forward to a relaxing beach vacation. As promised, the resort is beautiful and the beaches pristine. After the first day of lounging on the beach, they return to their room. They're surprised to see a note lying on their bed.

"The management regrets to inform you that there will be a severe tropical storm in the area. Please be advised that you will be required to evacuate by bus to a safe area. Please bring your belongings, a blanket, and a pillow. We will be leaving from the lobby of the hotel in two hours."

The buses take about 50 guests and hotel staff to a shabby school about 30 minutes away. The humidity is high and the school smells like mold. The staff tells the guests that the air conditioning in the school doesn't work very well, but they will try to keep everyone comfortable. Cots are set up in a large room that serves as a cafeteria and gymnasium.

Sandy and Brice try to keep a positive attitude, and the hotel staff seems very well organized. The first meal consists of a cold chicken salad, salsa, and chips. The hotel provides cans of beer and soda. A few of the quests start singing campfire songs, and the group remains festive. However, after a few hours, the rain picks up. Then the electricity goes off. The mood of the refugees grows darker with the darkening sky. Hours pass and the sounds of wind, rain, and thunder are interrupted by loud crashes. People huddle together; some cry; others pray. A few exhausted children sleep.

By morning, the intensity of the storm lessens. But the people are told that it's not yet safe to return to the beach area and that the airports are closed. Brice tells a staff member that he must get in touch with his family. The staff member tells him that communication is impossible. They serve cold hard rolls and canned juice for breakfast. Staff inform them that water is getting scarce and that they must ration it. As the day wears on, anger and irritability rise. Some people get sick. The smell gets worse and worse. The third and fourth days pose almost unbearable challenges from the lack of electricity, food, water, and sanitary conditions.

Finally, the buses come back and the tourists are returned to a devastated hotel. Windows are shattered and the halls are flooded. Sandy and Brice can barely walk, having suffered from food poisoning. Yet they feel lucky to be alive.

Sandy and Brice realize that even when you try your best to avoid risks, bad things happen. In looking back, they believe they gained maturity and closeness from the adversity. Their new marriage flourishes. And they face the coming years with greater acceptance of uncertainty and appreciation for every day of their lives.

Imagining and Dealing with the Worst

Hopefully, you've looked at how realistic your worries about natural disasters are, and you've done what you can do to plan. Nevertheless, you may find yourself worrying more than you'd like to.

Our first recommendation is to carefully read Chapters 5, 6, 7, and 8 to understand how your thoughts and the words you use influence your anxiety. Then you can apply that information to your worries about natural disasters. The following sections show you how to make that application to this issue.

If you or someone you care about does experience a natural disaster, you'll probably feel increased anxiety and distress. If your distress is mild, Chapters 5, 6, 7, and 8 may help you deal with it. If distress is severe and continues, please consider seeing a mental-health professional.

Rethinking uncertainty and anxiety

The anxious mind tries in vain to eliminate all uncertainty from life. Unfortunately, living a life without a reasonable degree of uncertainty would result in more misery than you think. Consider the following list of risks, many of which you probably take every day. Imagine trying to live life without any of these risks at all.

- Leaving your house
- Driving your car
- Breathing without a mask (unless a pandemic is active)
- Not decontaminating every single surface you contact
- Eating food that hasn't been boiled
- Opening your mail (it could have anthrax in it)
- Going shopping
- Walking across a street
- Riding a bike
- Taking a shower (poses a significant risk of falls)

Of course, we realize that if you suffer from significant anxiety, you probably do try to avoid at least a few of these risks. But you're taking many such chances regularly. Even if you wear latex gloves every day, you can't prevent contact with all germs, natural disasters, or accidents.

Even though you may think otherwise, *acceptance* of risk and uncertainty paradoxically helps anxiety abate. See Chapter 13 for more about accepting anxiety.

Rethinking your ability to cope

Most people with anxiety disorders gravely underestimate their ability to cope in the face of unexpected challenges. They see themselves as easily overwhelmed and lacking either the will, skills, or resources to deal with adversity. For example, they say to themselves, "I couldn't stand that," "I can't take it," or "I'd fall apart if that happened to me!" Yet when they actually encounter what they fear, inevitably, they do cope.

In Chapter 5, we provide a list of five questions for helping you deal with some pretty difficult worst-case scenarios. We suggest answering these questions for your fears of natural disasters. First, we show you the questions, and then we illustrate their use with an example.

- ✔ Have I ever dealt with anything like this in the past?

- ✔ How much will this affect my life a year from now?

- ✔ Do I know people who've coped with something like this, and how did they do it?

- ✔ Do I know anyone I could turn to for help or support?

- ✔ Can I think of a creative new possibility that could result from this challenge?

In the next example, a resident of Southern California attempts to answer the coping questions to help her deal with her fear of earthquakes.

> **Lynne** moves from London to San Diego to take an academic position at the University of California. She loves her new job and the sunshine. Lynne rents a small apartment within biking distance of her office. One day as she walks across campus, she's surprised by a sudden feeling of unease. She feels like she's stepping onto an unsteady boat. The sensation passes quickly. When she arrives at her office, she notices that some of the pictures are slightly tilted. She asks a nearby student whether she has just experienced her first earthquake. The student laughs and says, "Oh, that little sway was just a tremor, nothing like a *real* earthquake. Just wait until you're in a big one; it's totally awesome."
>
> "Awesome? Are you kidding?" Lynne trembles, her heart races, and she begins to sweat. She hadn't considered the reality of earthquakes in California. She wonders if she can possibly cope. She recalls having used coping questions to deal with her anxiety about moving. Now she returns to these questions to help her calm her newly heightened fears about earthquakes.

Have I ever dealt with anything like this in the past?

No, I haven't. I don't think I can stand this. Maybe I need to quit and go back to dreary London.

How much will this affect my life a year from now?

Well, if I live through an earthquake, I guess I may be okay. If I don't, then I'll be dead.

Do I know people who've coped with something like this, and how did they do it?

I guess about 36 million or so Californians have lived through a few earthquakes and haven't moved out. They must have accepted the risk and learned to live with it.

Do I know anyone I could turn to for help or support?

I can ask people I know about earthquake safety and get more involved in the local neighborhood so I meet some of my neighbors.

Can I think of a creative new possibility that could result from this challenge?

I realize that lots of people come to the University of California from other countries around the world. Maybe I can start a group for new residents. We can socialize a bit and have speakers about adjusting to America, including earthquake safety. It will be a great way to meet new and interesting people and provide a way for me to expose myself to my fear.

Lynne learns to accept the risk of earthquakes and the questions help her to stop feeling helpless and anxious. See Chapter 5 for examples of how these questions can help you ponder and cope even with the possibility of an unexpected event that results in death.

Going right at your worries

Exposure — facing your fears gradually over time — is probably the most powerful approach to dealing with fear and anxiety (Chapter 8 covers exposure in detail). We suggest applying this technique to your fear of natural disasters. Don't worry — obviously, we're not going to recommend that you actually chase tornadoes or set forest fires and walk into them.

When dealing with a fear of natural disasters, the best exposure strategy is called *imaginal exposure,* which includes constructing a staircase of fear and imagining the worst-case scenario (see Chapter 8). You can use imaginal exposure as an alternative approach to using the coping strategy questions (see the preceding section). Alejandro's story demonstrates how someone can apply imaginal exposure to an intense fear of earthquakes.

Alejandro lives in San Francisco. He worries about earthquakes. Rightly so, because San Francisco sits in a zone that poses a high risk for major earthquakes. Alejandro has taken all the usual, appropriate preparations, such as knowing how to shut off his utilities, securing water heater tanks, maintaining fire extinguishers, knowing evacuation routes, keeping emergency supplies, and such.

Nevertheless, he worries about earthquakes a lot. He jumps whenever he hears a rumble of thunder or an unexpected noise. His mind starts to dwell on horrible images of death and destruction, and then he quickly tries to think about something else.

Because he very much wants to continue living in San Francisco, Alejandro decides to see a psychologist. The psychologist suggests using imaginal exposure. At first, the strategy sounds to Alejandro like the psychologist is recommending that he do more of what's already scaring him — imagining scenes of horror and destruction. But the psychologist explains that imaginal exposure is different in a crucial manner. Imaginal exposure asks you to break your fears down into steps and gradually confront each one in your mind.

He tells Alejandro that he will hold the image of each step in his mind until his anxiety reduces by up to 50 percent. They start with the easiest step and work up from there. Figure 15-1 shows what his staircase of fear looks like:

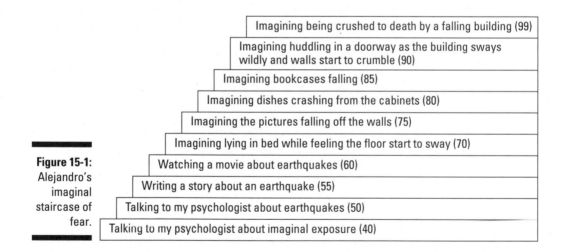

Figure 15-1:
Alejandro's
imaginal
staircase of
fear.

Imagining being crushed to death by a falling building (99)

Imagining huddling in a doorway as the building sways wildly and walls start to crumble (90)

Imagining bookcases falling (85)

Imagining dishes crashing from the cabinets (80)

Imagining the pictures falling off the walls (75)

Imagining lying in bed while feeling the floor start to sway (70)

Watching a movie about earthquakes (60)

Writing a story about an earthquake (55)

Talking to my psychologist about earthquakes (50)

Talking to my psychologist about imaginal exposure (40)

Note that some of Alejandro's steps occur solely in his imagination, and a few involve taking direct actions. By the time Alejandro has worked through his staircase of fear, his anxiety about earthquakes bothers him much less than it used to.

Doing Your Part to Improve the World

A number of research studies have shown that when people take charge of challenges and do something active, they cope better than if they cope passively. *Passive copers* usually do little more than try not to think about what worries them — this approach actually makes things worse for them.

On the other hand, *active copers* look for direct actions they can take to make themselves feel empowered. No, you can't actually do something to prevent most natural disasters like earthquakes, tsunamis, and volcanoes, but you can influence the environment for the better and/or improve the lives of other people who are threatened by disaster. Doing either of these things is likely to make you feel less like a helpless victim and more in charge of your concerns.

If you decide to volunteer to either help the environment or victims of disasters (see the next two sections), you may encounter some difficulty or disappointment at first. Sometimes, volunteer organizations consist largely of people who've been with the organization a long time and who may not immediately welcome new members. It may take some time to win them over. In other cases, you may discover that your skills don't fit well with the group. Or you may find that your own shyness inhibits your efforts at first. So we recommend that you give any such effort the time it takes to get over these concerns. You can also shop around until you find a comfortable fit.

Helping the environment

Maybe you're thinking that you, as one person, can't do much to affect the environment and natural disasters. But when millions of individuals each take steps to reduce the wear and tear on our planet, it adds up. So taking action can help reduce your anxiety about natural disasters. You become part of the solution, not part of the problem.

First, consider all the ways you can decrease your own carbon footprint. Turn that thermostat down a little in the winter and up in the summer. Run your dishwasher only when it's totally full. Use electronic bill paying instead of paper. Change your light bulbs as they burn out to long-lasting, energy-efficient bulbs. Search the Internet for a lot more ways to reduce your carbon footprint.

In addition, consider volunteering to help with the environment. Join a neighborhood trash-pickup effort. Volunteer for a conservation project. Help maintain a public park trail. Get creative; you'll come up with other possibilities.

Volunteering in disasters

One way to feel more empowered is to become involved in planning for and providing service in the face of natural disasters. Your local Red Cross has many opportunities for volunteers. You can offer to answer phones, file papers, or provide direct assistance to people affected by disasters. The Red Cross offers training and education to help people gain the skills necessary to help others. Volunteering gives back. Helping others can help you feel more powerful and less anxious.

Chapter 16

Staying Healthy

· ·

· ·

Contaminants in our food supply, poisons in the water, baby bottles that leak cancer-causing chemicals, stealthy antibiotic-resistant germs — have we got your attention? Oh wait, how about pesticides, black mold, asbestos, and lead paint? Invisible perils fill the world. No wonder many people worry about getting sick.

In this chapter, we talk about normal health concerns versus over-the-top health anxiety and worry. We point out that accepting a certain amount of risk is essential to maintaining emotional balance and a sense of well-being. We show you how to make an objective appraisal of your personal health risk factors and how to design a health action plan that makes sense.

Figuring Out the Connection between Worry and Health

Imagine that you're in a crowded subway. The brakes come on unexpectedly and the car stops in the dark tunnel. An announcement comes on stating that because of an electrical problem, there will be a delay of up to an hour. You hear a collective chorus of sighs and mutterings. Then you notice the coughing and sneezing. You realize you've been holding onto a sticky hand-rail that's been touched by hundreds of people that same day. The temperature starts to rise, and you begin to smell the sweat and body odor wafting through the air. You notice a slight feeling of nausea in your stomach.

There's no easy escape, and you begin to think that you may just come down with the flu or worse. And in fact, with all those people crammed together, surely one or two have something contagious. So if you find yourself worrying about illness in circumstances like these, you're not alone.

However, ask yourself this: Does your worry about getting contaminated in that subway car protect you from germs? Of course not.

Face it: Whether you're afraid of getting sick or not, germs waft through the air, oblivious to your concerns. That's the problem with most health anxiety. *Worry doesn't help keep you safe.*

The following signs indicate that your worries about health exceed the definition of *normal:*

- ✔ You spend hours each day worrying about your health.
- ✔ You frequently ask others for reassurance about your health.
- ✔ Your worries interfere with your day-to-day life.
- ✔ You frequently go to the doctor for minor symptoms and rarely receive a diagnosis.
- ✔ You take unusual precautions to protect yourself from germs.
- ✔ You feel that nothing you can do will keep you well.

People who constantly worry about their health are at higher risk for depression. If you (or someone you care about) lose interest in activities that were once pleasurable; have changes in energy, sleep, or appetite; and feel helpless or hopeless; please check it out with your medical provider or a mental-health professional.

Some people find that their worries about health spin out of control. They avoid crowded places. When venturing out, they wear surgical masks and carry disinfectants. Fear causes them to severely restrict their activities and interferes with their ability to enjoy life fully. These people have health anxiety. Some carry the diagnosis of generalized anxiety disorder (GAD) or obsessive-compulsive disorder (OCD) that's centered on health concerns. Others may have *hypochondriasis,* a persistent preoccupation with their belief that they have a disease, based on misinterpretations of symptoms, despite normal medical evaluations.

We don't mean to imply that you shouldn't take *reasonable* precautions to stay healthy. You *should* wash your hands after you use the restroom, after contacting obviously filthy surfaces, and before meals. Sometimes public health agencies may issue warnings to wash more frequently or even to wear masks in certain environments. And obviously, if you know someone who has a contagious disease, you'll probably want to avoid close contact with that person.

But if you're struggling to distinguish between what's reasonable and what's not, please see a mental-healthcare provider who can provide you with guidance. Distinguishing between GAD, hypochondriasis, and OCD that's focused on health worries requires an assessment by a mental-health professional.

Recalculating the Costs and Benefits of Health Worry

Take an honest look at your worry about health. Does your vigilance keep you safe? Maybe you believe that if you didn't worry so much you'd end up getting sick. Or perhaps your health worries extend to family members. Do you think that you are somehow responsible for keeping others safe and healthy?

How do you express your worries about health? Is it by frequent trips to the doctor, time spent thinking about your health, or frequently asking others for reassurance? Whatever your personal expression of health anxiety is, the following exercise will help.

Carry out a cost/benefit analysis of your health concerns. On a piece of paper, in your notebook, or in your computer file, write about your own health anxiety. Then, in a column on the left, write out all the benefits you believe that worrying about health gives you. Next, in a column on the right, write out all the possible costs your worry incurs. The following questions may help you discover the possible costs and benefits:

✔ How many times have I actually prevented what I fear the most?

✔ Does my worry really protect me in any way?

✔ How many times have I thought that I was sick when nothing was wrong?

✔ Is it possible that anxiety causes me to have other symptoms, such as stress and depression?

✔ If I do get sick, is there anything I can do to cope?

✔ How do others cope with what I'm worried about?

✔ Is there any evidence that I'm more likely to get sick than other people?

After completing the exercise, take another look at your answers. Decide for yourself whether your worry and anxiety keeps you safe. The following example of Arturo, a young man who worries excessively about getting sick from contaminated food, illustrates the cost/benefit analysis.

Arturo doesn't eat in restaurants because he worries about getting food poisoning. He believes that processing food increases the risk of industrial contaminants, rodent droppings, bacteria, or viruses entering into the food supply. Thus, he only eats fresh produce that he buys at a local food co-op. He then takes special care to make sure that the food he buys is clean. Because of his strict diet, Arturo is slender and generally healthy.

He spends more than three hours each day choosing and cleaning his food. Despite these precautions, he frets and worries. His peculiar habits keep other people from being close to him. His loneliness leads to depression. His primary-care doctor refers him to a psychologist who helps him develop the cost/benefit analysis shown in Table 16-1 regarding his concern about food contamination.

Table 16-1	Arturo's Cost/Benefit Analysis
Benefits	**Costs**
I don't eat contaminated food.	I'm lonely and sad.
I eat healthy food.	I spend too much time on cleaning.
I am slim.	Even though I avoid lots of foods, I'm still pretty anxious all the time.
I save money by not eating at restaurants.	My doctor said that chronic anxiety and depression can make me sick.
I believe my worry protects me.	No one can be safe all the time; I could get hit by lightning or something and die early anyway.

Arturo sees that his over-concern about food has both costs and benefits. He begins to understand that he can't stay completely safe all the time. And if he does get sick, it's likely that his illness can be treated. Furthermore, he sees that some of his perceived "benefits" for his worry are illusions. Thus, he could eat healthy food, stay slim, and still get sick whether he worries or not. He decides to take a chance and eat at a vegetarian restaurant with his cousin.

If you worry about your health, take Arturo's approach. Make lifestyle changes that matter and realize that excessive worries can, by themselves, make you sick. Seek professional help if your health concerns persist in spite of your best efforts.

Tabulating Risks of the Modern World

In the early 1900s, you were lucky to live to age 50. People died of contagious diseases like tuberculosis and influenza or infections caused by simple injuries. Heart disease, dementias, and cancers were less likely to be the cause of death only because people succumbed to infections before reaching old age.

Now, most industrialized countries boast a life expectancy well into the 70s. People over 100 are the fastest-growing sector of the world population, with expectations that this segment will be over 6 million strong by mid-century. Today, heart diseases and cancer have replaced contagious diseases as the most likely cause of death. Yet, it seems that as people live *longer,* they don't appear to be living *healthier.* The skyrocketing costs of healthcare not only reflect improvement in care but also the fact that many more people have chronic diseases. In the following sections, we take a look at when it makes sense to keep tabs on diseases and epidemics and when you can safely ignore them.

Examining the evolving realities of diseases and treatments

Paradoxically, longer life spans and modern medicine give people more to worry about all the time. Even though people live longer, in a sense, they're getting sicker. There are several reasons for this increase. First, more years of life equal more wear and tear on the body. Many diseases become more frequent with age, such as cancer, arthritis, dementia, and hormonal disorders, so obviously, in an aging population, the risk for getting sick is greater.

Second, so-called advances in technology and medicine allow doctors to find disorders they never looked for in the past, such as prostate cancer. Even though the vast majority of "sufferers" have relatively few symptoms and eventually die of other causes, we now worry about such cancer and often experience significant side effects from the treatment itself. Furthermore, we treat things we never used to see as problems. For example, what used to be considered normal aches and pains in the knee can now be seen on an MRI and diagnosed as osteoarthritis. Unfortunately, the surgical treatment of osteoarthritis has recently been found to be no better than a placebo — the treatment consisted of giving some patients a sham surgery (the patients thought they received surgery, but actually did not — the surgeons even cut open their knees and stitched them right back up).

On the other hand, screening can prevent diseases from even occurring in the first place. For example, the dreaded colonoscopy can detect benign polyps before they become cancerous. Removing these polyps stops colon cancer before it has the chance to take hold. That's wonderful.

Yet another interesting cost of medical advancement is the additional risk that some *treatments* carry. For example, acid reflux disease used to be called indigestion. Known to increase the risk of certain cancers, it's now vigorously treated with medication to reduce or eliminate stomach acid. However, stomach acid protects us against common bacteria such as salmonella. So people being treated for acid reflux may be at greater risk for food poisoning. Other medications such as antipsychotics (see Chapter 9) can help people with severe mental disorders but lead to weight gain and diabetes.

Another example can be found in the treatment of osteoporosis. Osteoporosis is defined as significant loss of bone density that results in an increased risk of bone fractures. This disorder can be successfully treated with medication. However, a rare side effect of long-term use of these medications results in collapse of bones (the very problem the treatment is supposed to deter).

Finally, definitions of disease have changed over time. Blood pressure is now considered high and treatable at lower levels than before; the cutoff for normal cholesterol has also dropped. The idea is to treat diseases early to prevent later problems. That can be a good idea, but what constitutes diseases sometimes gets out of hand, such as when normal sadness is defined as serious depression in need of medication.

Consider another example: Minor loss of bone density was once thought to be a common and normal result of aging. But today medical providers have started treating a "new" condition called *osteopenia* — a milder loss of bone mass than osteoporosis. Treating this newly diagnosed "disease" has led to a huge increase in sales of the drugs originally developed for osteoporosis. Because this disorder is usually found among younger people, the long-term effects of treatment with medication are not yet known.

Take the time to keep informed about the risks and benefits of treatments, and make modifications in your lifestyle as much as you can to stay healthy.

Weighing local versus global health risks

People who worry about their health sometimes focus on potential threats that are quite rare. Take some time and think about the risks of getting sick in your locality as compared to somewhere else in the world. For example, if you live in the United States or Canada, you're pretty unlikely to come down with malaria or typhoid fever. And if you live in a country where adequate care is available, getting sick is not necessarily a death sentence.

On the other hand, millions of people throughout the world lack basic sanitation, clean water, medical care, and food. These conditions breed and spread infections. Diseases that have been eliminated by improved sanitation or vaccines can be deadly when medical care is insufficient. Poverty, famine, disease, and violence shorten life spans to the mid or even early 30s in some countries.

Although your chances of getting the kind of diseases that regularly kill people in third-world countries are less than for those people who live in terrible conditions, people travel all over the world. And infectious diseases can catch a ride. The following example illustrates:

> **Leroy** travels to Indonesia. While there, he is bitten by a mosquito. He then travels to Paris for a short business trip. Sitting outside sipping wine at a French bistro, he is again bitten by a mosquito. That mosquito could infect someone in Paris with the tropical disease that Leroy carries. Leroy then returns to Chicago. Sitting outside on his deck on a hot summer evening, he gets bitten by another mosquito. That mosquito could possibly infect Leroy's neighbor. A couple of weeks later, Leroy comes down with fever, chills, and a horrible headache. In severe pain, he goes to the hospital and is diagnosed with malaria.

Leroy's story shows how diseases can spread. Although malaria is quite rare in most of the western industrialized world, between 350 to 500 million cases occur in Africa, Asia, the Middle East, and Central and South America. About a million people die from it each year, mainly young children in certain regions of Africa. Most people who get sick in the United States are people who travel to those regions. Fortunately, inexpensive medications that prevent malaria can be obtained before traveling to places where malaria is present.

So it's a good idea to take reasonable precautions when traveling. Reasonable precautions include making sure that you're up-to-date on vaccinations and checking with your medical provider if you're traveling out of the country.

Wear mosquito repellent when you're outdoors during a time that you might become infected by mosquito-borne diseases such as the West Nile virus, because this virus can occur almost anywhere on the planet.

The U.S. Center for Disease Control (CDC) maintains a Web site that includes up-to-date information about infectious diseases throughout the world. You can click on any country and find out whether there are any travel restrictions or warnings. Go to `http://wwwnc.cdc.gov/travel`.

Watching out for exaggerated claims

People pay attention to unexpected events. So when something predictable happens, it's less likely to be a focus of media scrutiny. For example, when an 88-year-old woman dies of a stroke in her sleep — unless she was rich or famous — there may be just a short obituary in the local paper. However, when a 3-year-old dies of a new type of flu that's spreading around the world, that's news. People talk about what's in the news and the media goes to great lengths to bring you complete coverage of the story, so your awareness of an event like a toddler's death from a new disease is heightened. As your awareness goes up, your anxiety likely does too.

We're not saying that the concerns about H1N1 flu (also known as swine flu) aren't legitimate, but the probability of dying from heart disease or an auto accident are much greater than dying of all but the most catastrophic of pandemics.

Taking an Inventory of Your Personal Health

Accidents happen, and people get sick. And eventually, as far as we know, everyone dies. Whatever your own personal beliefs are about what happens after death, most people don't look forward to dying. Some believe that people have a certain amount of time on this planet and what they do with their day-to-day lives doesn't much matter. But how you live your life greatly affects your health and comfort, no matter what happens in the end, whereas worry never kept anyone healthy. So we recommend that you take a careful look at your lifestyle and your known family health risks, take whatever steps you can to minimize those risks, and then make the best you can out of each and every day.

So far, no one has been able to predict the future. Live each day fully and to the best of your ability. Worry and regret do not lead to better health.

Checking out your lifestyle

In Chapter 10, we highlight some of the lifestyle changes that you might consider to improve your health and, hopefully, reduce your anxiety. Here we zero in on some of the health risks that may add to your worries. Many studies have looked at the factors that have the greatest impact on leading a long and healthy life. These studies follow people for decades and keep track of their health and habits. According to reports, more than a third to almost 90 percent of heart disease, cancer, diabetes, and stroke are caused by one or more of the following lifestyle choices:

- **Smoking:** If you don't smoke, don't start. If you've already started, quit. If people around you smoke, insist that they smoke outside. Secondhand smoke can hurt your health and the health of children. Make this a priority; get all the help you need.

- **Weight:** If you're overweight, face the fact. Excess weight can — and eventually will — make you sick. There are hundreds of free Web sites that can help you determine your body mass index. If you carry that extra weight around your belly, you're at higher risk for diabetes and heart attacks than if you carry it in your hips. Join a weight-loss group; talk to your doctor.

- **Poor diet:** Eat more fruits and vegetables and less saturated fat. Be aware that fiber keeps you full and keeps your digestive tract healthy.

- **Lack of exercise:** Get moving. Some exercise is better than no exercise, but exercising every day is best. Walk around briskly and get your heart pumping, dance, run, go to the gym. Weight-bearing exercise such as walking, running, or weight-lifting improves stamina, strength, and bone density.

- **High blood pressure:** Check your blood pressure. If you have high blood pressure, take medication and change your lifestyle to lower your risks.

- **Sun exposure:** Wear sunscreen if you're outside for a long time, especially in the middle of the day. Don't get sunburned.

- **Inadequate medical care:** Go to your doctor for regular checkups and talk to your doctor about any concerns that you have. Many diseases are treatable when caught early through screening tests.

Accepting your genetic risks

Although lifestyle changes can cut down most people's risk of getting sick, certain people have genetic predispositions that can't be overcome with good habits. For example, your family may have a high rate of cancer, heart disease, or diabetes. In such a case, your chances of getting sick are probably elevated, despite preventive care and good lifestyle choices. If that's the case, take the precautions that make sense, talk to your doctor, and learn as much as you can about the condition.

Designing a Health Action Plan

After you've looked carefully at your lifestyle and taken into account your genetic risks, decide what steps you can take to improve your chances of having a long, healthy life. Don't try and tackle everything at once; at first, just write down one or two small, achievable goals. The following examples can guide you:

- If you're inactive, don't plan on running the next marathon; start by walking 15 minutes a day, most days a week.

- If you have a family history of high cholesterol, get a referral to a dietician to talk about ways to improve your diet.

- Buy sunscreen and wear it every day. Daily use of sunscreen has the added benefit of keeping your skin looking young.

- Floss your teeth; it does more for your health than you think!

- Keep on trying to quit smoking. It may take lots of effort, but millions of people eventually do quit; you can too.

- Add one more serving of fruits and vegetables to your diet.

- Don't put off medical screening tests — especially mammograms and colonoscopies.

- If you do get sick, be hopeful and optimistic.

- Stay connected with friends and family.

- Accept the fact that life and death are part of this world.

When you've accomplished one or two goals, add a new one. Keep the process going until you've really improved your health; your anxiety will decrease as your body feels better.

Chapter 17

Keeping Out of Danger

· ·

In This Chapter

▶ Figuring out how dangerous your world is

▶ Staying as safe as you can

▶ Dealing with scary events

▶ Letting go of worries

· ·

*U*nexpected events frighten most people from time to time. Have you ever been in an airplane when turbulence caused a sudden dip of the plane as well as your stomach? Or watched in slow motion as another car careened across the road sliding in your direction? How about noticing someone wearing dark clothing, who's nervously glancing around, sweating, and carrying a large bag at a ticket counter? Do you get a bit jumpy in a strange city in the dark, not sure which way to go, with no one around, when a group of quiet young men suddenly appear on the corner? Boo. Sorry if we scared you.

This chapter is about true feelings of stark terror and the emotional aftermath of being terrified. First, we take a look at your personal risks — just how safe you are and how you can improve your odds. Then we discuss methods you can use to prepare or help yourself in the event that something terrifying happens to you. Finally, we talk about acceptance, a path to calmness and serenity in the face of an uncertain world.

Evaluating Your Actual, Personal Risks

Chapter 15 discusses the fact that the risk of experiencing natural disasters is quite low for most people. But lots of people worry about them nonetheless. Interestingly, the same can be said about risks of terrorism. Billions of dollars are justifiably spent battling terrorist activities, and according to a 2005 report in *Globalization and Health,* you're 5,700 times more likely to die from tobacco use than an attack of terrorism. Similarly, the journal *Injury Prevention* noted in 2005 that you're 390 times more likely to die from a motor vehicle accident than from terrorism.

However, your risk of exposure to some type of nonlethal, violent event is much greater. For example, around 3 million (about 1 percent) of all Americans will be involved in a serious motor vehicle accident in any given year. And about 1.4 million (slightly less than a half a percent) of the people of the United States alone will fall victim to some type of violent crime.

For those who sign up to serve and protect our country through the military, the risk of injury in combat varies greatly over time and also depends on the particular war. However, for someone in a combat zone, the risk of death pales in comparison to the chances that the person will experience serious injury or witness acts of severe violence to others — and then struggle emotionally afterward.

Any exposure to violence, including just witnessing it, poses a major risk factor for developing what's known as *post-traumatic stress disorder (PTSD)*. PTSD is a serious type of anxiety disorder that often follows exposure to one or more traumatic events. People find themselves having intrusive images of the event(s) and often work hard to avoid reminders of it. They also frequently lose sleep, become easily startled, and experience increased irritability (see Chapters 2 and 8 for more information about PTSD). The following section reviews what you can do to reduce your risks of experiencing trauma.

Maximizing Your Preparedness

No matter what your risks for experiencing violence, we advise taking reasonable precautions to keep yourself safe. A little preparation usually doesn't cost a lot in terms of either time or money. The key is making active decisions about what seems reasonable and then trying to let your worry go because you've done what makes sense. If, instead, you listen to the anxious, obsessional part of your mind, you'll never stop spending time preparing — and needlessly upset your life in the process.

Taking charge of personal safety

Chapter 15 lists important preparatory steps you can take in possible anticipation of natural disasters. Those same items apply to being prepared for terrorism and other violent situations. In addition, we recommend you consider a few more actions:

- ✔ Always have a stash of cash on hand.

- ✔ Have extra prescription medication for important medical conditions.

- ✔ Have a store of critical supplies, such as tissues and toilet paper.

- ✔ Have a multi-tool that can function as a screwdriver, can opener, knife, and so on.

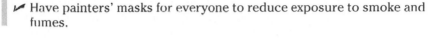

✔ Have some duct tape and plastic sheeting. Duct tape can fix a lot of things in a pinch and also serve to prevent windows from shattering. Plastic sheeting can be used to seal out toxic plumes.

✔ Have painters' masks for everyone to reduce exposure to smoke and fumes.

Always keep at least a three-day supply of food and water for each household member.

Avoiding unnecessary risks

The best way to minimize your risk of experiencing or witnessing violence is to avoid taking unnecessary risks. Of course, regardless of what you do, you can't protect yourself from life. People don't ask to be victims of crime, terrorism, or accidents, and you can't prevent such events from ever occurring.

But you don't have to ask for trouble either. We suggest the following, fully realizing that some of these may sound a little obvious. But because people often don't follow these suggestions, here they are:

✔ Wear seatbelts; need we say more?

✔ Hold onto purses or bags tightly when walking in crowded areas.

✔ If you have a wallet, carry it in your front pocket.

✔ If you're traveling, research the area for known risks. The U.S. State Department lists areas deemed unsafe for travel because of terrorism or other known risks at http://travel.state.gov.

✔ Make copies of your passport; give one to someone before you leave, and put another in your luggage separate from the bag you carry.

✔ Don't wear expensive jewelry when you travel.

✔ Don't drive in terrible weather conditions.

✔ Consider carrying a loud whistle in your purse or pocket.

✔ Heed the oft-given advice to report any unattended baggage in airports, train stations, or hotel lobbies.

✔ If you're in a hotel room, don't answer the door unless you know who it is. If you're not sure, call the front desk.

✔ If you do have to walk in an unsafe area, walk quickly and pay attention.

✔ Have your keys out and ready as you approach your car, and look before you get in.

✔ Try not to walk alone in dark, secluded areas.

Finally, don't limit your ability to enjoy life. Realize some risks are inevitable. Consider travel to places other than your backyard! Get to know some people from other cultures and lands. See some interesting landscapes. In other words, don't wall yourself off from the world.

Dealing with Trauma

We hope you're never a victim of nor a witness to severe violence, but we know it's a real possibility. Violence occurs in war, on the streets, and even in the workplace. So if you've recently been a victim, you may be experiencing some serious signs of anxiety or distress. That reaction is pretty normal. And the first thing we're going to tell you is that, *unless your symptoms are quite severe* and interfering greatly with your life, don't seek out mental-health treatment right away! That's because, in many cases, your mind's own natural healing process will suffice.

Furthermore, it's quite easy to interfere with natural recovery. For example, a single *debriefing session* often takes place after exposure to a traumatic event. In such a session, people are given basic information about trauma and its potential effects and are then encouraged to talk about how they're coping with it. But such a session may actually increase the risk of emotional symptoms occurring or continuing. If you're offered such a single-session intervention, we suggest skipping it unless it's obligatory. It's perfectly okay not to want to talk about the trauma right away.

So here's what we recommend you do first if you're unfortunate enough to witness or experience a highly traumatic event:

✔ Realize that it's normal to feel fearful and distressed.

✔ Talk to people you feel comfortable discussing the trauma with, but don't let yourself be pressured to talk by anyone.

✔ Ask yourself what you've done in the past to get through tough times, and see whether that helps you get through this one. For example, some people find benefit from spiritual counseling, prayer, turning to friends, or increasing exercise.

✔ If you're experiencing severe symptoms such as flashbacks, serious insomnia, significant irritability, or anxiety after a few months (even sooner if the symptoms are highly disturbing), consider seeing a mental-health professional for three or more sessions. Be sure to ask if your therapist uses *evidence-based* treatment (that is, supported by scientific research) for PTSD (see Chapters 2 and 8 for more information about PTSD).

In working on the ideas we discuss in the following sections, we strongly recommend that you do so *in collaboration with* a licensed mental-health professional who has experience treating PTSD.

Thinking through what happened

When people have been exposed to trauma, the experience never goes away. In other words, you can't ever completely erase the experience from your mind. But with help, the misery and pain can decrease, and life satisfaction can get much better.

Cognitive processing therapy (CPT) was developed by Patricia Resick and colleagues and has been shown to help some survivors get to a better place. With this approach, you take a hard look back and write a statement about the meaning that the traumatic event had for you in your life. In other words, describe how you think your life has changed:

- Do you feel responsible for the trauma?

- Do you feel unsafe everywhere you go?

- Have you changed the way you feel about yourself as a person?

- Are you angry, sad, or ashamed?

Your therapist will then help you explore your feelings and how your thoughts may be contributing to making things worse than they need to be for you. Among other things, your therapist may ask you these questions:

- How does this event affect the way you see yourself and the world?

- What would you tell a friend that this event meant about him or her as a person? Can you accept saying the same thing to yourself?

- Do you know anyone who has coped with something like this? If so, how did they do it?

- Do you believe that you're more unsafe than anyone else? If so, what is the evidence that you are?

- Did you *want* this traumatic event to happen to you? If not, can you stop blaming yourself?

- Is there anything shameful about having been a victim of trauma or violence?

- Can you think of a creative new possibility that could result from this challenge? For example, could you volunteer to help others in similar situations?

Finally, your therapist is likely to ask you to write about the actual traumatic event in great detail. Then you'll probably be asked to read that story out loud to yourself every single day for a period of time. As you do, don't try to squelch your emotions; instead, let the feelings flow. You can also embellish your story with more detail over time.

Some professionals consider this written account and the reading of the traumatic event to be a form of exposure therapy. Preliminary evidence suggests that this part of CPT may work as well as exposure, which we discuss in the next section. However, repeatedly reading your written account of the event may be somewhat less distressing than more direct exposure strategies.

Exposing yourself to the incident

Exposure therapy, as we describe in Chapter 8, has been supported by more research studies than any other approach for treating PTSD. Briefly, *exposure therapy* involves making extended contact with the traumatic event, usually through imagery. For example, a combat veteran may be asked to make an extensive list of all the details of his traumatic combat experiences. He would then be asked to list each detail and rate it for how much distress it causes him when he thinks about it.

The list is organized into a hierarchy, or what we call a *staircase of fear.* Starting with the least upsetting step, he would be asked to imagine it in detail until his anxiety and distress drop significantly. Then he would move on to the next step. See Chapter 8 for details and a specific example applied to PTSD.

The main problem with this approach lies in the fact that lots of trauma victims really don't want to revisit their trauma. Thus, the very idea of therapy elicits feelings of great distress. For some, exposure seems like adding more suffering to their already traumatized lives. For that reason, among others, far too many trauma victims fail to get treatment.

If you find that the prospect of exposure therapy seems completely overwhelming to you, consider seeking CPT first. Not every mental-health professional has been trained in both exposure therapy and CPT, so be sure to ask.

Accepting a Certain Degree of Uncertainty

Emotional distress stemming from traumas and violence presents a challenge, yet it's quite normal. It's important to realize that people can't control the emotions that arise from such causes. The more you can accept that fact, the more easily you'll be able to cope with life and whatever it deals you. The next two sections take a look at accepting uncertainty and risk.

Choosing to put yourself in high-risk situations

Some people, like police officers, emergency medical personnel, soldiers, and firefighters, choose to expose themselves to the best and worst of life. Their motives are positive: They may have a strong desire to help others, feel a deep sense of patriotism, or want to make a positive difference in the world. These people often become traumatized by the horrible events and disasters that they must deal with. And a good percentage of them end up with symptoms or a diagnosis of PTSD.

Those who fully understand and accept both the risks of the job and the fact that they may experience emotional distress from exposure to trauma just may be a little less vulnerable to traumatic events than those who see themselves as invincible. Paradoxically, the more you can accept whatever responses you have, the more easily you'll probably deal with them.

However, those who view themselves as indestructible may actually choose to go into their fields with an inflated sense of invulnerability. These people are more likely to have emotional pain from their experiences and refuse or shun help. They believe that part of their job is to handle whatever happens to them. Sadly, they're not immune to horror and trauma, yet they think that they should be.

If you or someone you care about has a front-line position in a field like medical care, law enforcement, or the military, you're at risk, just like everyone else, for getting a stress disorder from exposure to horrible events. This doesn't make you weak or less competent. You must bravely face your emotional pain and get help. Denying the emotional pain dulls your ability to continue to help others.

Experiencing danger in everyday places

A lot of people live lives in which they try to stay away from danger. But life happens to them as well. People are exposed to violence in places that were once considered safe: schools, churches, synagogues, mosques, parks, and the workplace. *Uncertainty in this world is certain.*

The only alternative to acceptance of risk and uncertainty is to devote your entire life to anticipating and avoiding risk. The problem here is that your efforts will still fail you. Even if you spend every waking moment trying to avoid risk, it won't work. So far we know of no one who has managed to avoid the ultimate risk of death.

The following story illustrates typical symptoms of PTSD following a motor vehicle accident, which is by far the most common avenue to getting PTSD in most parts of the world.

> **Lew** had always assumed, like most people do, that a green light signals it's safe to proceed through an intersection. He had driven with that assumption for 20 years without mishap. One day on the way to work, Lew drives through an intersection that he has safely traversed hundreds of times before. Suddenly, an SUV barrels through the red light and broadsides Lew's sedan. Lew suffers serious injuries. After several weeks in the hospital, he spends months in rehabilitation.
>
> When Lew returns to driving, he finds himself creeping through intersections with intense feelings of anxiety. He can barely make himself drive to work and back each day and avoids driving whenever possible. He frequently visualizes the accident, although he tries very hard not to. His body aches with tension. He wakes up in the middle of the night before he has to drive and can't go back to sleep. He's irritable and moody.
>
> Lew's doctor tells him that he now has high blood pressure and that he needs to reduce his stress. Lew worries about his worry but doesn't know what he can do about it. He thinks he may have to take a leave of absence from work. His supervisor is losing patience with him. Desperate, Lew makes another appointment with his doctor. This time, the doctor takes time to ask Lew about his symptoms. He refers Lew to a psychotherapist who specializes in working with people with PTSD.
>
> The therapist recommends exposure therapy (see the earlier section "Exposing yourself to the incident") involving a series of steps that start with talking about the accident and gradually increase in difficulty up to repeatedly driving through busy intersections. However, Lew can't get past the first couple of steps. He berates himself for failing to progress. Now Lew feels anger, not only about his accident but also toward himself.
>
> The therapist backs up and works on *acceptance*. He helps Lew to see that feelings are just feelings, not something to be avoided. He teaches Lew how to remain in contact with his emotions without judging them. Lew gradually learns to accept his emotions for what they are. Then the therapist works on CPT (see the section "Thinking through what happened"), and Lew makes excellent progress.

Unusual, unpredictable endings

Consider asking yourself how you could avoid these calamitous yet impossible-to-predict events. Please realize that we're not trying to be funny about or make light of tragic, violent, and horrific events. Our point is simply that you can never know how to predict and avoid the unpredictable. As we said, life has risks.

✔ A vacationing couple was left in the Great Barrier Reef off the coast of Australia when a dive boat crew member failed to count them upon returning to the boat — their bodies were never recovered.

✔ A surgeon in Houston was decapitated by an elevator door closing on his head.

✔ A 28-year-old woman died of drinking too much water in a radio station contest.

✔ An employee fell into a large tank of hot, melting chocolate and died after being knocked unconscious by one of the mixing paddles.

✔ A lawyer threw himself into a glass window to prove that the glass was unbreakable; unfortunately, he discovered that the windowpanes themselves broke out, and he fell from the 24th floor of the building.

✔ Every player on a soccer team in Africa was killed instantly by a forked bolt of lightning.

✔ A 24-year-old was trying to heat up a lava lamp on his kitchen stove; it exploded with such force that a shard of glass pierced his heart and killed him.

✔ Nine people were killed when over a million liters of beer burst out of a huge vat, causing a chain reaction that ripped open surrounding vats of beer and flooded the streets. The flood of beer filled surrounding houses and pubs, drowning those in its path. The BBC referred to the event as a beer tsunami; it's more commonly known as the London Beer Flood of 1814.

✔ And if you think the London Beer Flood sounds bad, there's always the Boston Molasses Tragedy. In 1919, 2.3 million gallons of molasses burst through a large storage tank and sent a wall of molasses about 15 to 20 feet high, wiping out homes and buildings and trapping people in the sweet goo. Twenty people were killed and about 150 injured. Months later, globs of molasses still clung to doors, sidewalks, and streets.

Part V
Helping Others with Anxiety

The 5th Wave   By Rich Tennant

"When I know he's had a rough day, I always put a few drops of lavender on the TV remote before he gets home."

In this part . . .

*I*f someone you care about has anxiety and worry, you naturally want to help. In this part, we detail what you can do. First, we help you find out whether your loved one suffers from anxiety, and then we show you how to talk about it. We also provide strategies for working together on the problem.

Today's kids appear more anxious than ever, about fears both real and imagined. We help you distinguish between normal and abnormal childhood fears. In the final chapter in this part, you discover how to prevent your children from developing abnormal fears and what to do if they have too much anxiety. We conclude by advising you when to seek professional help and telling you what to expect if you seek it.

Chapter 18

When a Family Member or Friend Suffers from Anxiety

In This Chapter

▶ Finding out whether your partner or a friend has anxiety

▶ Communicating about anxiety

▶ Coaching your anxious acquaintance

▶ Working together to fight anxiety

▶ Accepting your anxious friend or family member

*P*erhaps your friend, partner, or relative gets irritated easily, avoids going out with you, or often seems distant and preoccupied. Possibly he seems overly worried about sickness, money, or safety. Maybe he shuns physical intimacy. Or he may leave parties, concerts, or sports events early for no apparent reason.

You could easily take his behavior personally. You may think he doesn't love you, care about you, or is angry with you. And if these behaviors represent a recent change, it's difficult to know what's going on for sure. But it could be that your friend or partner actually suffers from anxiety.

This chapter helps you figure out whether someone you care about suffers from anxiety. We also help you communicate effectively with a loved one who has anxiety. With the right communication style, instead of provoking feelings of anger and resentment, you may be able to negotiate a new role — that of a helpful coach. You can also team up to tackle anxiety by finding ways to simplify life, have fun, and relax together. Finally, we explain how simply accepting your partner's anxiety and limitations leads to a better relationship and, surprisingly, less anxiety.

For convenience and clarity in this chapter, we mostly use the term "loved one" to refer to any partner, friend, or relative that you may be concerned about.

Discovering Whether Your Loved One Suffers from Anxiety

People who live together sometimes don't know each other as well as they think they do. Most people try to look and act as well adjusted as they can, because revealing weaknesses, limitations, and vulnerabilities isn't easy. Why do people hide their anxious feelings? Two big reasons for hiding them include

- **Fear:** Revealing negative feelings can be embarrassing, especially to someone with an anxiety disorder. People often fear rejection or ridicule, even though self-disclosure usually brings people closer together.

- **Upbringing:** Children may have been taught to repress or deny feelings by their parents. They may have been told, "Don't be such a baby," or "Boys don't cry." When taught to hide feelings, people grow up keeping concerns to themselves.

So how do you really know whether your loved one has a problem with anxiety? And does it matter whether you know or not? We think it does. Understanding whether your partner experiences anxiety promotes better communication and facilitates closeness.

The following list of indications may help you to discern whether your partner suffers from anxiety. Ask yourself whether your partner

- Seems restless and keyed up

- Avoids situations for seemingly silly reasons

- Ruminates about future catastrophes

- Can't ever seem to throw anything away

- Is reluctant to leave the house

- Spends inordinate amounts of time arranging things

- Has trouble sleeping or staying asleep

- Has trouble concentrating

- Has frequent nightmares

- Avoids situations or places reminiscent of a past traumatic event

- Is plagued with self-doubts

- Has episodes of noticeable shakiness and distress

- Is constantly on alert for dangers

- Seems unusually touchy about criticism

- Seems plagued by excessive superstitions

- Is overly worried about germs, contamination, or dirt

- Seems unusually concerned about health

- Has frequent, unexplained bouts of nausea, dizziness, or aches and pains

- Frequently rechecks whether the doors are locked or the coffee pot is turned off

- Constantly worries about everything

- Seems terrified by anything specific, such as insects, dogs, driving, thunderstorms, and so on

- Responds with irritation when pushed to attend social functions, such as parties, weddings, meetings, neighborhood functions, or anywhere you may encounter strangers (the resistance could be due to simple dislike of the activity, but carefully consider whether anxiety may lie at the root of the problem)

A couple of the symptoms in the preceding list (especially irritability, poor concentration, poor sleep, and self-doubts) can also indicate depression. Depression is a serious condition that usually includes loss of interest in activities previously considered pleasurable, changes in appetite, and depressed mood. See Chapter 2 for more information about depression. If your loved one seems depressed, talk with her and then consult with a mental-health practitioner or your family physician.

Now, if you answered yes to any of the questions in the preceding list (and your partner doesn't seem particularly depressed), we don't recommend that you approach your loved one and say, "Look at this list — you're a nut case! I knew it." That would be a really bad idea.

Instead, consider asking your loved one a few questions. This definitely shouldn't occur immediately following a conflict or argument. Possible questions to ask include:

- What's the biggest stress in your life lately?

- What worries you the most?

- Sometimes, when I go to events like this, I feel anxious. I'm wondering how you're feeling about going?

- How were you feeling when we left the party?

- How are you feeling about that problem?

- I've noticed you've had trouble sleeping lately. What's been on your mind?

Try to make your questions as nonthreatening and safe to answer as possible. In addition, try to ask questions that don't have a simple yes or no answer. For example, if you ask your partner whether she's anxious, she may reply with a simple "No," and then the discussion is over. But if you ask what worries she has, you may get a more complete response. Finally, asking "what" or "how" works better than asking "why" someone is feeling anxious — people often can't answer "why" they feel the way that they do.

Our list of questions for you about your loved one's anxiety and our list of questions to ask your loved one open the door to communicating about anxiety. After you broach the subject and confirm that the one you care about struggles with anxiety, you can build a plan from there. But you need to know how to keep the conversation going.

Talking Together about Anxiety

Talking about a loved one's vulnerability isn't always easy. Keeping a few ideas in mind may help. For example, if you find the conversation turning into an argument, it's not helpful. Back off. Your loved one may not be ready to face the problem. If so, you may want to check out the "Accepting Anxiety with Love" section later in this chapter.

Not every couple communicates easily about difficult subjects without arguing. If that's the case for the two of you, we suggest relationship counseling — reading a few pages about talking together won't solve fundamental communication problems. But if you're able to talk together about anxiety without experiencing a communication breakdown, we have some general guidelines for you in the following sections.

If your loved one has a problem with anxiety, you may find yourself feeling oddly ambivalent about helping. Sometimes, those confusing feelings come from the fact that seeing one's partner improve can upset the power balance in a relationship. If you prefer being the boss in your relationship, you may feel uncomfortable seeing your partner get better and become more equal to you. If you see that struggle in yourself, we suggest you seek relationship counseling. You're likely to discover that a more equal relationship feels better than your unconscious mind thinks it will.

Helping without owning the albatross

The first order of business in a discussion of your partner's anxiety is to show empathetic concern. That means putting yourself in your partner's shoes and seeing the world through his eyes. Then you can try to understand the source of the worry.

However, expressing empathy and concern doesn't mean that you need to solve the problem. You can't. You may be able to help, as we show in the "Guiding the Way" section later in this chapter, but you don't control the emotions of other people — they do.

Realizing that helpers don't own the responsibility for making change happen is important. Otherwise, you're likely to become frustrated and angry if and when efforts to change stall. Frustration and anger only make overcoming anxiety more difficult.

Avoiding blame

Just as you don't want to blame yourself by owning the problem when your partner becomes anxious, it's equally important to avoid blaming your partner. Your loved one developed anxiety for all the reasons we list in Chapters 3 and 4. Nobody asks for an anxiety disorder. Nobody wants one, and change is difficult.

People sometimes get upset when they try to help and the response they get consists of resistance and a lack of gratitude. But your loved one may resist your help because anxiety is like an old habit. It may not feel good, but at least it's familiar. When you start to work on reducing anxiety, anxiety typically increases before it gets better.

Therefore, make every effort to avoid blame and be patient. Success and failure aren't up to you. You want to help, but if change doesn't happen, it means nothing about you.

When help turns into harm

People with anxiety desperately seek ways to alleviate their distress. One common way is to ask for reassurance. If it's your partner who has anxiety, of course you want to help by giving that reassurance. For example, people who have a great fear of illness often ask their spouses if they look okay or if they're running a temperature. Unfortunately, reassuring your partner makes anxiety increase over time.

How can something designed to alleviate anxiety create more anxiety? Well, the immediate reduction in anxiety reinforces or rewards the act of seeking assistance. Thus, giving reassurance teaches the recipient to look for answers elsewhere, rather than to depend on his own good sense. Both dependency and anxiety thereby increase.

Asking for reassurance can take many forms. Sometimes, it's hard to spot. In Table 18-1, we give you some examples of reassurance requests and alternative ways to handle them. The first column gives a brief description of the basis for the fear or anxiety and the reassurance request, and the second column gives you an alternative response to offering reassurance.

Table 18-1	Responding to Reassurance Requests
Ways Your Loved One May Seek Reassurance	*New Ways of Responding*
Someone with generalized anxiety disorder may be worried about being late and ask, "Do you think we'll be on time?" or "When will we be there?" or "Do you think that we left enough time for traffic?"	"You never know," or, "I can't really predict the future."
A person with obsessive-compulsive disorder (OCD) who worries about locking the doors asks, "Do you think I locked the doors?" or "Could you check and see if I locked the doors?"	"Checking to see if doors are locked doesn't help you, so I'm not going to respond."
A loved one with OCD who worries about contamination asks, "Do you think it's safe to use that restroom?"	"We talked about the fact that I can't answer questions like that."
A loved one with agoraphobia asks, "Do you think I'll be able to handle going to the game with you?"	"I don't know; I guess we'll just have to try it and find out."
Someone with a fear of flying asks, "Do you think the weather will be okay for this flight?"	"Gosh, it's pretty hard to predict the weather."
A person who has social anxiety asks, "Will you make sure that I know the names of everyone there?"	"Well, I may not know all the names and I may not always remember them. You can always tell people you've forgotten their name."
A loved one who worries about getting sick asks, "Do you think I may be getting sick?"	"I really don't know. We've talked about me letting you handle this worry."

If you've been in the habit of giving your partner frequent, large doses of reassurance, don't suddenly stop without discussing the issue first. Otherwise, your partner is likely to think you've stopped caring. You need to let your partner know and come to an agreement that eliminating unnecessary reassurance is a good idea. Then, agree that you'll reassure once on any given concern, but when asked repeatedly, you'll simply smile and say, "We agreed that I can't answer that."

The following anecdote demonstrates how reassurance can aggravate anxiety and how alternative responses can help. At first, James hooks Roberto into feeling overly responsible for his insecurity and anxiety. Roberto provides more and more reassurance, and James keeps getting worse. A psychologist suggests a new response.

> **James** and **Roberto** have lived together for the past three years. Both graduate students, they lead busy lives. Lately though, James has stopped attending social events, complaining of fatigue. Roberto finds himself going alone and misses James's company.
>
> Roberto receives an announcement that he's the recipient of this year's Departmental Dissertation of the Year Award. Of course, he wants James to attend, but James fears sitting alone and feeling trapped. Roberto reassures James that the auditorium is safe and that he could get out if he needed to by sitting on the aisle. James still resists, so Roberto suggests they get Brenda, a good friend of theirs, to accompany him.
>
> Finally, after considerable cajoling and reassurance, James agrees to go to the event. He spends the time in the audience clinging to Brenda. He feels momentarily comforted by Brenda's presence and reassurances that everything will be okay. But he believes he couldn't have made it through the awards ceremony without her there to hold his hand.
>
> As each new outing comes up, it seems that James requires more reassurance and attention. James withdraws, becoming more isolated, and his anxiety increases.
>
> Then James finally sees a psychologist who suggests enlisting James's friends to help out. He asks them to provide James new, alternative responses to his reassurance seeking. At the next event, Roberto insists that James go on his own. When James asks Roberto, "Do you think I'll fall apart?" Roberto tells him, "You'll just have to try it and find out."

Initially, Roberto fell into the trap of not only being empathetic but also owning James's problem. His "help" only served to increase James's dependency. James eventually learns to rely on his own resources and feels empowered by doing so.

Unfortunately, when you own your partner's problem by giving too much reassurance and excessive help, it usually just makes things worse. Dependency, avoidance, and anxiousness all deepen. It's a matter of balance. Give truly needed help and show real concern, but avoid going too far.

Guiding the Way

Assuming you've had a healthy discussion with your partner about her anxiety problem, you may be able to help further. But first, take a look at yourself. If you also wrestle with anxiety, do all that you can for yourself before trying to tackle your partner's anxiety.

After you take care of your own anxiety, you may want to consider coaching your partner to overcome her anxiety. A coach is a guide who encourages, corrects, and supports. Part of the job of a coach requires modeling how to handle stress and worry. You can't do a good job of modeling if you're quaking in your boots.

Coaches can help carry out one of the most effective ways of overcoming anxiety: gradual exposure. *Exposure* involves breaking any given fear into small steps and facing that fear one step at a time. If any given step creates too much anxiety, the coach can help devise ways of breaking the task into smaller pieces. The following sections offer points to keep in mind when you're helping a loved one overcome her anxiety.

In all but the mildest cases of anxiety, a professional should oversee the coaching process. Be sure to read Chapter 8 for important details about exposure prior to attempting to help your partner carry out an exposure plan. If your partner resists or argues with you, consult a professional. Of course you want to help, but it isn't worth harming your relationship to do so.

Professional coaches have emerged in large numbers over the past decade. These people vary widely in their training and experience. You may want to use one of these folks to help carry out an exposure plan, but you don't want one of these people to diagnose an anxiety disorder or design a treatment plan from beginning to end. The only exception to this rule of thumb is a coach who also happens to be a licensed mental-health professional.

Coaching the right way

So exactly how does a coach help a loved one who has problems with anxiety? In most cases, coaches help the one they care about carry out exposure tasks. In other cases, coaches simply provide encouragement and support on the sidelines. Our discussion here focuses on the former role.

Generally, your participation in coaching would first come as a suggestion from the therapist working with your loved one. However, you may bring up the possibility yourself. In either case, you only want to serve as a coach if your partner clearly expresses an interest in and a desire for your assistance.

Coaching won't work if your partner doesn't feel ready to tackle her anxiety. Coaching also won't work if your loved one doesn't want your involvement. In fact, the effort could easily harm your relationship if you push your help too hard.

Not everyone is cut out to be a coach. Coaching requires significant patience, compassion, and time. If you don't have those things in abundance, don't agree to be a coach. Perhaps you can help your loved one in other ways, such as by taking on a few extra household tasks or simply by being an interested, supportive bystander.

Assuming you choose to accept the position, coaching requires you to take the following actions to be the best coach you can be:

✔ **Define your role:** Come to a clear understanding of how much and what type of input your loved one and her therapist want. Do they want you to be involved in the planning? How so? Ask whether they want you to simply observe the exposure activities or actively encourage carrying out the tasks involved with exposure. Make sure they're specific about what they want you to do. For example, ask whether you should stand next to your partner, hold a hand, or stand a few feet away during exposure tasks.

✔ **Encourage while keeping emotions in check:** Because you care so much, it's really easy to let your emotions guide your behavior while you coach. You want to encourage, but do so gently and calmly. Be careful not to

   • Push too hard. If your partner says "enough," it's enough.

   • Become too enthusiastic about progress. Your partner may feel it as pressure.

   • Get angry or argue. Remember to accept whatever your partner is able to do.

   • Become tearful or discouraged.

   • Feel overly involved with the process.

   • Start losing sleep.

If the coaching process causes you to become overly emotional or upset, back off. You may not be the right person for this job. That doesn't mean you don't care; in fact, you may simply care too much to be a good coach.

✔ **Avoid excessive responsibility:** Your loved one must develop an exposure plan, usually in concert with a therapist. You may help the one you care about develop a few details of the plan, but don't take on the full responsibility for designing an exposure hierarchy. People who have problems with anxiety frequently feel insecure and ask for excessive help and reassurance. Don't be pulled in by your loved one's insecurity.

✔ **Stick with the plan:** Resist the temptation to improvise. After a plan is in place, stick to it. If changes need to be made, consult with your loved one or have her discuss it with her therapist. Don't throw in surprises.

✔ **Remain positive:** Coaches need to avoid criticism and judgment. Your loved one won't be spurred on by negative comments from you. People work hard for praise and become immobilized and defensive in response to criticism. Avoid saying anything like, "You *should* be able to do this," or, "You aren't working hard enough."

✔ **Maintain realistic expectations:** After the plan is in place, expect your partner to have ups and downs. Some days go better than others. Small steps eventually go a long way. But you must always remember that determining how the plan plays itself out isn't up to you.

✔ **Execute the game plan:** After an exposure plan has been developed, the next step is to begin with relatively easy tasks. A good coach provides support and feedback. In addition, the coach can model, reward, and focus attention. Here are a few additional tips:

- Before asking your loved one to carry out a step, see whether she wants you to model the task first. If you model, showing a small amount of anxiety yourself is fine if you feel it.

- Practice going through the steps with imagery first. In other words, describe the scene in detail and have your loved one imagine it first. Don't carry it out in real life until your partner feels more comfortable with the imagery. You can consult Chapter 8 for details about using your imagination through exposure as well.

- Set up some rewards for success at a few intervals along the hierarchy. Do something you can enjoy together. You can also give some honest praise for success; just be sure not to sound patronizing or condescending.

- If the person you care about appears anxious at any step but not overwhelmed, encourage staying with that step until the anxiety comes down 50 percent. Obviously, don't absolutely insist, just encourage. Remind your partner that anxiety comes down with enough time.

Looking at a coach in action

Coaching someone you care about can seem overwhelming. The following example about Doug and Rosie helps you see how one couple worked through a mild case of anxiety with the help of a good game plan.

Doug and **Rosie** have dated for over a year. In all that time, they've never gone to a movie together because Rosie wrestles with a mild case of agoraphobia. Although she's able to go most places and do what she needs to in life, she dreads going anywhere that makes her feel trapped, especially movie theaters. She fantasizes that she'll need to get out, but she won't find her way to an exit because of the crowd and the darkness. She imagines that she would trip over people, fall on her face, and desperately crawl through the darkened theater.

Doug realizes that Rosie makes one excuse after another to avoid going to movies, even though she enjoys watching them on television. Gently, he asks Rosie, "Some things make me a little anxious — heavy traffic or big crowds — what makes you anxious?" Rosie confesses that crowded movie theaters make her feel closed in and trapped.

Several days later, Doug sees a copy of *Overcoming Anxiety For Dummies* in a bookstore and buys it with Rosie in mind. He starts reading, paying particular attention to Chapter 8 about exposure. Doug and Rosie have a productive discussion about her concerns and decide to face them. Doug volunteers to coach.

First, together they devise a staircase of fear, which breaks down the feared situation into small steps. (See more on the staircase of fear in Chapter 8.) Rosie's staircase of fear consists of the 12 steps shown in Figure 18-1.

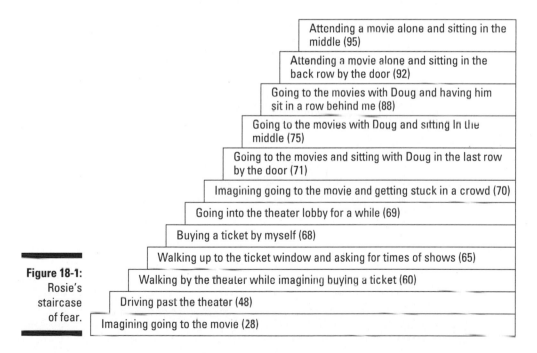

Figure 18-1: Rosie's staircase of fear.

Attending a movie alone and sitting in the middle (95)

Attending a movie alone and sitting in the back row by the door (92)

Going to the movies with Doug and having him sit in a row behind me (88)

Going to the movies with Doug and sitting in the middle (75)

Going to the movies and sitting with Doug in the last row by the door (71)

Imagining going to the movie and getting stuck in a crowd (70)

Going into the theater lobby for a while (69)

Buying a ticket by myself (68)

Walking up to the ticket window and asking for times of shows (65)

Walking by the theater while imagining buying a ticket (60)

Driving past the theater (48)

Imagining going to the movie (28)

Doug plays a role in most of Rosie's tasks. He helps her write a script for the imagined scenes. He reads the script out loud to Rosie while she closes her eyes and tries to picture the experiences. She rates her level of anxiety, and during the first few steps, he stays with her until her anxiety goes down.

Not only does he accompany her to the movies, but he also celebrates her successes and encourages her when she starts to falter. He holds her hand on the easier items and gives less support toward the end. Gradually, Rosie feels less anxiety when watching movies with Doug.

It takes attending a number of movies with Doug before she agrees to the final tasks of going by herself. In fact, they begin enjoying their nights at the movies and find that they both love talking about their experiences afterwards over coffee and dessert. Although Rosie balks at going to the theater by herself, her comfort level has increased over the last few months.

Rosie and Doug drive to the theater together on her last two items, but he chooses a movie playing on a different screen. Although Rosie feels frightened, she sticks it out. She feels good about her accomplishment, and the two of them become closer.

Rosie's fear of the movies had not yet reached the level of severely interfering with her life. Therefore, it was a good choice for a relatively simple exposure plan. Had Rosie not dealt with her fear in this early stage, it would likely have spread from fear of movies to fear of other crowded places.

Most people with fears, obsessions, or compulsions need to develop a plan with the help of a therapist. However, the example of Rosie and Doug can serve as an illustration of how a simple plan can be carried out without a therapist.

Teaming Up against Anxiety

One way you can help your partner overcome anxiety is to collaborate on ways to decrease stress in both your lives. With a little ingenuity, you can explore a variety of solutions that are likely to feel good to you even if you personally don't suffer from anxiety at all. For example:

- ✔ **Take a stress management class at a local center for adult continuing education.** These classes help people make lifestyle changes and set goals. Many of the ideas make life more fun and interesting in addition to reducing stress.

- ✔ **Take regular walks with your partner.** It's a great way to reduce stress, but even if you don't have much stress, strolling under the sky together is a wonderful time to talk and is great for your health.

✔ **Take a yoga, Pilates, or tai chi class together.** Again, even if you don't have anxiety, these classes are terrific for balance, muscle strength, flexibility, and overall health.

✔ **Explore spirituality together.** You may choose to attend a church, a synagogue, or a mosque, or scope out a less traditional method of communing with a higher power, such as immersing yourselves in nature. Thinking about things bigger than yourselves or the mundane events of the world provides a peaceful perspective.

✔ **Look for creative ways to simplify your joint lives.** Consider looking for help with household chores if you both work. Carefully analyze the way that you spend time. Make sure that your time reflects your priorities. See Chapter 10 for more ideas.

✔ **Do something good.** Consider jointly volunteering for a worthwhile cause or charity. Many people feel that such work enhances the meaning and purpose of their lives. Look at animal shelters, food banks, hospitals, and schools as possibilities. Even an hour every other week can make a positive difference.

✔ **Get away.** Take a vacation. You don't have to spend much money. And if you don't have the time for a long vacation, go away for an occasional evening at a local hotel. Getting away from texting, telephones, e-mails, doorbells, and other endless tasks and demands, even for a night, can help rejuvenate both of you.

Accepting Anxiety with Love

It may seem rather counterintuitive, but accepting your loved one's battle with anxiety is one of the most useful attitudes that you can take. Acceptance paradoxically forms the foundation for change. In other words, whenever you discuss your loved one's anxiety or engage in any effort to help, you need to appreciate and love all your partner's strengths and weaknesses.

You fell in love with the whole package — not just the good stuff. After all, you're not perfect, nor is your loved one. You wouldn't want perfection if you had it. If perfect people even existed, we can only imagine that they would be quite boring. Besides, studies show that people who try to be perfect more often become depressed, anxious, and distressed.

Therefore, rather than expecting perfection, accept your loved one as is. You need to accept and embrace both the possibility of productive change as well as the chance that your partner may remain stuck. Accepting your partner is especially important when your efforts to help

✔ Result in an argument

✔ Seem ineffective

    ✔ Aren't well-received by your partner

    ✔ Seem merely to increase your partner's anxiety even after multiple exposure trials

What does acceptance do? More than you may think. Acceptance allows you and your loved one to join together and grow closer, because acceptance avoids putting pressure on the one you care about. Intense expectations only serve to increase anxiety and resistance to change.

Acceptance conveys the message that you will love your partner no matter what. You'll care whether your partner stays the same or succeeds in making changes. This message frees your loved one to

    ✔ Take risks

    ✔ Make mistakes

    ✔ Feel vulnerable

    ✔ Feel loved

Change requires risk-taking, vulnerability, and mistakes. When people feel that they can safely goof up, look silly, cry, or fail miserably, they can take those risks. Think about it. When do you take risks or try new things? Probably not around an especially critical audience.

Giving up anxiety and fear takes tremendous courage in order to face the risks involved. Letting go of your need to see your partner change helps bolster the courage needed. Letting go of your need includes giving up your ego. In other words, this is not about you.

When you take on the role of a helper, it doesn't mean that your worth is at stake. Of course, you want to do the best you can, but you can't force others to change. Your loved one ultimately must own the responsibility.

Chapter 19

Recognizing Anxiety in Kids

. . . .

In This Chapter

▶ Seeing what's making kids so scared

▶ Knowing when to worry about your kids' anxiety

▶ Recognizing the usual anxieties of childhood

▶ Looking at the most common anxiety disorders among kids

. . . .

Many adults can recall childhood as being a time of freedom, exploration, and fun. Not too many years ago, kids rode bikes in the street and played outside until dark. Kids walked to school — with other kids.

Now, anxious parents wait with their children at bus stops until they're safely loaded. Parents rarely allow kids to leave the home without adult supervision. Parents worry about predators, kidnappers, and violence. They feel understandably protective. However, anxiety spreads from parents to their children. No wonder so many children experience anxiety.

Some anxiety is typical at certain ages. In this chapter, you discover the difference between normal and problematic anxiety in kids. We explain that some childhood fears are completely normal, while others require intervention. Then we take a look at the symptoms of anxiety disorders in children. (We devote Chapter 20 to ways you can ease your child's anxiety. If you're concerned about a particular child, we urge you to seek professional diagnosis and treatment.)

Separating Normal from Abnormal

Childhood anxiety has grown to epidemic proportions during the past 40 to 50 years. Numerous studies confirm this alarming development, but one in particular is a shocker. Psychologist Jean Twenge compared symptoms of anxiety in today's kids with symptoms in seriously disturbed kids receiving hospital treatment in 1957. She reported in the *Journal of Personality and Social Psychology* (December 2000) that boys and girls today report a greater number of anxiety symptoms than psychiatric inpatient children in 1957.

Should these findings cause alarm? We think so. The statistics are bad enough in their own right, but when you consider the fact that anxiety disorders often precede the development of depression later on, it raises concerns that the consequences of childhood anxiety could worsen in the years to come.

So what's going on? Why do our children experience emotional turmoil? Of course, we all know the complexities and tensions of the world today — longer work hours, rapidly developing technologies, violence on television, and even terrorism. We also suspect that certain types of parenting hold partial responsibility, as we discuss in Chapter 20.

For the moment, what you as a parent need to know is how to distinguish the normal anxieties of childhood from abnormal suffering. Realize that the vast majority of kids feel anxious at various times to one degree or another. After all, one of the primary tasks of childhood is to figure out how to overcome the fears that life creates for everyone. Successful resolution of those fears usually results in good emotional adjustment. You just need to know whether your children's fears represent normal development or a more sinister frame of mind that requires help. Look at Table 19-1 to get an idea of the anxiety that you can expect your children to experience at one time or another during their youth.

Table 19-1	Does Your Child Have an Anxiety Problem?	
Anxiety Problem	*When Anxiety Is Normal*	*When Anxiety Should Go Away*
Fear of separation from mother, father, or caregiver	Common between the ages of 6 months and 24 months. Don't worry!	If this continues with no improvement after 36 to 48 months, then you have some cause for concern.
Fear of unfamiliar adults	Common from 6 to 10 months.	Don't be too concerned unless you see this after 2 or 3 years of age. And don't worry about a little shyness after that.

Anxiety Problem	When Anxiety Is Normal	When Anxiety Should Go Away
Fear of unfamiliar peers	Common from age 2 until around 3 years old.	If this continues without showing signs of reducing after 3 years, you have some cause for concern.
Fear of animals, darkness, and imaginary creatures	Common between ages 2 and 6 years.	If these fears don't start to decline by 6 years of age, you have cause for concern. Many kids want a night light for a while; don't worry unless it's excessive.
School phobia	Mild to moderate school or day-care phobia is common from ages 3 to 6; it can briefly reappear when moving from elementary to middle school.	This should decline and cause no more than minimal problems after age 6. A brief reemergence at middle school is okay, but it should quell quickly. If not, it's a concern.
Fear of evaluation by others	This fear almost defines adolescence. Most teens worry a fair amount about what others think of them.	It should gradually reduce as adolescence unfolds. But it's not uncommon for it to last through the late teens.

Table 19-1 gives you some general guidelines about so-called normal childhood fears. However, independent of age, if fears seem especially serious and/or interfere with your child's life or schoolwork in a major way, they may be problematic and warrant attention. In addition, other anxiety problems we describe in the section "Inspecting the Most Common Childhood Anxiety Disorders," later in this chapter, are not particularly normal *at any age*.

If you have any doubts about the seriousness of your children's anxiety, you should consider a professional consultation. A mental-health counselor or your pediatrician should be well-equipped to handle your questions, quite possibly in a single visit. Anxiety problems sometimes predate other emotional difficulties, so you shouldn't wait to get them checked out.

Sleep terror in children

Childhood sleep disorders, one of the most common complaints brought to pediatricians, can disrupt the whole family. Children usually outgrow sleep disorders, such as bedwetting, frequent awakenings, and problems going to sleep.

Sleep terror, especially strange and frightening to parents, is relatively common, occurring among 1 to 6 percent of all kids; the incidence among adults is less than 1 percent. Sleep terror tends to present itself about an hour and a half after going to bed. The child typically sits up suddenly and screams for up to half an hour. During the episode, the child is actually asleep and is difficult to awaken and comfort. Children don't remember their sleep terror in the morning. Sleep terror most often occurs when children are between ages 4 and 10. By the time a child is a teenager, it usually disappears.

Direct treatments for sleep terror are unavailable as yet. But then again, because children don't remember it, sleep terror usually doesn't cause the children who have it any daytime distress. Too little sleep may increase the likelihood of sleep terror, so parents should make sure their children get enough sleep. And stress may also contribute to sleep terror, so parents should attempt to alleviate stress and other anxieties in their children.

Inspecting the Most Common Childhood Anxiety Disorders

Some fear and anxiety are normal for kids. You can probably remember being afraid of the dark, monsters, or ghosts. However, other types of anxiety, though not always rare, do indicate a problem that you should address. We briefly review the more common types of problematic anxiety in kids in the following sections.

Leaving parents: Separation anxiety disorder

As we show in Table 19-1, kids frequently worry about separations from their parents when they're as young as 6 months to perhaps as old as 4 years of age. However, significant fear of separation past about the age of 4, accompanied by the following, warrants intervention:

- ✔ Excessive distress when separated from caregivers or anticipating such separation
- ✔ Exorbitant worry about harm to parents or caregivers
- ✔ Obstinate avoidance of school or other activities because of worries about separation

- Refusal to go to bed without being near a parent or caregiver

- Frequent nightmares about separation

- Frequent physical complaints, such as headaches, stomachaches, and so on, when separated from parents

Among the various anxiety disorders, *separation anxiety disorder (SAD)* is relatively common in kids, but that doesn't mean it's normal. The average age at which it seems to start is around 7 to 8 years. The good news is that a large percentage of those with separation anxiety disorder no longer fulfill the diagnostic criteria for the disorder after three or four years.

WARNING!

The bad news is that quite a few of these kids go on to develop other problems, especially depression. For that reason, we suggest prompt intervention if it persists longer than a month or two and interferes with normal life.

The following story about Tyler and his mother Julie illustrates a typical presentation of separation anxiety in the form of a school phobia. Note that school phobia often also includes an element of social phobia (see the section "Connecting with others: Social phobia" later in this chapter).

> **Julie** doesn't know what to do about her 7-year-old son, **Tyler.** Every day, she battles with him about going to school. At first, she thinks he's really sick, so she takes him to the pediatrician. After a complete physical, the doctor reassures her that Tyler is healthy. The doctor encourages Julie to send Tyler to school and warns that if she doesn't, Tyler's behavior is likely to escalate.
>
> "My stomach hurts," whines Tyler. "I don't want to go to school."
>
> "Now sweetie, you've missed so many days," soothes Julie, "you really should go today; you're not that sick."
>
> "But my stomach really hurts; it really, really does Mommy." Tyler begins to sob. "Besides, the other kids don't like me."
>
> "You will go to school today," Julie says firmly, grabbing Tyler by the hand. Tyler plants his feet and pulls away, screaming. Julie can't believe what he's doing. He actually seems terrified; Julie's never seen him behave this way. Frantically, Tyler runs to his bedroom and hides in his closet. Julie finds him huddled, sobbing.
>
> Tyler suffers from school phobia, a common but serious childhood anxiety disorder involving anxiety about both separation from parents and social worries.

Wisely, Julie decides to seek further professional help. Most school counselors have had lots of experience in dealing with school phobias. See the sidebar "Getting back to school" for a typical treatment strategy.

Getting back to school

School phobia is a relatively common separation anxiety in childhood. The treatment for school phobia involves getting the child back to school as soon as possible. Children with school phobia often have parents who are slightly anxious themselves and care deeply about their kids. The first step is to convince the parents that they must be firm in their commitment to return the child to school.

A good way to calm the child and get him back to school is to allow for one brief contact between parent and child each day for a few weeks. The parent carries a cellphone. With agreement from the child's teacher, the child receives a get-out-of-class pass (usable only once each day) that allows the child to call his parent. The parent then speaks to the child for only an agreed-upon two minutes. The child is encouraged to save the pass for times of great distress and praised when he doesn't use the pass at all during a day.

This pass, allowing a parental phone call, gradually fades to one call every other day, one call a week, and so on. After the first few days, if the parents and teachers remain supportive and firm, the problem usually vanishes. If this strategy fails, there are many other techniques for overcoming school phobias. Consult a mental-health professional who specializes in child anxiety.

Sometimes, what appears to be a school phobia is actually a result of a child having been bullied at school. School counselors and teachers can help sort this out for you. Be sure to ask them to check into this possibility.

Worrying all the time: Generalized anxiety disorder

Based on what we know today, *generalized anxiety disorder (GAD)* is fairly common among kids and more common among older kids than younger ones. It most often develops at the onset of puberty or shortly thereafter and is characterized by

- ✔ Excessive anxiety and worry about school, friendships, or family problems
- ✔ Physical symptoms, such as stomachaches, headaches, or loss of appetite
- ✔ Difficulty concentrating and/or irritability
- ✔ Problems sleeping, restlessness, or agitation

Focusing on phobias: Specific phobias

Most young kids at one time or another exhibit fear of the dark or monsters in the closet. So don't worry if your child has these fears unless the fear becomes so intense that it disrupts daily living in a significant way. The typical age of onset of a *real* phobia (as opposed to the earlier, minor fears) is about age 8 or 9.

Specific phobias are exaggerated, intense fears that cause a child to avoid a particular object or situation. See Chapter 2 if you want more information on this type of anxiety.

Connecting with others: Social phobia

Some kids are just plain shy. They're born that way, and relatives often make comments like, "He's just like his dad was at that age." Sometimes, shyness decreases with age, but when shyness swells and causes a child to fearfully avoid social encounters in everyday life, your little one may have a problem.

Social phobia usually doesn't manage to get diagnosed until around 10 years of age. Signs generally appear at a younger age, but parents often have trouble distinguishing it from shyness until then. You can pick up on it sooner if you observe your children carefully. If their fears of unfamiliar peers or adults show no improvement whatsoever by age 3 or so, you may want to check with a professional to determine whether the problem is serious. See Chapter 2 for more information about social phobia.

Anxious repetition: Obsessive-compulsive disorder

This type of anxiety is somewhat less common than SAD, GAD, specific phobias, and social phobia. Nevertheless, almost 1 in 50 teens has *obsessive-compulsive disorder (OCD)*. Often beginning in childhood, OCD develops on average at around age 10. However, it can occur as early as 4 or 5 years of age; boys tend to get it earlier than girls do.

Obsessions are recurring, unwanted thoughts that your child can't stop (see Chapter 2 for more details). Some of the most common obsessions among children include

- Excessive fear of intruders
- Fear of germs
- Fear of illness
- Fixation on certain numbers

Compulsions involve rituals or various behaviors that your child feels compelled to repeat over and over. Common childhood compulsions include

 ✔ Arranging objects in a precise manner

 ✔ Excessive hand-washing

 ✔ Hoarding items of little value

 ✔ Repeatedly counting stairs, ceiling tiles, and steps taken while walking

Many children perform a few harmless rituals that involve magical thinking, such as not stepping on sidewalk cracks. However, any child that exhibits serious signs of OCD should be evaluated. It doesn't matter at what age it shows up, because OCD tends not to improve without treatment. The good news is that treatment really works!

Rare anxieties among children

A few anxiety disorders that occur in adults show up infrequently in children:

 ✔ **Agoraphobia** is often a response to panic and involves avoidance of places or situations in which you feel no escape is readily available.

 ✔ **Panic disorder** involves a sudden onset of intense fearfulness, terror, and physical symptoms. It usually doesn't appear until late adolescence or later.

 ✔ **Post-traumatic stress disorder** is a response to some traumatic event in which the person develops *hyper-arousal* (a heightened state of alert), intrusive thoughts about the event, and avoidance of any reminders of the event.

See Chapter 2 for more details on all these anxiety disorders. If any of these anxieties show up in your children, we recommend a professional consultation.

Post-traumatic stress disorder among children

Although thankfully rather rare in children, PTSD symptoms are slightly different among kids than adults. Like adults, children can get PTSD from abuse or other directly experienced trauma. (PTSD among New York City kids spiked after the September 11 terrorist attacks. Fourth and fifth graders were particularly affected.) Also, similar to adults, kids can develop PTSD from witnessing trauma happening to others, such as seeing a parent beaten.

Children with PTSD become restless, agitated, irritable, and unfocused. Instead of having nightmares and intrusive thoughts, children may act out their terror in play. They may have bad dreams, but these usually don't have content specifically relevant to the trauma. Like adults, they become anxious and alert to any possible sign of danger. They also tend to overreact to trivial incidents, such as being bumped into or criticized.

Chapter 20

Helping Kids Conquer Anxiety

- -

In This Chapter

▶ Bringing up calm kids

▶ Helping anxious children change

▶ Finding professional help if you need it

- -

We think it's pretty tough being a kid today. We picked up our grand-daughter at school the other day. Before leaving, we wrote her name on a big sign and placed it on the dashboard. We waited in a line of minivans and SUVs for more than 30 minutes while teachers walked around with bull-horns calling out children's names so that the drivers could identify them-selves. The children waited like cows in a secure, fenced-in area. Most of the vehicles in line had DVD players hanging like the screens in taxicabs — separating the adults from the kids, who become immobile prisoners in compli-cated car seats. Wow, just getting picked up from school can arouse anxiety.

How can parents and other concerned adults help children navigate this complex world without developing anxiety? In this chapter, we give parents and caregivers some guidance on how to prevent anxiety from taking root. But some kids will have anxiety despite parents' best intentions, so we also provide tips on ways to help those kids who do. Finally, we take a look at signs that indicate the possibility that a child needs professional help, who to seek for such help, and what to expect from mental-health professionals.

Nipping Anxiety in the Bud

How does anxiety begin? The risk for developing anxiety begins at concep-tion. That's right, studies of twins have demonstrated that almost half of what causes anxiety lies in your genes. However, that's just the beginning. Many other factors come into play, and you can do much about these factors, as we explain in this section.

Anxiety's brain chemistry

Recent research at Columbia University explored the effect of the brain chemical *serotonin* (a neurotransmitter thought to influence mood), which is produced naturally in the body, on the development of anxiety. Experimenters bred mice that lacked important receptors for serotonin, which left them unable to use this important neurotransmitter. They found that mice between 5 and 20 days old without the ability to process serotonin developed mouse anxiety as adults. But when they raised mice with normal serotonin receptors and later depleted the mice of serotonin when they had reached adulthood, the mice didn't develop anxiety.

What does this research have to do with anxious kids? It points to the importance of biological factors in the development of anxiety. Even prenatal and early infantile experiences may affect emotional well-being long into the future. Perhaps treating childhood anxiety early can help to prevent future problems.

More research is needed to understand how all this works. However, we know that biological interventions (such as medications) affect serotonin levels, and it appears that behavioral strategies, such as those described in this book, also alter brain chemistry in productive ways.

Early mastery experiences

When a hungry or uncomfortable baby cries out and parents respond by feeding or comforting, the baby experiences a beginning sense of mastery. In other words, what the baby does results in a predictable outcome. This early opportunity can be repeated thousands of times over the next few years in various ways. For example, the toddler discovers how to use language to make requests that then get rewarded. If parents respond unpredictably and chaotically to an infant's attempts to control his or her environment, anxiety is likely to increase.

So to decrease the probability of anxiety, responding predictably to young children is imperative. For young infants, parents should respond with reasonable consistency to most of their distress. Later, predictability is still important but should occur only to age-appropriate distress or requests. In other words, you wouldn't want to reinforce a 2-year-old's temper tantrums by caving in.

As your children grow older, you should provide as many opportunities as possible for them to experience a feeling of mastery. You can do this by

- Involving them in sports
- Interesting them in hobbies that require some skill
- Playing games of skill, such as puzzles or Scrabble

✔ Making sure that they have the chance to experience success at school and getting immediate help if they start struggling with their studies

✔ Training them to have good manners and social skills

Fine-tuning emotions

One of the most important tasks of childhood consists of learning how to control emotions, tolerate frustration, and delay gratification. Again, young infants need prompt gratification. However, with increasing age, the world tends to look unfavorably upon those who demand instant gratification and rejects those who can't keep a reasonable lid on their emotional outbursts.

You can help your child learn these crucial skills of emotional regulation. Helping children express emotions without letting them run out of control involves a few basic steps:

✔ **Validate your children's emotions.** When children feel distressed, anxious, or worried, validate their emotions. You do that by saying,

   • "I see that you're a little afraid of . . ."

   • "You seem worried about . . ."

   This validating statement should also try to help your children connect the feeling to what's going on.

✔ **Don't deny your children's feelings.** To the greatest degree possible, don't deny the feeling or try to take it away. In other words, you don't want to say, "You shouldn't be scared," or, worse, "You're not really afraid."

✔ **Don't overprotect.** No one likes to see children feel fearful or anxious. However, they need to figure out how to deal with most fears on their own. If you try to solve all their problems or keep them from all worries and danger, you're doing more harm than good.

✔ **Help your kids learn to calm down.** You can teach them to take a few slow, deep breaths or count to ten slowly. You can also explain that extreme anxiety and fear will lessen eventually.

✔ **Praise your children.** When they make efforts to overcome anxieties, praise your kids. However, don't punish them for failing to do so.

✔ **Don't provide unnecessary reassurance.** Making comments such as, "There's nothing to be afraid of" is unnecessary. Kids need to find out how to handle a little stress and anxiety on their own. Don't constantly reassure them or you'll create a surefire path to anxiety.

Inoculating against anxiety

Experiencing certain situations, activities, animals, and objects commonly turns into a phobia. The following list of children's fears shows that children experience fears that are often similar to those that adults experience:

- ✔ Airplanes
- ✔ Being alone
- ✔ Dogs
- ✔ Heights
- ✔ Rodents
- ✔ Snakes
- ✔ Spiders and insects
- ✔ Thunder and lightning

If you want to prevent your children from acquiring one of these common phobias, you can inoculate them. You do that by providing safe interactions with the potentially feared event or object — prior to any fear developing. Try the following activities:

- ✔ Take your kids to a museum or zoo that offers hands-on experiences with snakes and insects.
- ✔ Climb a mountain together.
- ✔ Watch a storm from the safety of your living room couch. Discuss how lightning and thunder work.
- ✔ If you don't have a dog or cat of your own, go to the pound and visit puppies and kittens.

Research has proven that this method works. For example, studies have shown that children bitten by dogs don't develop a phobia as readily if they have had past, positive experiences with dogs. Children who fly at an early age rarely develop a phobia to flying. The more experiences you provide your children with, the better their chances are of growing up without phobias.

If you're somewhat phobic yourself, try not to make faces or get too squeamish when you inoculate your kids against phobias. Don't say, "Oooh, how gross!" Even if you feel nervous, try not to show it.

Taking precautions via parenting style

Parents can set children up to develop an anxiety disorder, or parents can help to prevent anxiety, depending on their parenting style:

✔ **Permissive parents** engage with their kids and show concern and caring. But permissive parents hate confrontation, and they abhor seeing their kids feel bad. Therefore, they set low expectations for their children, and they don't push them to act mature or try new things.

✔ **Authoritarian parents** represent the opposite extreme. They demand, direct, and expect instant obedience from their children. They control every detail of their children's lives and tend to be overly structured and hostile.

✔ **Authoritative parents** take the middle road. These parents set reasonable limits and boundaries. They're flexible and aware of their kids' developmental stage. They try to help their kids understand the reasons behind their expectations for good behavior, although they don't spend a whole lot of time *reasoning,* or debating, with their kids.

Keep reading for more details about how each of these parenting styles affects a child's anxiety level.

Permissive and authoritarian parenting

Both the permissive and the authoritarian types of parents fuel anxiety in children. The following story is about both types. The mother demonstrates permissive parenting, and the father is an authoritarian.

> Four-year-old **Nancy** screams with terror. Her parents rush into her room to see what's wrong. "There's a bad man in my room; I saw him," she cries.
>
> Nancy's mother hugs her, strokes her hair, and tells her, "Everything will be okay now that Mommy's here."
>
> Her dad turns on the light. He checks her closet and under her bed and snaps, "There's nobody here. Just stay in your bed and go to sleep. Don't be such a baby."

When this scene reenacts itself night after night for six weeks, Nancy's dad becomes increasingly annoyed and speaks harshly to her about what he calls her silly fears. At the same time, her mother overprotects Nancy. Her mom even starts to sleep in her room to make her feel safe. Her fears only intensify. Poor Nancy receives mixed messages from her parents, and neither message helps.

Authoritative parenting

A different kind of parenting can help your kids deal with anxiety better. It's called *authoritative* (as opposed to authoritarian) parenting. Authoritative parents provide clear expectations for their children. They encourage their kids to face challenges. They validate their children's feelings of anxiety but urge them to deal with them. They aren't harsh or punitive, but they don't overprotect. Using Nancy's story again, the following demonstrates how authoritative parents would deal with Nancy's anxieties.

Four-year-old **Nancy** screams with terror. Her parents rush into her room to see what's wrong. "There's a bad man in my room; I saw him," she cries.

Nancy's mom gives her a quick hug and says, "You sound afraid, sweetie."

Her dad turns on the light, checks the closet and under the bed, and says, "Nobody's here, honey. But if you'd like, we can leave a night light on."

Nancy says, "Please don't leave me alone. Can't Mommy just stay here with me tonight?"

Nancy's mom tells her, "No, you need to handle this yourself. I know you're worried, but it will be okay." They turn the night light on and tell her, "Here's your bear; he'll keep you company. We'll see you in the morning."

Nancy cries softly for a few minutes and falls back to sleep.

Nancy's parents were lucky that she only cried for a short period of time. They felt a bit guilty for letting her cry but realized that Nancy needs to learn that she can handle a little anxiety on her own. Some kids aren't so easy.

Perhaps your child keeps on crying and won't stop. Well, sometimes that happens. Occasionally, you may need to hang in there for an hour or two. The first night is usually the worst. Don't give up. Eventually, the vast majority of kids start falling asleep sooner. If that doesn't happen after four or five nights in a row, you may need to consult a professional.

Helicopter parenting

The term *helicopter parenting* has gained popularity in the past decade. Think of a helicopter hovering over you, following you throughout each day as you go about your business. Specifically, these parents direct their kids' lives, run interference for them whenever they can, and try to shield them from all bad feelings. Thus, a helicopter parent will complain to teachers about grades or assignments, argue with coaches, and confront their children's peers when a conflict occurs.

It's bad enough when helicopter parents hover in this manner during elementary school. But some of these folks never stop. They continue to prevent their teens from experiencing the consequences of their own behavior and misjudgments. Some of these parents even write their kids' college papers for them. In fact, a few colleges have found that parental interest is so intense that parent-teacher associations (PTAs) have sprung up on campus.

Helicopter parents often have high expectations of their kids, unlike permissive parents. However, they're similar to permissive parents in that they can't stand seeing their kids feel frustration or upset. The problem with both types of parents is that they fail to teach their kids how to deal with life's difficulties. Anxiety often results.

Helping Already Anxious Children

If you have a child with anxiety, don't make yourself anxious by blaming yourself for the problem. Multiple factors probably went into making your kid anxious (for more information, read Chapter 3). And you probably weren't able to read this book prior to your child developing anxiety, so you didn't know what you could do to prevent it. So now what do you do? Read on.

Helping yourself first

If you've traveled on a commercial flight, you've probably heard flight attendants instruct you about how to deal with the oxygen masks should they drop down. They tell you to put the mask on yourself prior to assisting your child. That's because if you don't help yourself first, you won't be in any condition to help your child.

The same principle applies to anxiety in your kids. You need to tackle your own anxiety prior to trying to help your children. Children learn many of their emotional responses by observing their parents; it makes sense that anxious parents more often end up with anxious children. The nice part of getting rid of your own anxiety first is that this is likely to help your children, as well as give you the resources for assisting with their worries.

You can do this by reading this book for yourself. Pick and choose the strategies that best fit your problem and personality. However, if the ideas you choose first don't seem to work, don't despair. The vast majority of the time, one or more of the techniques that we describe does help.

If you find that reading this book and trying our recommendations don't reduce your anxiety as much as you'd like, consider consulting a mental-health professional who's trained in cognitive behavioral therapy.

Modeling mellow

If you don't have a problem with anxiety or if you've overcome your excessive worries for the most part, you're ready to teach by example. Children learn a great deal by watching the people they care about. You may recall a time when your child surprised you by repeating words you thought or wished he hadn't heard. Trust us, kids see and hear everything.

Therefore, take advantage of every opportunity to model relatively calm behavior and thinking. Don't invalidate your child's anxiety by saying it's a stupid or silly fear. Furthermore, demonstrating complete calm is not as useful as showing how you handle the concern yourself. Table 20-1 shows some common childhood fears and how you can model an effective response.

Table 20-1	Modeling a Better Way
Fear	*Parental Modeling*
Thunderstorms	"I understand a thunderstorm is coming tonight. Sometimes, I get a little nervous about them, but I know we're safe at home. I'm always careful to seek shelter during a thunderstorm. But I know that thunderstorms can't really hurt you when you're inside."
Insects	"I used to think that insects were gross, awful, and scary, but now I realize that they're more afraid of me than I am of them. Insects run away from people when they can. Sometimes, they're so scared that they freeze. I admit that I still use plenty of tissue to pick them up, and that's okay. Let me show you how I do it."
Heights	"I sometimes feel a little nervous looking down from high places. Here we are on the top of the Washington Monument. Let's hold hands and go to the window together. You can't fall off, and it can't hurt you. Looking down from heights is kind of fun. The scariness is kind of exciting after you get used to it."
Being alone (don't say this unless your child expresses anxiety about feeling safe alone)	"Your father's going on a trip tomorrow. I used to feel afraid staying at home by myself, but I realize that I can take pretty good care of myself and of you. We have a security door, and if anyone tries to get in, we can always call the police. Our dogs are pretty good protection, too. Do you ever get scared? If you do, we can talk about it."

Leading children through anxiety

As we discuss in Chapter 8, gradual exposure to whatever causes anxiety is one of the most effective ways of overcoming fear. Whether the anxious person is a child or an adult, the strategy is much the same. Therefore, if you want to help your children who already have anxiety, first model coping as we describe in Table 20-1. Then, consider using *exposure,* which involves breaking the feared situation or object into small steps. You gradually confront and stay with each step until anxiety reduces by 50 percent or more.

Read Chapter 8 for important, additional details about exposure. However, keep a few things in mind when doing this as a guide for your child:

- **Break the steps down as small as you possibly can.** Don't expect your child to master a fear overnight. It takes time. And children need smaller steps than adults. For example, if you're dealing with a fear of dogs, don't expect your child to immediately walk up to and pet a dog on the first attempt. Instead, start with pictures and storybooks about dogs. Then progress to seeing dogs at a distance, behind an enclosed fence. Gradually work up to direct contact, perhaps at a pet store.

- **Expect to see some distress.** This is the hard part for parents. No one likes to see their kids get upset. But you can't avoid having your kids feel modest distress if you want them to get over their anxiety. Sometimes, this part is more than some parents can handle. In those cases, a close friend or relative may be willing to pitch in and help. At the same time, if your child exhibits extreme anxiety and upset, you need to break the task down further or get professional help.

- **Praise your child for any successes.** Pay attention to any improvement and compliment your child. However, don't pressure your child by saying that this shows what a big boy or girl he or she is.

- **Show patience.** Don't get so worked up that your own emotions spill over and frighten your child further. Again, if that starts to happen, stop for a while, enlist a friend's assistance, or seek a professional's advice.

The following story shows how parents dealt with their son's sudden anxiety about water. Kids frequently become afraid when something unexpected happens.

Penny and **Stan** plan a Caribbean vacation at a resort right on the beach. The brochure describes a family-friendly atmosphere. They purchase a snorkel and diving mask for their 3-year-old, **Benjamin,** who enjoys the plane ride and looks forward to snorkeling.

When they arrive, the hotel appears as beautiful as promised. The beach beckons, and the ocean water promises to be clear. Penny, Stan, and Benjamin quickly unpack and make their way down to the beach. They walk into the water slowly, delighted by the warm temperature. Suddenly, a large wave breaks in front of them and knocks Benjamin over. Benjamin opens his mouth in surprise, and saltwater gags him. He cries and runs back to the shore, screaming.

Stan immediately pulls Benjamin back into the water. He continues to scream and kick. Penny and Stan spend the rest of the vacation begging Benjamin to go into the ocean again to no avail. The parents end up taking turns babysitting Benjamin while their vacation dream fades.

At home, Benjamin's fear grows, as untreated fears often do. He fusses in the bath, not wanting any water to splash on his face. He won't even consider getting into a swimming pool.

Benjamin's parents take the lead and guide him through exposure. First, on a hot day, they put a rubber, inflated wading pool in the backyard. They fill it and model getting in. Eventually, Benjamin shows a little interest and joins them in the pool. After he gets more comfortable, the parents do a little playful splashing with each other and encourage Benjamin to splash them. He doesn't notice that his own face gets a little water on it.

Then his parents suggest that Benjamin put just a part of his face into the water. He resists at first, but they encourage him. When he puts his chin into the water, they applaud. Stan puts his face entirely under water and comes up laughing. He says that Benjamin may not be ready to do that. Benjamin proves him wrong. Benjamin and Stan take turns putting their faces into the water and splashing each other. What started out as fear turns into fun.

The parents provide a wide range of gradually increasing challenges over the next several months, including using the mask and snorkel in pools of various sizes. Then they go to a freshwater lake and do the same. Eventually, they take another vacation to the ocean and gradually expose Benjamin to the water there as well.

If Benjamin's parents had allowed him to play on the beach at the edge of the water instead of insisting that he get back in the water immediately, he may have been more cooperative. They could have then gradually encouraged him to walk in the water while watching for waves. That way, they may have been able to enjoy their vacation. They made the mistake of turning a fear into a power struggle, which doesn't work very well with children — or, for that matter, with adults.

Relaxing to reduce anxiety

Children benefit from learning to relax, much in the same way that adults do. We discussed relaxation methods for adults in Chapters 12 and 13, but kids need some slightly different strategies. That's because they don't have the same attention span as adults.

Usually, we suggest teaching kids relaxation on an individual basis rather than in groups. Kids in groups tend to get embarrassed. They deal with their embarrassment by acting silly and then fail to derive much benefit from the exercise. Individual training doesn't usually create as much embarrassment, and keeping kids' attention is easier.

Breathing relaxation

The following directives are intended to teach kids abdominal breathing that has been shown to effectively reduce anxiety. Feel free to use your own creativity to design similar instructions. Say the following to guide your child through each step:

1. **Lie down on the floor and put your hands on your tummy.**

2. **Pretend that your stomach is a big balloon and that you want to fill it as full as you can.**

3. **Breathe in and see how big you can make your stomach.**

4. **Now make a whooshing sound, like a balloon losing air, as you slowly let the air out. Excellent.**

5. **Let's do it again.**

   Breathe in and fill the balloon. Hold it for a moment and then let the air out of your balloon ever so slowly as you make whooshing sounds.

Repeat these instructions for eight or ten breaths. Tell your kids to practice this exercise daily.

Relaxing muscles

An especially effective way of achieving relaxation is through muscle relaxation. The following series of directives may help a child relax. Again, feel free to use your creativity. Have your child work each muscle group for about ten seconds before relaxing. Then relax for about ten seconds. Talk your child through the exercises as follows:

1. **Sit down in this chair, close your eyes, and relax.**

2. **Pretend the floor is trying to rise up and that you have to push it back down with your legs and feet.**

   Push, push, push.

3. **Okay, now relax your legs and feet.**

   Notice how nice they feel.

4. **Oh, oh. The floor is starting to rise again. Push it back down.**

5. **Good job, now relax.**

6. **Now tighten your stomach muscles.**

   Make your stomach into a shield of armor, strong like Superman. Hold the muscles in.

7. **Good, now relax.**

8. **One more time; tighten those stomach muscles into steel. Hold it.**

9. **Great, now relax.**

   See how nice, warm, and relaxed your stomach feels.

10. **Now, spread your fingers and put your hands together in front of your chest. Squeeze your hands together. Push hard and use your arm muscles, too.**

    Pretend you're squeezing Play-Doh between your hands and make it as squished as you can.

11. **Okay, now relax. Take a deep breath. Hold it.**

12. **Now let the air out slowly.**

13. **Again, spread your fingers wide, and squish Play-Doh between your hands. Hold it.**

14. **Great. Now relax.**

15. **Pretend you're a turtle. You want to go into your shell. To do that, bring your shoulders way up high and try to touch your ears with your shoulders. Feel your head go down into your shell. Hold it.**

16. **Okay, now relax.**

    See how nice, warm, and relaxed your shoulders and neck feel.

17. **One more time now. Be a turtle and go into your shell. Hold it.**

18. **Good. Now relax.**

19. **Finally, squish your face up like it does when you eat something that tastes really, really bad. Squish it up tight. Hold it.**

20. **Okay, now relax. Take a deep breath. Hold it.**

21. **Now let the air out slowly.**

22. **One more time. Squish your face up real tight. Hold it.**

23. **Relax. Good job! See how limp and relaxed your body feels.**

    When you feel upset or worried, you can do this all by yourself to feel better. You don't have to do all the muscles like we did. You can just do what you want to.

Imagining your way to relaxation

One way to help your child relax is through reading books. Before bed, kids find stories very relaxing. Reading rids their mind of worries and concerns from the day. You can also find various books and tapes specifically designed for helping kids relax. Unfortunately, some of the tapes use imagery of beautiful, relaxing scenes that kids may find rather boring.

Rather than beautiful scenes of beaches and lakes, kids can relax quite nicely to more fanciful scenes that appeal to their sense of fun and joy. The scenes don't need to be about relaxation per se; they just need to be entertaining and pleasant. Again, the point is to provide engaging alternatives to worries and fears. One great idea comes from one of our clients and that client's mother. You can design your own book with your child. This child, with a little help from her mom, wrote and illustrated each page of her own relaxation book as in the following excerpt, titled "Imagine Unicorns and Smiling Stars":

> Close your eyes and relax.
>
> Imagine unicorns dancing.
>
> Imagine outer space. Look at the planets spinning and floating.
>
> Imagine smiling stars. See how happy they are.
>
> Imagine blue moons. See the moons smiling.
>
> Imagine nice aliens. They like you.
>
> Imagine spaceships soaring.
>
> Imagine unicorns dancing in outer space with smiling stars, blue moons, and friendly aliens in their spaceship soaring.
>
> Now, relax. Dream wonderful dreams.

Exorcizing anxiety through exercise

Exercise burns off excess adrenaline, which fuels anxiety. All kids obviously need regular exercise, and studies show that most don't exercise enough. Anxious kids may be reluctant to engage in organized sports. They may feel inadequate or even afraid of negative evaluation by others.

Yet it may be more important for anxious kids to participate in sports for two reasons. First, sports can provide them with important mastery experiences. Although they may feel frustrated and upset at first, they usually experience considerable pride and a sense of accomplishment as their skills improve. Second, aerobic activity directly decreases anxiety.

The challenge is to find a sport that provides your child with the greatest possible chance of at least modest success. Consider the following activities:

✔ **Swimming:** An individual sport that doesn't involve balls thrown at your head or collisions with other players. Swimmers compete against themselves, and many swim teams reward most participants with ribbons, whether they come in first or sixth.

✔ **Track and field:** An individual sport that has a wide variety of different skill possibilities. Some kids are fast and can run short dashes. Others discover that they can develop the endurance to run long distances. Still others can throw a shot put.

✔ **Tennis:** A low-contact and relatively safe sport. Good instruction can make most kids adequate tennis players.

✔ **Martial arts:** Good for enhancing a sense of competence and confidence. Many martial arts instructors have great skill for working with uncoordinated, fearful kids. Almost all kids can experience improvements and success with martial arts.

✔ **Dance:** A sport that includes many variations, from ballet to square dancing. Musically inclined kids often do quite well with dance classes.

In other words, find something for your kids to do that involves physical activity. They can benefit in terms of decreased anxiety, increased confidence, and greater connections with others. Don't forget to include family bike rides, hikes, or walks. Model the benefits of lifelong activity and exercise.

Getting Help from Others

The goals of childhood include learning how to get along with others, learning self-control, and preparing for adult responsibilities. Children make progress toward these goals by interacting with friends and family as well as by attending school. If anxiety interferes with these activities, then consultation and professional treatment may be needed. In other words, if a child can't play, learn, or participate in activities because of worries, it's time to get help.

Who to get help from

We recommend that parents first turn to their child's medical doctor to make sure there are no physical reasons for a child's anxiety. Certain medications prescribed for other conditions can cause a child to feel anxious. The physician may decide to switch medications first. If the culprit is anxiety, rather than a drug or physical problem, the medical provider may have recommendations for mental-health providers. The following tips may help you search more effectively.

- ✔ Call your health insurance plan to see what type of coverage you have for your child's mental-health care. Your company may have a list of providers in your area.

- ✔ Call providers and ask whether they have experience and training in treating childhood anxiety. The therapy can seem like play to your child, but therapy should be based on an approach that has been shown to help children overcome anxiety. We generally recommend practitioners trained in cognitive or behavioral strategies because their effectiveness has been supported most consistently by research.

- ✔ Make sure the provider you choose has office hours that can accommodate several appointments. Although the treatment may be relatively brief, don't expect it to happen in one or two sessions.

- ✔ Ask what state license your provider holds. Don't seek help from someone without a license to practice mental-health counseling. Professionals who usually treat children may be clinical psychologists, social workers, counselors, or school psychologists.

Psychiatrists can also be involved in treating childhood anxiety disorders; however, they usually prescribe medication. We recommend that treatment for anxiety, especially for children, begin with psychotherapy rather than medication. We take this approach because of unknown side effects of long-term use of medication and the great potential of relapse when medication is stopped. In contrast, the new ways of thinking or behaving learned through psychotherapy can last a lifetime.

If your insurance doesn't pay for psychotherapy, consider this: A study reported in the *Journal of Abnormal Psychology* (2008) found that the medical costs of anxious children were almost 21 times higher than those without anxiety. Covering effective treatment for anxious children is cost-effective for health insurance companies. Your medical provider may be able to advocate with your insurance company using this argument. Treating anxiety early can save considerable money and suffering in the long run.

What to expect at the first session

Generally, the first session is a time for your child's therapist to learn about the problems your child is having. You can expect lots of questions. Parents are almost always invited into the first session to provide information. You may want to prepare for the first appointment beforehand by keeping a journal of what you're concerned about. For example, consider taking notes on the following questions:

- ✔ **What happens?** Does your child avoid certain situations? Is anxiety getting in the way of her schoolwork or her play with other children? Is she getting bullied at school?

- ✔ **When do your child's symptoms crop up?** Is he fine at home with familiar people and afraid at school? Does he get worse when he's worried about a test or when meeting new people? Are there particular times when his anxiety seems better or worse?

- ✔ **How long have you noticed these symptoms?** Have there been any changes in the family, such as the birth of a child, death, or divorce? Has your child experienced any trauma?

- ✔ **Do other members of the family have problems with anxiety?** If so, what sorts of problems?

- ✔ **Has your child experienced any recent health problems or hospitalizations?**

Generally, what a parent or child says to a therapist is held in strict confidence with only a few limitations. One important limit to confidentiality with professionals is that they're required to report suspicions of child abuse. Another limit is that they must report cases involving children who appear to represent an imminent threat to themselves or other people.

What happens in therapy?

For young children, much of the work is likely to focus on the parents. In other words, the therapist spends much of the time teaching the parents things they can do to facilitate their child's progress. This focus doesn't mean the parents caused the problem, but they often can do much to alleviate it.

Older children and teenagers spend more time in discussions with the therapist, and parents' involvement varies more widely. In either case, you can expect the therapist to give tasks to both parents and their kids to be carried out in between sessions. You should expect the therapist to discuss what the specific goals of the sessions are, as well as detailed plans for getting there. However, you shouldn't expect therapists to reveal details of what is discussed in sessions with your child. Kids need to feel safe in revealing whatever they want to their therapists. Parents are, however, entitled to progress updates.

More often than not, childhood anxiety can be expected to *improve* significantly (not necessarily resolve entirely) within six months or so of treatment. If that doesn't seem to be happening, discuss it with the therapist and consider getting a second opinion.

Part VI
The Part of Tens

The 5th Wave   By Rich Tennant

"Right now I'm managing my anxiety through medication, meditation, and limiting visits from my pain-in-the-butt neighbor."

In this part . . .

We offer ten quick ways to defeat anxious feelings on the spot. In case your anxiety comes back, we review ten ways of dealing with relapses. Also, be sure to take a look at the ten indications that you may need professional help. Finally, we include an appendix where we recommend books and Web sites that you can turn to for more help in dealing with your anxiety.

Chapter 21

Ten Ways to Stop Anxiety Quickly

Sometimes you need quick, temporary relief from anxiety. With that in mind, this chapter describes ten assorted therapies from our anxiety/ stress reduction first-aid kit. Select one or more when worry and stress start to get out of hand.

Breathing Out Your Anxiety

Anxiety makes breathing shallow and rapid. And rapid, shallow breathing has a way of increasing anxiety — not a useful cycle. Try this quick, easy-to-learn breathing technique to restore a calming pattern of breathing. You can do this anytime, anywhere. It really works. Give it a try.

1. **Inhale deeply through your nose.**

2. **Hold your breath for a few seconds.**

3. **Slowly let your breath out through your lips while making a slight sound — hissing, sighing, or whatever.**

4. **Repeat Steps 1 through 3 for a minimum of ten breaths.**

Talking with a Friend

Anxiety is a lonely feeling, and loneliness increases anxiety. Research shows that social support helps people deal with almost any type of emotional distress. So don't hesitate to reach out to friends and family. Find a trusted person to confide in. You may think that no one would want to hear about your troubles, but we're not talking about whining and complaining. We're talking about sharing what's going on with you.

No doubt you would do the same for someone else. You likely know some folks who want you to call them in troubled times. If you find yourself without friends, call upon a minister, priest, or rabbi. If you have no religious connections, call a crisis line. You can also see Chapter 23 for signs that you may need professional help.

Exercising Aerobically

Anxiety floods the body with adrenaline. Adrenaline, a chemical produced by your body, causes your heart to beat faster, your muscles to tighten, and various other body sensations that feel distressing. Nothing burns off adrenaline faster than aerobic exercise. Good examples include jogging; a long, fast walk; dancing; rope jumping; and tennis.

Soothing the Body

The most distressing aspect of anxiety is the way that it makes your body feel — tense, queasy, racy, and tight. Quick ways to temporarily break through the tension include the following:

✔ Soaking in a hot bath for a good while.

✔ Taking a long, hot shower.

✔ Enjoying a 15-minute massage, such as in a chair or on a mat with an electronic heating and vibrating massager. Of course, if your budget allows for a longer massage performed by a professional masseuse, that's great too!

Drinking Tea

Keep a selection of herbal teas in your cupboard. Certain teas, like chamomile, reportedly have relaxing properties. Stay away from caffeinated teas, however, especially if caffeine bothers you.

When you feel anxious, heat up a favorite tea. Hold the cup in your hands and breathe in the warm scent. Spend a couple of moments enjoying the comfort of sipping tea. Concentrate on the soothing sensation and the luxury of sitting quietly.

Challenging Your Anxious Thinking

The way you think strongly influences the way you feel. Anxious people inevitably think about things in ways that increase their anxiety. One of the best ways of dealing with anxiety is to examine the evidence for your anxious thoughts.

First, write down what you're worried about. Afterwards, ask yourself some questions about those thoughts, such as

✔ Is this worry truly as awful as I'm thinking it is?

✔ Could some evidence contradict my anxious thoughts?

✔ In a year, how important will this event be to me?

✔ Am I making a dire prediction without any real basis?

After answering these questions, try to write down a more realistic perspective. See Chapter 5 for discovering more about how to write out your anxious thoughts, analyze them for distortions, and replace them with more realistic, calmer thoughts.

Listening to Music

Sounds influence the way you feel. Think about it. If you listen to fingernails scraping across a blackboard, how do you feel? Most people (us included) report that it gives them a creepy, anxious feeling. Just as unpleasant sounds jangle the nerves, soothing sounds can calm you.

Select music that you find relaxing. Get comfortable and close your eyes. Turn the volume to a comforting level. Relax. Listen.

Finding Distractions

In general, avoiding your anxiety isn't a good idea. But until you discover better ways of dealing with it, sometimes distractions can help. Remember, they're just a temporary bandage and won't last. However, once in a while, distraction helps. Consider the following:

✔ A good book

✔ A movie

✔ Television, mindless as it may be

✔ Video games

Having Sex

If you have an available, willing partner, sex is a wonderful way to relax. It can certainly take your mind off anxiety! And, like aerobic exercise, it burns off adrenaline. What a perfect combination.

On the other hand, some anxious people get anxious about their sexual performance. If that's you, don't try this strategy — at least until you overcome your anxiety about this issue. And, if you don't have an available, willing partner, we don't recommend hiring one.

Staying with the Moment

What are you worried about? Chances are it's something that hasn't even happened yet and may never occur. The fact is, almost 90 percent of what people worry about never actually happens. And if it does occur, it rarely ends up being as catastrophic as the worriers predict.

Therefore, we suggest that you focus on the here and now. What are you doing? Look around you. Notice how the air feels as it goes in and out your nose. Feel your feet and the muscles in your legs as you sit. If you still feel anxiety, study it. Notice the various sensations in your body, and realize that they won't kill you. They'll pass eventually as you observe them. If you accept feeling just a bit anxious, the feelings abate more quickly than if you tell yourself that you must get rid of them at once. Read Chapter 13 for more ideas about mindful acceptance.

Enjoy the moment.

Chapter 22

Ten Ways to Deal with Relapse

*I*f you're reading this chapter, you've probably made some headway with your anxiety. Maybe, after all your hard work, you've experienced a setback, or perhaps you're worried about one. Not to worry. We have ten ideas for you to use when anxiety pops back.

Expecting Anxiety

Perhaps you've worked hard to overcome your anxiety, and now your hard work has paid off. You've beaten it. Congratulations! But alas, one day you wake up suddenly with anxiety staring you in the face. You turn it into a catastrophe and assume that you've failed.

Oh, get real. You'll never totally annihilate anxiety. That is, until you stop breathing. It's bound to show up from time to time. *Expect* anxiety. Look for its early warning signs. But don't compound matters by getting anxious about your anxiety. If you understand that anxiety happens, you can lessen the impact.

Counting the Swallows

The proverb "One swallow doesn't make a summer" reflects the fact that a single sign doesn't necessarily indicate that something more is inevitable. Anxiety has an ebb and flow. Having an anxious episode or two doesn't mean that you're back to square one. You figured out how to handle some of your anxiety, and that knowledge can still help you. You don't need to start all over again. You do need to move forward and reapply what you practiced. Thinking of minor setbacks as catastrophes will only increase your anxiety and immobilize your efforts. Regroup, reorganize, and go back at it!

Checking Out Why Anxiety Returned

Minor relapses are a great opportunity to discover what gives you trouble. Figure out what events preceded your latest bout of anxiety:

- ✔ Have you had some recent difficulties at work, such as deadlines, promotions, problems with co-workers, or financial setbacks?
- ✔ Have you had recent problems at home, such as divorce, problems with a child, or other stressors?

If so, understand that an increase in your anxiety is a natural response and likely to be temporary. Use the new information about your anxiety triggers to challenge your anxious thinking, as we describe in Chapters 5 and 7.

Seeing a Doctor

If you've looked high and low for situations or events that may have set off your relapse and can't come up with anything at all, consider making an appointment with your primary care physician. Anxiety can have a number of physical causes, such as side effects from prescription medication or over-the-counter medications and supplements, excessive caffeine, and physical problems (see Chapter 3). Don't try to diagnose yourself. If you experience anxiety with absolutely no apparent cause, please get a complete physical checkup.

Revisiting What Worked Before

If anxiety creeps back into your life, review the strategies that worked for you previously. Some of those techniques may need to become lifelong habits. Keep relaxation in your life. Exercise on a regular basis. Review Chapters 5, 6, and 7, and do a few of the exercises from time to time.

Anxiety isn't a disease that you can cure with a one-time injection, pill, or surgery. Anxiety is a natural part of life. When it mushrooms to a distressing degree, you merely need to reapply your strategies for managing it.

Doing Something Different

We've presented a variety of strategies for overcoming anxiety. Most likely, you've picked a few that have felt compatible with your lifestyle. Now consider looking at some ideas you haven't yet attempted. We urge you to do something different. Take a look at the list that follows, and choose one you haven't gotten around to trying yet:

- Rethinking your anxiety (see Chapters 5, 6, and 7)
- Facing fear head-on (see Chapter 8)
- Engaging in relaxation strategies (see Chapter 11)
- Exercising (see Chapter 10)

If you've simply dabbled at one or more of these techniques, pursue it more aggressively and see whether it works better that way. Anything in this book that you haven't tried yet is worth considering.

Getting Support

You don't have to face anxiety relapses alone. Talking with others helps you deal with emotional distress. A great source of such support can be found in your local newspaper. Most city newspapers list support groups for just about everything: various health concerns, emotional problems, relational problems, and, of course, anxiety.

But what if you live in Pie Town, New Mexico: population 55? Pie Town may not have an anxiety support group. But all is not lost. You can go to an Internet search engine, such as Google (www.google.com), and enter "chat rooms for anxiety." You'll find more than enough interesting sources of support. Try out a few and see whether you can find a group that feels compatible. Millions of people suffer from anxiety, and they have great advice and support to offer you. You don't need to suffer alone.

The best support groups give you ideas for coping. Beware of groups that seem to encourage whining and complaining.

Considering Booster Sessions

If you've seen a professional and later experience an unexpected increase in your anxiety, think about calling for a few booster sessions. Your therapist isn't going to think you failed. Usually, a second round of therapy helps and doesn't take as long as the first. In addition, some people like to check in every few weeks or months as a kind of prevention. Again, anxiety isn't a disease with a single, one-shot cure.

On the other hand, if you've never seen a professional and you experience a relapse, you should consider it now. If you've had previous success on your own, you're likely to improve rapidly with a little assistance.

Looking at the Stages of Change

Any kind of change involves a series of steps or stages. These stages don't necessarily occur in a straight, linear fashion. As we discuss in greater detail in Chapter 2, these stages include

- **Pre-contemplation:** Not even thinking about change. Obviously, you're not in this stage if you're reading this book.
- **Contemplation:** Thinking about change but not being ready to do something about it.
- **Preparation:** Making plans to do something about your problem.
- **Action:** Meeting the problem head-on.
- **Maintenance:** Continuing your efforts to deal with your problem.
- **Termination:** Only a lucky few reach this point; you no longer even have to think about your problem.

Relapse can occur during any of these stages. For example, you may move back from action to contemplation or even pre-contemplation. Just remember, it's normal. Stepping back for a while doesn't mean that you can't gather the resources to make another run at the problem. Most people who succeed have to try a number of times before they get there.

Accepting Anxiety

With this tip, we come full circle — back to the top of the list: Anxiety happens. It will return. Welcome it with open arms. It means that you're still alive! Appreciate the positive aspects. Anxiety tells you to pay attention to what's going on around you. Go with the flow.

We're not suggesting that you need to feel horrendous amounts of anxiety, but a little anxiety is unavoidable. And anxiety, when not overwhelming, may help mobilize your resources during difficult challenges.

Chapter 23

Ten Signs That You Need Professional Help

Some people find that self-help is all they need. They read about good ways of dealing with their anxiety, and then they apply what they've discovered. Voilà! Their anxiety gradually fades to a manageable level.

However, no self-help book is intended to completely replace professional help. And anxiety sometimes requires the assistance of a professional, just like complicated tax matters may call for a certified public accountant or deciding to draw up a will may send you to an attorney. We hope you understand that seeking a mental-health professional's assistance is a reasonable choice, not a sign of weakness.

This chapter tells you how to know whether you should consider professional assistance for yourself or someone you care about. It's not always an obvious decision, so we give you a list of indicators. And if you still aren't sure, you can always talk with your primary care doctor, who should be able to help you decide.

Having Suicidal Thoughts or Plans

If you find yourself thinking about harming yourself, get help now. Take these thoughts very seriously. Call the national suicide hotline at 1-800-SUICIDE (1-800-784-2433). If your thoughts become overwhelming, call 911 and get to an emergency room. Help is available. And when you do access professional help, be honest about your thoughts; hold nothing back. A professional can help gather other options and solutions that seem out of reach when someone is feeling tremendously anxious or depressed.

Feeling Hopeless

From time to time, everyone feels defeated. But if you begin to feel hopeless about getting better, thinking that the future looks bleak and you can't do much to change it, get professional help. Feelings of hopelessness put you at greater risk for suicide. You need to know that you *can* feel better. Let others help you.

Handling Anxiety and Depression

You may be experiencing depression mixed with anxiety if you find yourself having some of the following symptoms:

- Feeling sad most of the day
- Losing interest or pleasure in activities
- Change in weight
- Changes in your sleep patterns and habits
- Decreased interest in sex
- Feeling keyed up or slowed down
- Feeling worthless
- Feeling excessively guilty
- Poor concentration
- Thoughts of death

If you do have anxiety and depression, seek professional help. Depression is a treatable condition. Having the energy to fight both can be hard. You may also want to pick up a copy of our *Anxiety and Depression Workbook For Dummies* (Wiley).

Trying to No Avail

Perhaps you've read this book and given the recommendations your best shot at overcoming anxiety, but for whatever reason, they just haven't worked. That's okay. Don't get more anxious because you didn't get rid of worry and stress. Something else may be going on. Get an experienced mental-health professional to help you figure out the next step.

Struggling at Home

You're anxious. The anxiety causes you to be irritable, jumpy, and upset. You hold it together at work and with strangers, but you take it out on the people you care about most, your family. Then you feel guilty, which increases your anxiety. If this sounds like you, a professional may help you decrease the tension at home and ease the pathway to finding peace.

Dealing with Major Problems at Work

Maybe you have no one at home to take out your anxiety on, or perhaps home is the haven away from stress. If that's the case, work stress may overwhelm you. If you find your anxiety exploding at work, consider professional help.

First, anxiety sometimes causes irritability and moodiness with co-workers or bosses; such behavior can cause plenty of trouble. Anxiety can also rob you of your short-term memory, make it difficult to focus, or make decisions feel overwhelming. So if anxiety affects your job performance, get help before you hit the unemployment line.

On the other hand, if you're out of work, take a look at Chapter 14 for ideas.

Suffering from Severe Obsessions or Compulsions

Obsessive-compulsive disorder (OCD) can be serious. See Chapter 2 for more information about OCD. The problem is that people with the disorder often don't seek help until their lives are taken over by unwanted thoughts or repetitive actions. Most people with OCD need professional help. If you or someone you love has more than mild OCD, get professional help. Also, consider reading *Obsessive-Compulsive Disorder For Dummies* by yours truly (Wiley).

Understanding Post-Traumatic Stress Disorder

You feel agitated and keyed up. Were you also exposed to a traumatic event that resulted as follows?

- At the time, you felt helpless and afraid.
- Later, you try not to think about it.
- In spite of your efforts not to think about it, the thoughts and images keep on popping up.

If so, you may have *post-traumatic stress disorder* (PTSD). See Chapter 2 for a complete description of PTSD. The treatment of PTSD is probably best done by an experienced professional. Many people with PTSD try to tough it out and live life less fully because of their stubbornness.

Going through Sleepless Nights

Is anxiety keeping you awake? That's quite common. If your sleep doesn't improve after working on your anxiety awhile, be sure to read Chapter 10 about sleep. Too many sleepless nights make it hard to function and more difficult to help yourself in the fight against anxiety. If you sleep poorly night after night and awaken tired, check it out with a professional. You may be experiencing depression along with anxiety.

Getting High

Sure, a beer or three can seemingly soothe the soul, but excessive drinking or drug abuse is a common problem among those with anxiety disorders. It makes sense; anxious feelings are uncomfortable. What begins as an innocent attempt at feeling better can become another big problem later on. If you find yourself consuming too much alcohol or another drug to calm your feelings, get professional help before the crutch turns into an addiction.

Finding Help

In the days of high-cost healthcare, you may not always have as much free-dom to consult any professional you want. However, whether you receive a restricted list of professionals from your insurance company or not, it's still a good idea to check out one or more of the following:

✔ Ask the insurance company or the state licensing board for the specific profession or license of the referred professional.

✔ Ask your friends if they know of someone whom they had a good experi-ence with.

✔ Ask your primary care doctor. Family physicians usually have a good idea about excellent referrals for various types of problems.

✔ Talk to the professional before making an appointment. Ask about his experience with treating anxiety and what approach he takes. Ask about whether you'll receive a scientifically verified approach for dealing with anxiety.

✔ Call the psychology department of your local college or university. Sometimes they have referral lists.

✔ Call or use a search engine on the Web to find your state psychological, psychiatric, or counseling association. Or check out national consumer organizations. (See the appendix in the back of this book for more information.)

Appendix

Resources for You

* *

*I*n this appendix, we provide some books and Web sites for finding out about and overcoming anxiety as well as other emotional difficulties. These are only a few of the many excellent resources available to supplement the information in this book.

Self-Help Books

Anxiety and Depression Workbook For Dummies, by Charles Elliott and Laura Smith (Wiley Publishing, Inc.)

The Anxiety and Phobia Workbook, by Edmund Bourne (New Harbinger Publications)

Anxiety Free: Unravel Your Fears Before They Unravel You, by Robert Leahy (Hay House)

Borderline Personality Disorder For Dummies, by Charles Elliott and Laura Smith (Wiley Publishing, Inc.)

Changing For Good: The Revolutionary Program that Explains the Six Stages of Change and Teaches You How to Free Yourself from Bad Habits, by James Prochaska, John Norcross, and Carlo DiClemente (William Morrow & Co., Inc.)

Depression For Dummies, by Laura Smith and Charles Elliott (Wiley Publishing, Inc.)

Feeling Better, Getting Better, Staying Better: Profound Self-Help Therapy for Your Emotions, by Albert Ellis (Impact Publishers, Inc.)

The Feeling Good Handbook, by David Burns (Plume)

Full Catastrophe Living: Using the Wisdom of Your Body and Mind to Face Stress, Pain, and Illness, by Jon Kabat-Zinn (Bantam Dell Publishing Group)

Get Out of Your Mind and Into Your Life: The New Acceptance and Commitment Therapy, by Steven Hayes (New Harbinger Publications)

Mastery of Your Anxiety and Worry: Workbook (Treatments That Work), by Michelle Craske and David Barlow (Oxford University Press, USA)

Mind Over Mood: Change How You Feel by Changing the Way You Think, by Dennis Greenberger and Christine Padesky (The Guilford Press)

Mindful Recovery: A Spiritual Path to Healing from Addiction, by Thomas Bien and Beverly Bien (Wiley Publishing, Inc.)

Obsessive-Compulsive Disorder For Dummies, by Charles Elliott and Laura Smith (Wiley Publishing, Inc.)

The OCD Workbook: Your Guide to Breaking Free from Obsessive-Compulsive Disorder, by Bruce Hyman and Cherry Pedrick (New Harbinger Publications)

Reinventing Your Life: The Breakthrough Program to End Negative Behavior . . . and Feel Great Again, by Jeffrey Young and Janet Klosko (Plume)

Seasonal Affective Disorder For Dummies, by Laura Smith and Charles Elliott (Wiley Publishing, Inc.)

The Shyness and Social Anxiety Workbook: Proven, Step-by-Step Techniques for Overcoming Your Fear, by Martin Antony and Richard Swinson (New Harbinger Publications)

Why Can't I Get What I Want?: How to Stop Making the Same Old Mistakes and Start Living a Life You Can Love, by Charles Elliott and Maureen Lassen (Davies-Black Publishing)

The Worry Cure: Seven Steps to Stop Worry from Stopping You, by Robert Leahy (Three Rivers Press)

Resources to Help Children

Cat's Got Your Tongue? A Story for Children Afraid to Speak, by Charles Schaefer (Magination Press)

Freeing Your Child From Obsessive-Compulsive Disorder, by Tamar Chansky (Three Rivers Press)

SOS Help for Parents, by Lynn Clark (SOS Programs & Parents Press)

Talking Back to OCD, by John March with Christine Benton (The Guilford Press)

Up and Down the Worry Hill: A Children's Book about Obsessive-Compulsive Disorder and its Treatment, by Aureen Pinto Wagner (Lighthouse Press)

What to Do When You Worry Too Much: A Kid's Guide to Overcoming Anxiety, by Dawn Huebner (Magination Press)

Accessing Web Sites to Discover More about Anxiety

Type the word "anxiety" into a search engine, and literally thousands of sites pop up. Be careful. The Web is full of unscrupulous sales pitches and misinformation. Be especially cautious about official-sounding organizations that promote materials for sale. Don't be fooled by instant cures for anxiety.

Many Web forums host chat rooms for persons with anxiety concerns. Feel free to access them for support. At the same time, realize that you don't know who's sitting on the other end. They may be uneducated about anxiety or, worse, trying to take advantage of a person in distress. Don't believe everything you read.

Here's a list of a variety of legitimate Web sites that don't sell snake oil:

- **The Academy of Cognitive Therapy** (www.academyofct.org) is a group that certifies experts in the field of cognitive therapy. They promote evidence-based treatment and maintain a list of certified mental-health professionals through the world.

- **The American Psychiatric Association** (www.psych.org/public_info) has information for the public about anxiety and other mental disorders.

- **The American Psychological Association** (www.apa.org/pubinfo) provides information to the public about treatment and interesting facts about anxiety and other emotional disorders.

- **The Anxiety Disorders Association of America** (www.adaa.org) lists self-help groups across the United States. They also display a variety of anxiety screening tools for self-assessment. On their site you can find an online newsletter and a message board.

- **The Association for Behavioral and Cognitive Therapies** (www.abct.org) is a large professional organization that focuses on research-validated treatment approaches for people with emotional disorders. We often refer people to their extensive list of qualified therapists.

- **The International OCD Foundation** (www.ocfoundation.org) has an annual conference and provides considerable information about the assessment and treatment of obsessive-compulsive disorder. It also has a message board and provides an opportunity to ask experts questions.

- **The National Alliance on Mental Illness** (www.nami.org) is a wonderful organization that serves as an advocate for people and families affected by mental disorders. Information is available about causes, prevalence, and treatments of disorders for children and adults. This group also offers support groups across the country.

- **The National Association of School Psychologists** (www.nasponline.org) maintains a site with information and fact sheets for parents and teachers.

- **The National Institute of Mental Health** (www.nimh.nih.gov) reports on research about a wide variety of mental-health issues. It also has an array of educational materials on anxiety. It provides resources for researchers and practitioners in the field.

- **PsychCentral** (www.psychcentral.com) has an abundance of psychology-related resources, blogs, and free information. We happen to write a blog called "Anxiety & OCD Exposed" on this site. Feel free to send us feedback or ask questions through this Web site.

- **WebMD** (www.webmd.com) provides a vast array of information about both physical and mental-health issues, including information about psychological treatments, drug therapy, and prevention.

Index

exposure therapy, 258
first action recommendation, 256
medication and, 147
staircase of fear, 258
talking about, 256
terrorizing, 51
thinking through what happened, 257–258
writing about, 258
trazadone (Desyrel), 150
treatment, health risks of, 248
tricyclic antidepressants. *See also*
    antidepressants; medications
dosing, 152
side effects, 151, 152
time for effectiveness, 151
types of, 152
triggers
agoraphobia, 135
anxious feelings, 70–71
anxious thoughts, 71–72
defined, 71
panic attack, 26, 135
profile example, 72
tracking, 73–74

• U •

uncertainty
constant, 206
danger, 258–260
rethinking, 237–238
tolerating, 205–206
unpredictable endings, 261
untreated anxiety, effects of, 15
"upping the ante," 142–143
*U.S. Bureau of Labor Statistics, Occupational
    Outlook Handbook,* 225

• V •

vacations, 277
vagus nerve stimulation (VNS), 162–163
valerian, 160, 177
Valium (diazepam), 154
valporic acid (Depakote), 157
venlafaxine (Effexor), 150
victim words. *See also* worry words
defined, 90
examples, 94, 98

reasons for, 94
refuting, 98–99
replacements, 98–99
as self-fulfilling prophecies, 98
tracking, 94–95
use of, 93–94
violence, exposure risk, 254
Vistaril (hydroxyzine), 155
visual imagery, 199
vitamins, 161
VNS (vagus nerve stimulation), 162–163
volunteering
benefits of, 241
in disasters, 242
in helping environment, 241
jointly, 277
vulnerability schema. *See also* anxious
    schemas
balanced assumptions, 119–120
characteristics of, 119
cost/benefit analysis, 113
defined, 103
evidence collection, 120
profile example, 112–113

• W •

walking
mindful, 216–217
with partner, 276
Web sites, resource, 321–322
WebMD, 322
weight, health risk, 251
Welbutrin (bupropion), 151
whining and complaining, 16
whirlpools, 192
whole body relaxation. *See* progressive
    muscle relaxation
words
critical, 90, 92–98
for feelings, 68–69
worry, 89–99
workaholism, as feeling avoidance
    method, 66
worries
deconstructing in thought therapy, 78–84
future, 212–215
health, 243–246
job, 221–226
writing about, 59–61